THE FRENCH MENU COOKBOOK

THE
FRENCH MENU
COOKBOOK

A Revised and Updated Edition
of a Culinary Classic by

RICHARD OLNEY

with illustrations by Judith Eldridge

DAVID R. GODINE · PUBLISHER · BOSTON

This revised edition first published in 1985 by

David R. Godine, Publisher, Inc.
306 Dartmouth Street
Boston, Massachusetts 02116

Originally published in 1970 by Simon and Schuster

Library of Congress Cataloging-in-Publication Data

Olney, Richard, 1927–
The French menu cookbook.
1. Cookery, French.   2. Menus.   I. Title.
TX719.O45   1985   641.5944   85-70146
ISBN 0-87923-579-9
ISBN 0-87923-613-2 Ltd

First printing

Printed in the United States of America

In memory of Madeleine Decure,
Georges Garin, and
Odette Kahn

CONTENTS

CONTENTS

Contents

Two Informal Spring Dinners

Four Simple Spring Menus

SUMMER MENUS · 245

Two Summer Dinners

A Semi-Formal Summer Dinner

Four Simple Summer Luncheons à la Provençale

CONTENTS

THE FRENCH MENU COOKBOOK

Preface

In revising *The French Menu Cookbook,* I have concentrated on the introductory sections, expanding, in particular, the chapters on Wine and on Mechanics, Aromatics, and Basic Preparations. The menus themselves have not been altered, but, when possible, procedures and presentations have been simplified.

Emphasis throughout the book has been placed on the importance of tactile sense, which I consider to be a sort of convergence of all the senses, an awareness through touching but also through smelling, hearing, seeing, and tasting that something is "just right" — to know by seeing the progression from the light, swelling foam of an initial boil to a flat surface punctuated by tiny bubbles, by hearing the same progression from a soft, cottony, slurring sound to a series of sharp, staccato explosions, by judging from the degree of syrupiness or the smooth, enveloping consistency on a wooden spoon when a reduction has arrived at the point a few seconds before which it is too thin, a few seconds after which it may break or burn; to know by pinching and judging the resilience of a chop or a roast when to remove it from the heat; to recognize the perfect amber of a caramel moments before it turns burnt and bitter; to feel the right liquid flow of a crepe batter and the point of light but contained airiness in a mousseline forcemeat that, having absorbed a maximum of cream to be perfect, would risk collapsing through any further addition. . . .

The maniacal precisions of weights, measures, and oven temperatures imposed on modern cookbooks serve mainly to soothe feelings of insecurity in the timid cook; a blind respect for them will discourage self-confidence and the development of tactile sense, which go hand in hand. Food should be an expression of a cook's personality; a recipe executed by two individuals, in each of whom may reside a finely developed tactile sense, will produce, thanks to individual sensibilities, two different dishes, each of which may be flawless.

French Food and Menu Composition

Good and honest cooking and good and honest French cooking are the same thing. Certainly there are national dishes, just as there are regional dishes — sage and onion stuffing and apple pie will remain forever British and American (although there is nothing unique about the former except for the choice of herb, and the latter is nothing but a *tarte aux pommes* with a lid), as will *beurre blanc* remain French — but it is comforting to realize that the principles of good cooking do not change as one crosses frontiers or oceans and that the success of a preparation depends on nothing more than a knowledge of those principles plus personal sensibility.

A meat stew, for instance, is usually a preparation of pieces of meat seared in fat, enough flour to bind the sauce, one or several aromatic elements, and liquid, all gently cooked until done. In France, depending on the meat, the fat, the aromatic elements, the liquid, and finally (having nothing at all to do with the preparation) specific garnishing elements, the stew may assume any one of dozens of names. Color some onions in lard, remove them and fry floured pieces of chuck in their place, return the onions, and moisten with water — in short, reduce each element to its simplest and most economical version — and you have an old-fashioned beef stew that housewives in a dozen different countries consider to be their personal heritage. The steps in its preparation are identical to those for *boeuf bourguignon, carbonade, gibelotte de lapin, navarin de mouton,* or *coq au vin*. Scalloped potatoes and *gratin dauphinois* are the same thing, as are creamed eggs and onions and *oeufs à la tripe;* pot roast is a rustic *boeuf à la mode,* and boiled meat and vegetable dinners or the endless soups that our grandmothers prepared are to be found in French cuisine as *potées* and *garbures*.

A menu composed of preparations that are not in themselves French may remain totally French in spirit, for it is the degree to which a menu is based on a sensuous and aesthetic concept that differentiates a French meal from all others. It may be served under the simplest and most intimate of circumstances, but its formal aspect is respected, and its composition — the interrelationships and the progression of courses and wines — is of the greatest importance.

Classical French cooking — that which from the beginning made France's reputation abroad — is naturally eclectic. It was, and is, created by men —

professional chefs. It is refined and, in execution, often involved. In the hands of a loyal artisan it can be very good indeed; in the hands of a great chef it can be sublime.

The concept of a great meal in France has altered greatly since the nineteenth century, when menus sometimes counted twenty or thirty courses and a dozen wines. Around the turn of the century, refining and simplifying forces worked hand in hand. Auguste Escoffier was influential and his great manual, *Le Guide Culinaire,* first published in 1902, remains the professional's standard reference book today. Later, simplification took another leap (though this time the refining element was less in evidence) when people slowly pulled themselves together after World War II, not to take up life where it had been left off, but to plunge into a nervous, active world that occasionally bordered on hysteria. The elaborate, leisurely luncheon disappeared and a simple dinner became the important meal of the day. Today, a meal organized at a great Paris restaurant by the Club des Cent or the Académie des Gastronomes may begin with an hors d'oeuvre or directly with a fish course, followed by meat, cheese, and dessert, and be accompanied by three wines. Before the war, this would have been unthinkable.

In contrast to the classical cuisine of professional kitchens are the traditions in regional cooking — as various as the provinces are numerous, but all related in character in the sense that each is the direct outgrowth of the combined wealth and poverty of the immediate countryside and the limitations of the kitchens. It is essentially peasant cooking, elaborated by generations of women who were never far from the kitchen and whose imaginations were forced into flower through necessity and limited means.

Nearly all French country cooking traditions are based on the use of the fireplace. Quantities of utensils were designed to be embedded in hot ashes, recipes *"en papillote"* were originally conceived to be cooked under hot ashes, and preparations that today are held for many hours at a bare simmer in a cool oven or over very low heat were once half buried in ashes for the night and forgotten until it was time to serve them. As the coals never died from autumn till spring, a bed was always ready if there were meats or vegetables to be grilled, and it was merely a question of adding a couple of logs to produce the heat necessary to turn a roast on a spit before the flames. Rapid gratins and glazes were produced by heating a shovel in the hot coals and holding it directly over the surface of the dish (the ancestor of the salamander). *Crème brûlée,* in certain provinces, is still known as *crème à la pelle* — "shovel custard." Slow gratins were made in special copper pans designed to be placed on tripods over the coals, their high-sided lids, concave at the center, to be filled with hot coals.

The only ovens were bread ovens, the door often opening from the back wall of a fireplace. Enormous, brick-lined, and igloo-shaped, they were heated by beds of coals, constantly fed by broom or other sweet-scented kindling over a period of several hours. When the bricks were sufficiently heated, the ovens were swept clean; they retained sufficient heat for many hours of baking. Isolated farms had their own ovens but small villages had community ovens that were heated once a

week, to which all the villagers brought their risen bread dough as well as other preparations to be baked as the ovens cooled.

The term *cuisine bourgeoise* nowadays is used to describe a certain kind of preparation. As a rigidly defined aspect of a way of life it no longer exists as a category apart. It is richer than regional cooking in the sense that it uses more expensive products, yet it is also less imaginative. It is based on stock; hence the kitchens were always full of boiled meats, and it was accepted tradition, even with distinguished guests, to place a platter of boiled meats at table at the same time as the soup and leave it throughout the service. (In restaurants it was the kitchen help who nourished themselves on boiled meats.) Braised dishes like *boeuf à la mode* are typical. "Vulgar" elements such as offal were eschewed. Veal liver and sweetbreads were, however, considered elegant fare and, curiously, a stew of calves' eyes was acceptable. *Cuisine bourgeoise* is, like regional cuisine, also a woman's cooking (though it was not the mistress of the house but servants who executed it), but much in it has been borrowed from professional classical cuisine. The food prepared by Françoise and caressingly described by the narrator in *A la Recherche du Temps Perdu* is exemplary *cuisine bourgeoise*.

As for *la nouvelle cuisine,* it has several times been "invented" of recent centuries, sometimes baptised *"la cuisine nouvelle"* or *"la cuisine moderne."* Bizarre marriages and simplistic methods are always part of the baggage. That which is valuable is rarely new and is eventually reintegrated into the mainstream of tradition, while the rest is blessedly forgotten.

MENU COMPOSITION

A perfect meal can be many things — a plate of lentils with a boiled sausage, a green salad, a piece of cheese, and a bottle of cool young Beaujolais — or nothing but a composed salad and any light young wine.

A dinner that begins with a soup and runs through a fish course, an entrée, a sorbet, a roast, salad, cheese, and dessert and that may be accompanied by three to six wines presents a special problem of orchestration. The desired result is often difficult to achieve. Each course must provide a happy contrast to the one preceding it; at the same time, the movement through the various courses should be an ascending one from light, delicate, and more complex flavors through progressively richer, more full-bodied, and simpler flavors. The wines, too, should be flattered by — and should flatter — the courses they accompany while relating to one another, as well, in a similar kind of progression (except that, with wine, increasing complexity seems to be the most exciting formula).

A semiliquid sorbet, more tart than sweet, often with a Champagne base, refreshes the palate halfway through this progression, and a green salad serves the same purpose before relaxing into the cheese course, which is normally accompanied by the fullest-bodied of the red wines, and, finally, the dessert, neither heavy nor oversweet, but light and delicate, slightly less sweet than the intricate and voluptuous Sauternes that may accompany it.

This is obviously not the only way to conceive a menu. Essentially the only thing to remember is that the palate should be kept fresh, teased, surprised, excited throughout a meal. The moment there is danger of fatigue, it must be astonished or soothed into greater anticipation until the moment of release and postprandial pleasures.

In organizing a menu, consider its presentation — the eye must be flattered as well as the palate. Don't serve tomato sauces in red plates or spinach on a green platter. Never serve a roast's garnish on the same platter; a roast is sufficiently handsome to be presented alone and, should it slip while being carved, artichoke bottoms and stuffed mushrooms should not be there to fly in all directions. Don't sprinkle large handfuls of parsley indiscriminately over everything. Don't follow one white-colored sauce with another, or a gratin of fish by a gratin of meat, even though the underlying sauces may be very different. Rustic preparations are generally best, and look best, served directly from the earthenware vessels in which they were cooked. Elegant preparations should be elegantly presented, on condition that the quality in no way suffers as a result. (Cold food lends itself best to fanciful dress, but however it is presented, food should always look like food.)

A menu must be conceived also in terms of one's time and work. Never try to serve a meal in which every course requires last-minute preparations. When a dish calls for a number of ingredients to be added at intervals, combine in advance all those elements to be added at the same time. In this way you have only one article to think of rather than five or six, a couple of which might otherwise be forgotten in last-minute confusion. Many dishes are at least as good reheated — prepare these on the preceding day. Others can be prepared ahead of time except for finishing the sauce. Think everything out ahead of time. When preparing something that is new to you, don't read the instructions only once or try to cook as you read; memorize the instructions before attacking.

Avoid repetition. If there are mushrooms in the fish sauce, don't add *duxelles* to the meat stuffing; if one of the main dishes is rich in cream, don't serve a sweet based on whipped cream, or a *sabayon* or custard sauce with dessert if another sauce is thickened with egg yolks. Don't serve rice with the fish and potatoes with the meat, or watercress with the roast and a green salad after. Don't serve a gratin based on Gruyère and include the same cheese on the cheese platter. The juxtaposition of cold and hot, rough and smooth, crisp and creamy, sauced and dry should be considered.

For the most part, it seems best for a simple meal to include only one sauce and for a more complex menu to be limited to two, which should be very different in character, or perhaps three if one includes a sauced dessert.

The selection on a cheese platter depends on the wine chosen to accompany it. Cheese's reputation as a perfect partner to wine is perhaps based as much on the numbing, deforming effect of sharp or otherwise strongly flavored cheeses on indifferent wines, masking their faults and making them easier to drink, as on a delicate cheese's aptitude to throw into relief a wine's finesse. Good wines whose qualities lie more in ruggedness and strength than in nuance — Châteauneuf-du-Pape, Gigondas, Barolo, and California Zinfandel, for instance — may nonetheless go well with such cheeses, whereas a fine old Médoc or Burgundy would suffer badly. Gruyère, fresh Parmesan, fresh Cantal, or relatively mild Cheddar are good, all-round wine cheeses. Fresh or semifresh, properly drained, unpasteurized farmers' goat cheeses can be exquisite with fresh, young wines, red or white. Reblochon, Saint-Nectaire, and Taleggio are among the most dependable of the soft fermented cheeses (Pont l'Eveque that has never known refrigeration, perfectly matured in a cellar to a creamy, not quite runny consistency, can be one of the great cheeses but is increasingly hard to find, and Camembert, which must be an *artisanal* farmer's product to be good, is now nearly all industrially produced); Maroilles and Livarot are too violent and aggressive for most wines. Blue cheeses, too, are difficult, although rough, young, and rustic reds can sometimes withstand the attack; the Sauternais often place a Sauternes on Roquefort; old vintage port, sometimes served in conjunction with Stilton, is no doubt best appreciated on its own after a meal.

Very rich desserts should follow only the simplest of meals; on most menus, something light and playful in spirit is best. Lots of air, in the form of a soufflé or a mousse, is usually appreciated; ices are refreshing. If serving a dessert wine, avoid chocolate, ice creams, and ices.

Pomerol produces only red wine. The merlot grape dominates, followed by cabernet franc and cabernet-sauvignon. Vieux Château Certan has more of the latter than most. The properties are small by comparison to others in the Bordelais; the quality is high and generally consistent from one growth to another. The growths have never been classified.

Wine

To analyze a wine, the taster takes no food, for the palate must remain virgin, unaffected by other flavors. But wine's principal role is to give pleasure, and that role is best played at table in the context of a menu; when the two are carefully chosen, the wine and the food enhance each other, each subtly altering the other. Any wine that is honestly made can be perfect of its sort; the line separating great wines from others is tenuous — mostly a matter of complexity, something more easily sensed than defined. A great wine partakes of the same mystery and inspires the same awe as a work of art. "With complex wine, simple flavors; with complex flavors, simple wine": as long as it is not taken too seriously, this is a good rule of thumb. Rarely is a great wine better served than by a plain roast; if its place is with the cheese course, sharp, extraordinarily stinky, or otherwise aggressive cheeses are best banned. The intoxicating essences melded from a multitude of aromatic vegetables, herbs, stocks, and marinades, typical of *daubes*, stews, and many other preparations, are too imposing — as is the exuberant note of much Mediterranean food, the sharpness of mustard or a vinaigrette, or the contrasts of sweet and savory preparations — to do justice to an intricate bouquet and elusive taste sensations; a robust, fruity, but uncomplicated wine, easy to drink but undemanding, will taste better, and so will the food.

THE WINE IN YOUR GLASS

Wine is made from more than 3,000 varieties of the European wine grape, *Vitis vinifera,* fewer than two dozen of which are designated as "noble," or apt under ideal conditions to be transformed into complex wines of great subtlety, capable of evolving in depth with age. Millennia of shifting adaptations, mutations, and clonal survivals have altered or reinforced varietal characters and definitively established each variety in the climate, soil, and subsoils of its predilection. Among the most exalted expressions of these varietal-regional alliances are: cabernet-sauvignon in Bordeaux's Graves and Médoc areas, pinot noir and chardonnay in Burgundy's Côte d'Or, syrah in the northern Rhone valley, and riesling in the German Rheingau. These and other varieties have been transplanted to the far corners of the world, often with surprising results, but the sublime heights sometimes reached by a noble variety in its elected milieu have so far remained serenely unchallenged.

Up to a point, the quality of a wine is directly but inversely related to the quantity; this is measured in one-hundred-liter units — or hectoliters — per hectare, an area of about two-and-a-half acres. It is not unusual for anonymous wines, industrially produced, to surpass 150 hectoliters to the hectare; the production of fine wine varies, for the most part, between twenty-five and fifty hectoliters per hectare. None of the noble-grape varieties are huge producers, but a number of restraints must nonetheless be imposed on the vines, of which radical winter pruning and "cluster thinning," the removal during the summer of excess bunches of grapes in formation, are among the most important. It is often said that a vine must be made to suffer to give its best; crowding will force the roots to penetrate more deeply in search of nourishment, diminishing the production of each vine — thus, 10,000 vines per hectare will yield only the same harvest as 5,000 but will give better wine.

Vines from the plains planted in rich soil produce flat, boring wine; the best wines come from the hillsides — gentle slopes or steep inclines, usually with southern or eastern exposures — where drainage is good but soil compositions are often so poor as to be useless for other agricultural pursuits. A vine must be eight or ten years old for its roots to have penetrated deeply enough to draw the maximum complexity of mineral nourishment from the earth's substrata; at forty years, production will have begun to decline but quality will continue to improve as long as the vine lives in good health. Today's grafted vines do not enjoy the same longevity as their pre-phylloxera forebears. (Since the nearly universal devastation of vinifera vines in the late nineteenth century by the American vine-root louse, *Phylloxera vastatrix,* which now permanently infests the soil of most of the world's vineyards, vinifera cuttings are grafted onto rootstocks developed from phylloxera-resistant American wild-grape species.)

The only wine from the Bordelais to be classified alone in a category apart, Yquem was classed in 1855 as premier cru supérieur, *followed by the* premier cru *and* deuxième cru *categories. The label gives no more information than that imposed by the law; since 1975 the mentions* "Sauternes Appellation Contrôlée" *and* "Mis en Bouteille au Château" *have been removed to another labeling strip.*

The nuance of color, the smell, taste, and texture of the wine in your glass depend not only on these general conditions. Microclimates, affording protection from winds or frosts, stones on the earth's surface storing the sun's heat to radiate it by night, the weather of the particular year, the care and rapidity with which the grapes are harvested and the weather at that time, the method of vinification, whether or not the wine has been raised in wood and for how long, whether or not it has been filtered, fined, or racked, and the conditions under which it has been bottled (despite the scoffing of enlightened persons, many serious growers will put their wine in bottles only in cool weather when the full moon has begun its decline and the barometer is high)   all of these details and more help form a wine's personality, which may or may not be developed to its fullest extent, depending on the cellar in which it has reposed, whether it has been decanted and permitted to breathe in advance, the temperature at which it is served, the size and shape of the glass from which it is drunk and the level to which it is filled, the wine that has preceded it, and the preparation that it accompanies.

HOW WINE IS MADE

The mechanical aspects of wine making have altered greatly in the last two decades. The use of easily cleaned, temperature controlled stainless-steel fermentation vats has become generalized, both industrially and on more rarefied levels. (Château Haut-Brion and Château Latour both have stainless-steel installations.) Most of the changes — refrigeration systems that hold wines at near freezing temperatures to precipitate out tartar crystals, centrifuges to whirl out other matter in suspension, various devices to filter what cannot be otherwise precipitated out   are destined to clarify and stabilize industrially produced wines as rapidly as possible; wherever they are made, these wines resemble one another, but inexpensive, bulk-produced wines today are a good bit more drinkable than they have been in the past. The violent treatments that permit bright, thirst-quenching little wines to be promptly marketed cannot be successfully applied to wines of greater potential that must evolve gently both in barrel and in bottle to give their best.

Perhaps the most significant change in wine making is a certain loss of provincialism among wine makers and oenologists, an awareness everywhere of what is happening in the world. The stubborn Burgundian peasant who continues to make wine exactly as his father and his grandfather did does not do so through ignorance of the most recent methods employed in California, Australia, or Bordeaux; he simply believes that his wine is better. He believes that the wild yeasts that inhabit his vines and his cellars are better than laboratory cultures. He knows that alcoholic fermentation — the transformation of the grape sugars by enzymes, generated as the yeasts feed and multiply, into approximately equal parts of alcohol and carbon dioxide — is a natural phenomenon that may be controlled but cannot be altered. And if he has inherited perfectly good old oak vats, he sees no reason to replace them with shiny stainless steel.

RED WINE

All grapes used for making high-quality red wine are white-fleshed and give transparent juice; for this reason, in traditional red-wine vinification, the grapes are crushed and propelled directly into vats, where the juice ferments in the presence of the skins, whose cellular structure is destroyed in the process of fermentation, releasing the coloring matter as well as certain aromatic elements and much of the tannin essential to the structure and longevity of complex red wines. The grape bunches may or may not be stemmed, all or in part, at the time

The Volnay community appellation *in the Côte de Beaune applies only to red wine. The Champans* climat *is a* premier cru *and its name may appear on the label in letters the same size or smaller than those of* "Volnay."

of the crushing, depending on whether the additional tannin of the stems is thought to improve the wine's aging potential.

Fermentation sets in within a few hours and after three or four days reaches the tumultuous phase and the point at which cooling devices may have to hold the heat below 90°F to prevent its paralyzing the yeasts before their work is finished. The pressure of escaping gas forces up a spongy mass, or cap, of skins and pulp that may be held beneath the surface by a wooden grid or, if permitted to float in an open vat, must be regularly punched down. The must, as the fermenting juice is called, is drawn from the bottom of the vat and pumped over the surface at intervals, aerating the contents to activate the yeasts and moistening the cap if it has been left floating. As sugar decreases and alcohol increases, the multiplication of the yeasts rapidly diminishes, the violence of the escaping gas subsides, and the cap of pomace sinks to the bottom. The alcoholic fermentation is usually finished in a week's time; the new wine may be drawn off immediately or the vat may be covered or sealed to maintain a protective blanket of carbon dioxide while the skins continue to macerate for another week or two, increasing the tannic intensity of the wine. When the wine is drawn off, the pomace is pressed and this press wine is, except in rare instances, mixed with the free-run juices (*vin de goutte*).

It is tannin that gives many fine wines an astringent harshness in youth; if the wine maker's aim is to create a supple, quaffable wine to be drunk young, he will want an attractive color with as little tannin as possible. To this end, he may draw the half-fermented must into another vat as soon as the color is deep enough and finish the fermentation out of contact with the skins; or he may heat the freshly crushed grapes, freeing the pigment, before pressing them and fermenting the colored juice apart. Another method, carbonic maceration, commonly used with wines labeled *primeur,* consists in placing the whole, unbruised grape bunches in sealed vats under carbon-dioxide pressure for a couple of weeks, during which time a partial fermentation, with an accompanying loss of malic acid, occurs within the whole berries, which are then pressed so that the juices may finish fermenting apart.

A secondary fermentation — once thought to have been the tail end of the alcoholic fermentation, thrust back into action by a mysterious sympathy between the wine in barrels and the flowering vines — is now recognized to be a completely separate process that rarely takes place until the alcoholic fermentation is finished, and that, without the interference of the technician, waits until the cold winter months are over to go into action. Malolactic fermentation — the breaking down, through the action of lactic bacteria, of the wine's malic acid into lactic acid and escaping carbon dioxide — produces a natural deacidification essential to the quality of the wine. By drawing the finished wine directly into other vats and heating the vinification cellars, this fermentation is usually now launched promptly after the alcoholic fermentation. Some growers, however, are loath to heat their cellars, and in so doing diminish natural humidity and dry out the precious wood in which the wine lives; they prefer to wait for spring and let nature take its course.

While lesser wines often never see wood, most others, before being put into bottles, pass a period of settling and evolution in wooden casks, or tuns, that can vary from six months to several years, one-and-a-half to two years representing the average. During this time the wine must be regularly topped up to keep it from contact with acetic bacteria, always present in the air and ready to turn wine to vinegar. Solids slowly fall out of suspension, leaving the wine clear. Most wines are regularly racked, the clear wine drawn from one barrel to another, leaving the lees behind, and often they are fined by the addition of egg white or another albuminous substance to precipitate any remaining solids. Wines raised in large tuns are often filtered instead of being fined. As with other sophisticated procedures, racking, fining, and filtering are eschewed by some growers, in the belief that they emasculate the wine, robbing it of certain nuances.

The first growths of Bordeaux and the greatest Burgundies are raised only in new oak, a material that not only infuses supplementary tannins into the wine but is a powerful seasoning agent as well. Few wines have the muscle or depth to support this treatment, and many growers prefer to use only a proportion of new oak in combination with used barrels, or even none at all. (A number of California vintners, wishing to emulate nothing of a lesser stature than first growths, have discovered their wines to be thrown out of balance by the aggressive, harsh presence of new French oak.)

In the Côte de Beaune, Burgundy's greatest white wine, Le Montrachet, straddles the border between the villages of Puligny and Chassagne, both of which have added the wine's name to their own. Puligny produces almost exclusively white wine, of which Les Combettes is one of half a dozen celebrated premiers crus, whereas Chassagne produces almost twice as much red as white.

WHITE WINE

Outside of Champagne, where the pinot noir grapes are picked when only just ripe and pressed immediately, without first being crushed, to draw off a clear juice untainted by the color of the skins, white wines are rarely made with red grapes. The white grapes used for making white wine are usually crushed without stemming and pressed immediately, and the juice is fermented out of contact with the skins. At the time of pressing, the must is treated with sulfur dioxide (often used also in red-wine vinification), not only to protect the juice from harmful bacteria but, because it temporarily paralyzes the yeasts, to permit the heavier solids to fall out of suspension before the relatively clear liquid is run off into casks or vats to ferment.

White wines are fermented at lower temperatures than reds to retain their fresh fruit aromas. This has never been a problem with traditional vinification in 225- or 228-liter casks, the loss of heat from such small volumes being so great that the temperature rarely rises above 68°F. As volume increases, however, so do the heat and the difficulty in controlling it; until recently, bulk production of white wines never gave satisfactory results. Today, inexpensive, refreshing white wines are common thanks to technological innovations permitting fermentation in vast stainless-steel tanks at strictly controlled temperatures, usually around 60°F in European countries; in California, much lower temperatures often produce a rather spiky, aggressive fruit that rarely appeals to the European palate.

White wines that are fermented in casks are also raised in casks and receive the same treatments as red wines; the greatest Bordeaux and Burgundy whites are also raised in new oak.

ROSE WINE

Rosés are made from red grapes or a combination of red and white and are vinified like white wines. Those with only a delicate blush of pink are sometimes called *vins gris* and are made by crushing and pressing the grapes immediately. Deeper nuances are obtained by leaving the crushed grapes to macerate for a few hours before pressing them and fermenting the juice; these wines, in certain regions, are known as *vins clairets*.

SPARKLING WINE

Good sparkling wines are all made by the Champagne method: a mixture of sugar, yeasts, and wine is added to a vat of finished wine just before bottling, to induce a second fermentation in the bottle, imprisoning carbon dioxide in the wine. The sediment resulting from the bottle fermentation is drawn to the neck of the bottle by a process of repeated twists, known as riddling, which may take from several weeks to several months. The bottles are then stored neck end down until they are ready to be disgorged, the neck ends passed first through a refrigerated bath to freeze the plug of sediment. Upon a bottle's being opened, the plug is expelled by the pressure from within and replaced by an equivalent amount of clear wine, which may or may not be sweetened. The bottle is then promptly recorked, wired, and given a rest before being dressed for the market.

NOBLE ROT

Botrytis cinerea, when it attacks damaged, unripened grapes, is known as gray rot and can seriously compromise a vintage. When, however, under perfect atmospheric conditions — fine autumn days opening with morning mists — the ashen fungus attacks perfectly ripened, healthy white grapes, it is known as noble rot, and a magical thing happens: the grape berries wither and their chemical structure is altered, creating flavors reminiscent of no other wine. Partly because of the concentration of grape sugars through desiccation and partly because the mold has an inhibiting effect on the yeasts, fermentation is arrested before all of the sugars have been transformed into alcohol, and the wine remains sweet but vibrant, with delicately bitter overtones. A vine may produce a glass or so of such an unusual nectar. Germany's greatest wines and the wines of Sauternes owe their qualities to noble rot. Hungary's Aszu tokays are made by adding a paste of noble-rot grapes to a vat of normal must.

FLOR

Under certain circumstances, not all of which are well understood, wines may be left on ullage, in kegs that are never topped up, inviting a heavy veil of yeasts to form on the surface and thus shielding the wine from contact with air and warding off the attack of acetic bacteria, while at the same time breaking down any acetic acid already in the wine, to reduce volatile acidity. Like noble rot, flor imposes its own special flavor on any wine protected by it. Fino sherry is the best known example, hence the use of the Spanish *flor* in English. Known in French as *la fleur*, it also protects and nourishes the *vins jaunes* of the Jura.

Wines are fortified by the addition of brandy or other spirits, either (as with port) before the fermentation is finished, when they are said to be muted, the fermentation being arrested, leaving a high proportion of unfermented grape sugars in the wine, or (as with sherry) only after the alcoholic fermentation is finished, in which case the addition of spirits serves only to raise the level of alcohol without otherwise altering the structure of the wine. The wines of Madeira and Banyuls are fortified progressively both during and after the arrest of the fermentation.

In the context of a menu, fortified wines rarely find a place. Dry sherry is a good aperitif and is sometimes served with a soup, most often consommé. A vintage port that has passed the half-century mark or a vintage or *solera* Madeira from the last century can be the most sublime of after-dinner drinks, on condition that a Sauternes has not been served with the dessert.

GENERAL CONSIDERATIONS

The proportion of wines characterized as fine, great, or noble is infinitesimal by comparison with the others. Many wines are best drunk as young as possible and without too much thought. Some fine wines — whites or non-tannic reds — show well if drunk within the year following the vintage, while others are at their prime after a year or two, and still others may require five, ten, twenty, even thirty or forty years to reveal all their secrets. Some few from rare vintages, reposing in perfect cellars, may pass the century mark with perfect equanimity, assuming a complexity of bouquet — an ethereal presence — not permitted to those less favored or of commoner origins.

Especially in temperate and often difficult climates like those of Burgundy and Bordeaux, the vintage, or year, counts for a great deal in a wine's evolution and constantly deals surprises even to the most accomplished of wine makers. Different years develop more or less rapidly and often in unpredictable ways. Many vintages are declared great at their inception, but in the Bordelais, for instance, only some dozen years in the last two centuries have given birth to massive, dense, bigger-than-life clarets of the kind that, when proven, are always rated highest on the vintage charts; since 1929, only 1945 and 1961 have produced these slumbering giants. (It is recorded that the 1870 first-growth clarets were not ready for drinking until the late 1920s, and certainly the 1928s began to open out in breathtaking beauty only during the '60s, while many '61s are still in a state of uneasy awakening.)

At the other end of the scale lie the "disaster" vintages. They usually follow cold, rainy summers; at worst, the grapes are picked in the rain. Yet conscientious growers make good wine every year. All damaged or imperfectly ripened grapes will have been sacrificed and the remaining, healthy grapes will probably have had to be chaptalized (sugar added to the must to raise the alcohol level) to create a balanced wine; the wine will be light-bodied, light in color, and fast-maturing. Rather like a mirror image of the same wine from a better year, it may have lost some of the detail and depth but it will be a loyal reflection of style; such wines have great charm when drunk at the right moment — usually between three and eight years of age — and, thanks to the vintages' reputations, are exceptionally easy on the purse.

Between these extremes lie the surprises (not only the disappointments but the lean and pale austere wines for which no brilliant future was forecast but which, many years later, have mysteriously deepened in color and fleshed out, harsh angles softening into voluptuous contours) and the classics — the great but not quite mythic vintages, the average decent vintage, symbol of continuity, and the delicious, supple, non-tannic vintages, best in the fruit of their youth and always rated low on the vintage charts.

Because, in particular in the Bordelais, vintage-chart snobbism has such a radical effect on the entire market, but disproportionately so for the greatest growths, astute private buyers often adhere to a "value for money" policy, expressed thus: Buy minor growths from great vintages and great growths from minor vintages.

STORAGE

If wine is to be laid down, a good cellar is essential. It is a simple affair: above all, the temperature should be fairly constant the year round, ideally between 50 and 57°F; at somewhat higher temperatures — up to 62° or 65°F — a wine will evolve normally but much more rapidly and, over a period of years, in less depth. A cellar should be relatively humid and there should be some ventilation. If the floor is of beaten earth, the problem of insufficient humidity will not arise; concrete floors can be spread with a layer of sand and occasionally moistened with a garden sprinkler. Wooden racks or bins will rot in humid cellars; the best solution is a metal rack for easy access to bottles in small quantity and, for economy of space, labeled concrete bins for larger quantities. Foods that may lend an odor to the air should never be kept in a wine cellar, for the gentle evolution of a wine depends on a slow breathing process through the cork. (It is for this reason that half-bottles, bottles, and magnums — different capacities related to identical corks — age more and less rapidly.) Bottles must always be stored lying down; a cork that is not constantly in contact with the wine loses its resiliency, allowing air to enter and spoiling the wine.

Even wine-loving architects fail to provide decent cellars in modern homes and wonderful cellars have been destroyed in many old houses by central-heating installations. Space permitting, a cellar can be dug away from the house. A more common solution is to insulate a room and equip it with temperature and humidity control. For modest collectors or those who cellar most of their wine with a merchant, many firms now manufacture refrigerated, humidity-controlled units in which fifty to two hundred and fifty bottles may be stored at cellar temperature. Small quantities of wine meant to be stored for only a few weeks or months can be kept in a dark, cool corner — an unheated closet, for instance — without suffering noticeably.

TEMPERATURE AND SERVICE

Most white wines are served too cold and most red wines too warm. (The "room temperature" concept dates from the last century, when most rooms were closer to cellar temperature than to that of today's centrally heated houses.) A wine that is served too cold is paralyzed; too warm, it falls out of harmony, alcohol, tannins, and acids no longer forming a whole, and the alcohol becomes aggressive, the acidity overstated. A wine's ideal temperature has less to do with its color than with its specific structural components, its complexity, its age, and, to a certain extent, the time of the year. (A wine at 60°F will seem quite cool on a hot summer's day; in winter, the same wine would have to be served several degrees cooler to give the same impression of freshness.)

Coolness exalts the fresh, fruity scents and flavors of young wines and, at the same time, tempers their acidity; it will, however, exaggerate the astringency of tannic, red wines not meant to be drunk young. (Warmth, on the other hand, tempers the tannins and heightens the sharpness of acidity.) Most wines that take age well are thrown better into relief at more moderate temperatures. Sweet white wines, like Sauternes, made from nobly rotted grapes, can support lower temperatures than dry white wines of comparable complexity. Sparkling wines, whose bouquets are conferred by the continuing explosion of tiny bubbles on the wine's surface, need to be served chilled, not only for reasons mentioned above but also to restrain the bubbles' exuberance. It is not a bad idea to serve wines slightly cooler than the degree that you judge to be ideal; at normal room temperatures any wine will rapidly gain a couple of degrees when poured, but if it is already too warm, it will never cool off in the glass.

The greatest of white Burgundies and Graves, white Hermitage, Condrieu, certain California Chardonnays, and many light-bodied, fruity, and relatively non-tannic reds — *primeur* wines, Beaujolais, Chinon, Bourgueil, Bardolino, Valpolicella, California Zinfandels — are never better than when drunk at a cool cellar temperature (50° to 53°F). Ideal temperatures for other wines vary only by a few degrees up or down the scale — a couple of degrees less for crisp, flinty whites, a couple more for the great red Burgundies and most other reds, except for the most tannic and complex; 43° to 46°F for Sauternes and Champagne. I prefer to serve no wine at more than 60°F, reserving mature clarets and other especially tannic wines like Hermitage or Côte Rôtie for this treatment; some serious wine drinkers would raise this maximum temperature to 65°F.

Wines to be cooled or chilled should be brought as rapidly as possible to the desired temperature. (Any wine that is refrigerated at exceptionally low temperatures for long periods of time will go dead — it is said to be *cassé*, "broken.") A couple of hours in the refrigerator or half an hour in the freezer will do the trick, but an ice bucket, whether or not the wine has first been briefly refrigerated, is still the best method — packed with ice and water for chilled wines or filled with cold water, a handful of ice cubes added, for cool wines. Specially designed double-walled plastic containers are effective for keeping the temperature of an already cooled bottle constant.

DECANTING

Decanting has recently become a controversial subject. The non-decanters claim that decanting oxidizes all wines, that all oxidation is harmful to wine, and that, if decanting is absolutely necessary because of heavy sediment, it should be done only at the instant of serving.

The principal reasons for decanting are: 1) to separate the clear wine from the sediment, a deposit of tannins that is always present in old red wines; 2) to oxygenate the wine (oxygenation, the simple physical process of incorporating air into the wine, which helps release aromas, should not be confused with oxidation, a chemical change that in many instances destroys the bouquet, imposing tired, flat, often unpleasant odors of decay, and that can take place very rapidly with certain wines and only gradually and after many hours with others); 3) to

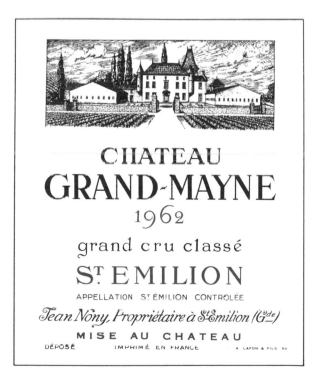

The Saint-Emilion classification (all red) dates from the mid-fifties and has been revised twice. About seventy growths are rated grand cru classé.

APPELLATION HAUT-MÉDOC CONTROLÉE

1973

CHÂTEAU CANTEMERLE

GRAND CRU CLASSÉ DE MÉDOC 73cl

Héritiers Pierre J. DUBOS, Propriétaires Macau-en-Médoc

Because it does not lie within one of the Médoc communities that possess their own appellations, Cantemerle takes the regional Haut-Médoc appellation. Wines from the northern part of the peninsula, beyond Saint-Estèphe, take the broader Médoc appellation. Classed fifth growth in 1855, Cantemerle deserves a better classification.

rid certain natural wines (that have not been stabilized by more or less sophisticated treatments) of a slight prickle caused by the presence of carbon-dioxide gas, the result of a fermentation in the bottle of remaining traces of residual sugar; 4) to rid a wine of tastes of reduction, more familiarly known as "bottle stink," a phenomenon that is not well understood (sometimes mysteriously described as "the opposite of oxidation") but that is undoubtedly rectified by a slight but genuine oxidation in a wine decanted in advance, after which its bouquet may swell and blossom normally; 5) to permit an old wine that, immediately after being uncorked, seems dead or mute, having neither odor nor any defined taste beyond a tannic presence, to open out: the oxidizing action, similar to the preceding instance, permits a miraculous change — what appears to be a thin and dusty skeleton slowly and inexplicably acquires flesh, freshness, depth, and complexity.

Uncorking a bottle in advance is harmless but it serves no real purpose; left for a day or two, of course, the wine might spoil, but a couple of hours' contact of air with the tiny surface in the neck of the bottle will not perceptibly affect it. Whether bottle stink or, more often, simply a mute refusal to reveal its message at the moment of uncorking is considered to be a fault or a natural quality in an old wine, only the complete aeration effected as the wine flows from bottle to decanter will bring it around, sometimes immediately, often only after two or three hours. The problem is that one cannot know; in tasting a series of old wines of similar origins, all decanted a discreet hour in advance, it is a near certainty that some will be in a state of perfection, others could profitably have been decanted an hour or two earlier, and some, whose seductive capacities may have peaked shortly after decanting, will have suffered from too deep a breath of fresh air. It is traditional to decant wines in Bordeaux, and the professionals, all with generations of experience behind them, disagree about whether it should be done one or two hours in advance or immediately before serving. In Burgundy, wines are rarely decanted, and no doubt rightly, for Burgundies seem to be more immediately susceptible to oxidation than most wines and less reticent to reveal themselves than many Bordeaux. It is not unusual for an undecanted old Burgundy to flower in all its fragile glory seconds after it has been poured and to show signs of fatigue before the bottle is finished.

White wines are not usually decanted. They, too, like to breathe, but will unfold with a bit of swirling in the glass; the occasional deposit of tartar crystals, being relatively heavy, does not disturb the wine.

An old red wine should be gently set upright a couple of days before serving; assuming the bottle to have been lying label side up, the sediment will slide down to the side of the punt opposite the label. Cut the capsule and remove it beneath the ridge at the lip of the bottle. Wipe the top of the bottle neck and the cork top clean with a cloth or paper towel, dampened if necessary. Hold the bottle firmly on the table surface so that it does not move while being uncorked (the perfect corkscrew has not yet been invented — the Screwpull is easiest for most people), remove the cork slowly with a regular movement, and, again, wipe the top and, with a corner of the towel, the inside of the neck to remove any fragment of cork that may cling there. If you are decanting several bottles, prepare them all to this stage before continuing.

Have at hand a glass and a lighted candle or small, upward-facing flashlight, over which the neck of the bottle may be held to check the wine's clarity. Holding the bottle at the labeled side, pour slowly at first, until the glug-glugging gives way to a smooth flow, then move decanter and bottle together over the light source so that, looking down at the neck of the bottle, the light passes through the flowing wine in a line to your eye; continue pouring, steadily but more rapidly, stopping the moment the first trace of sediment creeps into the neck from the shoulder of the bottle. Before returning the bottle to an upright position, pour a bit of the little remaining troubled wine into a glass so that it may be swirled, smelled, and tasted, to check its condition. If more than one wine has been decanted, the identifying corks are often hung, necklace-like, around the collar of the decanter with cork pins — tiny silver chains terminating in pins with which to pierce the ends of the cork; lacking these elegant devices, the cork can be affixed to the neck of the decanter with an elastic band.

If a bottle containing deposit has not been stood up in advance, it should be slipped, without altering its horizontal position, into a cradle; it may then be decanted from the cradle. If it is being poured directly into glasses, pour slowly and steadily with as little backward and forward movement as possible. Never disturb the sediment by twisting the bottle to free it of a drop of wine clinging to the lip; a folded napkin, placed in the cradle so that the neck of the bottle reposes on it, will absorb the droplet.

The glass from which one drinks should be uncut, undecorated, and uncolored so that the color of the wine may be properly admired. It should be relatively thin, stemmed, and large enough to hold from three to four fluid ounces when less than half filled. The form may be that of a tulip or a balloon — there are many variations on these two shapes, but the essential thing is that the circumference of the lip be somewhat smaller than that of the waist, so that when the glass is from one-third to one-half full, the wine may be swirled and the bouquet may develop in the space above. Certain traditional Burgundy glasses and larger versions of those known as *dégustation* should not be filled to more than an eighth of their volume; glasses of this format are perhaps a bit ostentatious. It is attractive but not necessary to serve white and red wines in differently shaped glasses.

The mechanics of wine-tasting may seem better suited to the laboratory or cellar than to the table but, to give wine its due, it should not be considered indiscreet in serious company to pucker one's mouth and suck air through the wine, letting it then spread to all corners of the mouth and tongue before swallowing it.

In selecting wines for a meal, it is logical to begin with the lightest and driest of whites to accompany hors d'oeuvre, light seafood dishes, etc., and work through richer, though still dry, white wines with hot sauced fish dishes and certain other white meats, vegetable gratins, cheese or other savory soufflés. In

A red from the northern Rhône valley, Côte Rôtie is a dense black-purple wine made from the syrah grape and a very small proportion — always less than ten percent — of the local white viognier grape. It has an intense, chewy fruit when young, evolves slowly, and lives long.

moving from a white to a red wine, neither should suffer by comparison (a light little thirst-quencher should not be followed by a venerable first-growth claret, for instance, nor a noble white Burgundy by a green little Beaujolais), and the red wine that follows another should be bigger of body and older. In short, work from white to red, small to large, simple to complex, and young to old. Switching regions from one color to another poses no problem, but a progression of wines of a single color is usually most successful if they are of similar styles and from the same region.

These general guidelines are not intended to command the respect of rigid laws; your palate must be the ultimate guide. It is good to remember that many light-bodied red wines can be served with perfect success with foods normally associated with white wine, that sweet white wines are considered by some to be fine accompaniments to game, or that a Château-Chalon can comfortably fill many a role normally attributed only to red wine. Assuming the dessert to be of the right character, one's pleasure is always enriched by finishing a meal with a great Sauternes of a respectable age.

SOME FRENCH WINES

Central and Southern France produce vast quantities of small wines, many of which carry the V.D.Q.S. (*vin délimité de qualité supérieure*) label of quality. They are often pleasant and very often hard to find outside their region of production. The few wines discussed on the following pages are among the best-known in France and the most widely exported. Nearly all fall under the control of the French Institut National des Appellations d'Origine (hence the term *appellation contrôlée* to be found on the labels, and its abbreviations, A.C. or A.O.C., for *appellation d'origine contrôlée*).

The official classifications of the great wines of Burgundy and Bordeaux, some based on rigorous codes of ancient tradition and others on recent legislation, must inevitably confuse and frustrate the novice wine lover, not because any single system of classification is in itself complicated, but because they all use the same hierarchical terms (*cru classé, premier cru classé, grand cru classé, premier grand cru classé*) with widely differing implications of value. In Burgundy, the highest accolade is *grand cru classé,* followed by a multitude of nonetheless very distinguished *premiers crus classés*. In the Graves region of Bordeaux, sixteen growths are soberly designated as *crus classés* with no further precision or differentiation of class within the group, whereas Saint-Emilion has created a dozen *premiers grands crus classés* (of which Châteaux Ausone and Cheval Blanc are distinguished by the addition of the letter A, the others carrying the letter B), followed by seventy-some *grands crus classés* plus a vast and shifting number of *grands crus*.

Premier cru classé is the highest distinction in the Médoc hierarchy, whose official classification, except for the elevation in 1973 of Château Mouton-Rothschild from second to first growth, has remained unchanged since 1855. The other *premiers crus classés* are Châteaux Lafite-Rothschild, Latour, Margaux, and the

Graves growth Château Haut-Brion (the only non-Médoc, thus distinguished by being classed twice over), followed by more than fifty second, third, fourth, and fifth *crus classés,* a number of the latter being easy equals to certain Saint-Emilion *premiers grands crus classés* and in a class equivalent to the Burgundian *premiers crus classés.*

Like that of the Médoc, the Sauternes classification dates from 1855: Château d'Yquem heads the list, classed as *premier cru supérieur,* followed by eleven *premiers crus classés* and thirteen *deuxièmes crus classés.*

Finally, to add to the confusion, the five first growths from the Médoc classification, the two *premiers grands crus (A)* from Saint-Emilion, Château d'Yquem, and Château Pétrus, from Pomerol (a region that has never been officially classified), are often unofficially grouped together, a sort of aristocratic *"bande à part,"* under the designation *les premiers grands crus de Bordeaux.*

BURGUNDIES

The red grapes of Burgundy are pinot noir and gamay noir a jus blanc; the white grapes are chardonnay, pinot blanc (a white mutation of pinot noir), and aligoté.

The generic *appellations* — wines that may come from anywhere in Burgundy — are: Bourgogne Aligoté, white wine made entirely or in part from the aligoté grape; Bourgogne, which, if white, is made from chardonnay or pinot blanc and, if red, from pinot noir (the exception being the unlikely instance of its coming from one of the Beaujolais community *appellations,* in which case the grape is gamay); Bourgogne Rosé (or *clairet*), made from pinot noir, and Bourgogne Passe-tout-grains, a mixture of gamay with one-third or more of pinot noir. Bourgogne Ordinaire and Bourgogne Grand Ordinaire are made from any combinations of Burgundy grapes.

A step up the ladder are the regional *appellations,* sometimes hyphenated with the word *"villages"* (Côte de Beaune-Villages, Beaujolais-Villages, etc.), in which case the grapes must come from certain specified communities within the region. Then come the community *appellations* and, finally, the *premiers crus* and the *grands crus,* each designating a specific vineyard, or *"climat,"* within a community.

The main body of the Burgundy vineyards extends from just north of Lyons to just south of Dijon. Isolated from the others, far to the northwest, are the chardonnay vines of Chablis. The Chablis *premier cru* and Chablis *grand cru* wines are typically steely, crisp, and clean, rigidly constructed, pale straw-colored wines with green reflections, often a bit hard at first, probably best drunk between four and ten years of age, although many can live much longer. A lesser *appellation,* Petit Chablis, is rarely exported.

At the southern extremity of Burgundy, the grape of Beaujolais is the gamay noir à jus blanc (so named to distinguish it from the red-fleshed gamay teinturier grapes). The generic Beaujolais and Beaujolais supérieur wines come mostly from the south; farther north, Beaujolais-Villages and the nine community *appellations* have more substance. Viticultural literature attributes different characters to each — although whether Saint-Amour is more delicate, Chiroubles and Fleurie more

A. ET P. DE VILLAINE

Propriétaires

Bourgogne

La Digoine

Appellation Bourgogne Contrôlée

BOUZERON

1983

Mis en bouteilles au Domaine

75 cl

The Bourgogne appellation can apply either to white or, as here, to red wine. Reds carrying this appellation that are made in the Mâconnais, the Chalonnais, or the Côte d'Or must be one hundred percent pinot noir. Bouzeron is at the northern extremity of the Chalonnais, at the entrance to the Côte de Beaune. La Digoine is the name of the parcel of vineyard, which is planted to the oldest vines on the domaine.

graceful, Morgon, Juliénas, Brouilly, or Côte de Brouilly firmer or grapier would be hard to say. Chenas may have a bit more muscle, thus forming a transition between the others and Moulin-à-Vent, which is proclaimed by many to be the finest of the Beaujolais because of its Côte d'Or-ish aspirations and thought by some to fall between two stools, possessing neither the fresh charm and immediacy of the lighter growths nor the extra dimension of a great wine.

The snowballing vogue of Beaujolais Primeur, clarified and stabilized by November 15, only a few weeks following the vintage, together with a seeming inability on the part of many growers to resist over-chaptalization, has robbed much Beaujolais of its typicity. Traditional Beaujolais, drunk young, with its exhilarating green fruit, refreshing light acidity, and supple descent (the inexpressive "quaffable" seems to be the best we can do in English to replace such French adjectives as *"gouleyant," "glissant,"* or *"coulant,"* all describing an irrepressible, sensuous, flowing quality), can still be found in certain Lyons bistros to wash down the food it likes best — rustic charcuterie, *"canaille"* salads of ears and feet, *andouillettes* and other variations on the theme of tripe.

The Mâconnais is an abundant producer; if many of the reds, mostly made from gamay, lack a certain delineation of character, certain whites, such as Mâcon-Villages or those that take a specific village name — Mâcon-Lugny or Mâcon-Viré, for instance — can be good, clean, refreshing wines at welcome prices. A more recent *appellation,* Saint-Véran, having acquired instant popularity, seems already on the verge of overpricing and overproduction. The Mâconnais's exceptional growth, Pouilly-Fuissé, has long been criticized for its prices and uneven quality, said to be a result of its popularity in America; at best, it is a vigorous and subtle wine with soft edges and a warm fruit. The small vineyard of Château Fuissé produces a remarkable example; Pouilly-Vinzelles and Pouilly-Loché are similar in style but often lack the fullness of a good Pouilly-Fuissé.

In the Côte Chalonnaise, except for generic *appellations,* pinot noir replaces gamay; the whites, like those of the Mâconnais, are made from chardonnay with some pinot blanc. The style of the wines, both red and white, is similar to that of many Côte de Beaune *appellations,* but because they are less celebrated, the prices are often advantageous. Rully and Montagny are known for their whites, Givry and Mercurey for their reds. Mercurey is by far the largest producer of the four community *appellations* and, like Givry, produces also some white wine that can be of outstanding quality. To the north, before entering the Côte de Beaune, the village of Bouzeron lends its name to an Aligoté, ideal as an aperitif and in a different league from most other Aligotés.

The greatest wines of Burgundy are from the Côte d'Or, a narrow strip of hillsides about thirty miles in length planted, with hardly a breathing space, to vines — pinot noir and chardonnay. The southern section, the Côte de Beaune, is separated from the Côte de Nuits, to the north, by a brief, vineless passage. Twenty community *appellations* are woven into the Côte de Beaune; the Côte de Nuits has seven. Each is broken down into an intricate mosaic of small vineyards known as *climats* — and a *climat* that is not divided among a number of proprietors is a rarity. Many *climats* are *premiers crus;* a few are *grands crus.*

The Côte de Beaune is known for light-bodied, sprightly, and supple red wines, often most seductive between four and six years of age, and for Burgundy's greatest whites. Typical of the red wines are Savigny, Beaune, and Pommard, all liberally sprinkled with first growths, and Volnay, whose graceful, filigree finish is often likened to that of delicate Musigny; from Chassagne-Montrachet, whose name is associated with white because of its *grands crus,* come some of the most ethereal and elegant of reds, be they first growths or the simple community *appellation.* The community of Beaune also produces a lovely white first growth, the Clos des Mouches, and certain first growths from the white-wine community of Meursault (Genevrières, Charmes, Perrières) — vibrant, completely dry, but with a voluptuous softness and a bouquet that recalls sweet fruits and hazelnuts — can rival those of Puligny-Montrachet; no wines can better accompany richly sauced fish dishes or white meats in creamy sauces. Half the communities of the Côte de Beaune are world-famous; others, however, are so little-known that they prefer to sell their red wine as "Côte de Beaune-Villages," while some, such as Auxey-Duresses, Monthélie, or Pernand-Vergelesses, may retain their *appellations,* offering wines of often comparable distinction at more modest prices than the better-known communities. Côte de Beaune-Villages is a mixture of two or more red wines from any of sixteen specific community *appellations* (excluding Pommard, Volnay, Aloxe-Corton, and Saint-Romain).

The red wines with the greatest depth and complexity come from the Côte de Nuits, which is often thought to produce only red. (In Nuits-Saint-Georges and in Morey-Saint-Denis, small quantities of unusual, firm white wine of great finesse are made from pinot blanc grapes, cloned from a mutation discovered among the red pinots in the Gouges vineyards at Nuits. A whimsical couple of casks of nonetheless wonderful chardonnay come yearly from the *grand cru* Musigny *climat,* and the Clos Blanc de Vougeot produces a fine, classical white from chardonnay.) Upon entering the Côte de Nuits from the Côte de Beaune, the first community *appellation,* Nuits-Saint-Georges, claims a host of first growths — les Saint-Georges, les Porrets, les Vaucrains, les Pruliers, les Cailles, les Chaboeufs, Clos de la Maréchale, and a couple of dozen others; beautiful wines, earthier, and, when young, easier of access than some of the more exalted *grands crus,* they can still profit from two or three more years in bottle than most of the

Like Vosne and Chambolle, the village of Gevrey, in the Côte de Nuits, has attached the name of its most celebrated growth to its own. The appellation *applies only to red wine.*

Côte de Beaune reds. Following Nuits, Vosne-Romanée, Vougeot, Chambolle-Musigny, Morey-Saint-Denis, Gevrey-Chambertin, and Fixin crowd in, one upon the other. Fixin, best known for its first growths, La Perrière and Le Clos du Chapitre, is the only community *appellation* whose wines may be used (along with those from four villages that have no *appellation* status) for the Côte de Nuits-Villages *appellation.* To the north of Fixin, Marsannay, the only remnant of what was once the Côte de Dijon, is known for its *vin rosé.*

PREMIERS CRUS AND GRANDS CRUS

A *premier cru* must always carry the community *appellation* on the label in letters at least as large as those used for the name of the *climat;* the community *appellation* may be followed by the words *premier cru,* with no further precision (which means either that the wine is an assemblage of more than one first growth or that the *climat* is not well enough known to warrant its mention), or by the name of the *climat,* with or without the mention *premier cru.*

Legislation concerning a *grand cru* from the Côte d'Or is unusual — it is its own *appellation;* only the name of the *climat* need appear on the label, accompanied by the comforting words *"appellation contrôlée."* Because a number of communities have added the name of their most celebrated growth to their own, a footing can sometimes be found in the wilderness, as with the *appellations* incorporating the word "Chambertin"; in neighboring Morey-Saint-Denis, nothing on the labels of Clos de la Roche or Clos de Tart will indicate their origins.

Except for white Musigny, all of the *grand cru* whites are far from the Côte de Beaune. Corton-Charlemagne shares the Corton hillside, near the Côte de Nuits boundary, with red Corton. The others form a single block of some seventy-five acres of vines and five *appellations* clustered around the borderline between the villages of Chassagne and Puligny, each of which has added the name of its shared, greatest growth, Montrachet, to its own. Bâtard-Montrachet lies also in both communities; Chevalier-Montrachet and Bienvenues-Bâtard-Montrachet are in Puligny, and Criots-Bâtard-Montrachet is in Chassagne. Whether the palm is given to Le Montrachet or to Chevalier-Montrachet makes little difference — the beauty of these wines can hardly be exaggerated.

A Côte de Nuits red grand cru, Clos de la Roche *is in the community of Morey-Saint-Denis, bordering on Gevrey-Chambertin, but it is its own* appellation.

The reds are no less magical. Corton is the only *grand cru* in the Côte de Beaune. The others form a chain, broken here and there by *premiers crus,* that stretches through the heart of the Côte de Nuits from Vosne-Romanée to Gevrey-Chambertin. The summits are Romanée-Conti, Musigny, and Chambertin-Clos-de-Bèze, but the others, for the most part, do not fall far behind. In Vosne, the two most revered growths, La Romanée-Conti and La Tache, are both "monopoles," a term indicating single ownership. The proprietor, the Domaine de la Romanée-Conti, also owns parcels of Richebourg, Romanée-Saint-Vivant, Grands-Echezeaux, and Echezeaux, the last two technically within the community of Flagey-Echezeaux, which does not enjoy *appellation* privileges. (Were they to be demoted from their stellar standing, they would fall into the Vosne-Romanée *appellation.*) La Romanée is the other *grand cru* of this cluster. For Burgundy, the *climat* of Clos de Vougeot, which swallows up most of the Vougeot *appellation,* is huge — about one hundred and twenty-five acres, divided among sixty, seventy, or eighty proprietors, depending on your sources — and its reputation is correspondingly equivocal. Chambolle-Musigny has Musigny to itself and shares Bonnes Mares with Morey-Saint-Denis, whose other *grands crus* are Clos de la Roche, Clos de Tart, Clos Saint-Denis, and Clos des Lambrays. In Gevrey, Chambertin and Chambertin-Clos-de-Bèze are traditionally given the edge on the seven other *grands crus,* the names of whose *climats* must precede the word Chambertin (Charmes-, Chapelle-, Griotte-, Mazis-, Mazoyères-, Latricières-, and Ruchottes-Chambertin). Mazoyères may also be called Charmes. A Gevrey-Chambertin first growth, the Clos Saint-Jacques, is considered the equal of a number of the *grands crus.*

It is hopeless to try to bring a virgin appreciation or even new adjectives to these wines. Two centuries of wine literature have repeatedly defined the great growths of Vosne-Romanée as harmonious, majestic, spicy, and velvety and those of Chambolle-Musigny (in fairness, this must include the exquisite first growths of Charmes and Les Amoureuses also) as delicate, silky, and lacy, their underlying force veiled by elegance; they are said to be feminine whereas the wines of Morey-Saint-Denis and Gevrey-Chambertin are described as masculine. Bonnes Mares is often cited as a growth whose style allies Musigny's suave tenderness with the firmness and sobriety of the other growths in Morey-Saint-Denis and those of Gevrey-Chambertin. The scent of violets recurs in descriptions of all these wines, augmented at times by cherries, strawberries, raspberries, licorice, truffles, hawthorn, reseda, roses, or wild mint. The barnyard nuance, around which the Burgundians have embroidered an admirable vocabulary, is more pronounced at the Gevrey-Morey end of the chain; these wines, in particular, accompany to perfection unadorned and unsauced roast game birds.

The reputations of the *grands crus* are consecrated by centuries of tradition; this means essentially that the soil structure and the microclimate of a given growth are capable, when other conditions comply, of producing a wine equal to its reputation. A guideline to quality in the Côte d'Or is more difficult than elsewhere because of the extreme fragmentation of ownership within the vineyards. Different strains of pinot noir may be planted from one fragment to another; the age of the vines varies; some growers regularly obtain less than the legal maximum yields and conscientiously eliminate all imperfect grapes (and, despite increasingly astute legislation designed to frustrate overproduction, there are those who continue to overfertilize and underprune); vinifications vary. Many small growers sell their wines to *négociants* who raise them in barrels and put them into bottle under their own labels. Some *négociants* will buy anything that carries an *appellation;* others are rigid in their selection. A simple community *appellation* or a *premier cru* from one grower or *négociant* may be better than a *grand cru* from another.

BORDEAUX

Vast quantities of inexpensive and drinkable wine are made in the outyling regions of the Bordelais, much of it labeled Bordeaux or Bordeaux Supérieur. On the whole, the reds are more interesting than the whites. From an interminable list of *appellations contrôlées,* some of the most interesting are: Graves de Vayres, Canon-Fronsac, Premières Côtes de Bordeaux, Côtes de Bourg, Premières Côtes de Blaye, Lalande de Pomerol, Saint-Georges-Saint-Emilion, and Montagne-Saint-Emilion. The vast region of Entre-Deux-Mers, once known for banal, vaguely sweet white wines, is planting increasingly to the sauvignon grape and now makes only dry white wine, usually crisp and clean and always inexpensive.

Bordeaux's great wines come from five regions that, geographically, can be reduced to two: Sauternes and Barsac form an enclave in the southern part of Graves, which is itself a prolongation, south from Bordeaux, of the Médoc; about twenty-five miles distant, across two rivers (the Gargonne and the Dordogne, which enclose Entre-Deux-Mers), Saint-Emilion and Pomerol lie together. Médoc, Saint-Emilion, and Pomerol are all red, Graves may be red or white, and Sauternes (of which Barsac is a part, having the right to either the Barsac or the Sauternes *appellation*) can apply only to luscious white noble-rot wines. Red wines from the Sauternes region or the dry white wines produced either in Médoc or Sauternes may be labeled only Bordeaux or Bordeaux Supérieur.

The principal red grapes are cabernet-sauvignon, cabernet franc, and merlot. Some vineyards in Médoc and Graves have a small proportion — rarely more than five percent — of the tannic and acidic, late-ripening petit-verdot, and malbec and carmenère have almost entirely disappeared. No legislation designates proportional plantings of grape varieties and they vary greatly from one chateau to another; Médoc and Graves vineyards average two-thirds cabernet-sauvignon with merlot dominating the other third; in Saint-Emilion and Pomerol, merlot is given the largest place, with cabernet franc assuming greater importance than cabernet-sauvignon.

The white grapes are sémillon and sauvignon. (Most growers are disenchanted with the once traditional muscadelle, which has been abandoned throughout the Graves region and nearly so in the Sauternais.)

A *cru,* or growth, in Bordeaux is a vineyard belonging to a single person or society. It is usually called a *château*, whether or not the property happens to harbor a structure of a certain élan. Most are vast by Burgundy standards. (Consider the loftiest reputation of the Côte de Nuits, La Romanée-Conti, with less than five acres of vines, as compared with its equivalent in the Médoc, Château Lafite-Rothschild, with two hundred and twenty-two acres.)

The Médoc is broken down into two regional *appellations,* Médoc, the farthest or northern half of the peninsula, and Haut-Médoc, within which there are six community *appellations:* Margaux, Saint-Julien, Pauillac, Saint-Estèphe, Moulis, and Listrac. Several hundred chateaux, scattered through all of these *appellations,* are unofficially classed as *crus bourgeois;* about a third of these have banded together to create Le Syndicat des Crus Grands Bourgeois et Crus Bourgeois du Médoc, within which members are classed as *crus bourgeois, crus grands bourgeois,* and *crus grands bourgeois exceptionnels. Bourgeois* growths, whether or not they adhere to the *syndicat,* can be very good wines at very good prices; it is a good level at which to become acquainted with the characteristic Médoc restraint and elegance, a chewy fruit usually associated with blackcurrants and a tannic structure that permits the wines to age well. Many are the equals of fourth or fifth growths from the official classification.

All of Médoc's sixty classed growths are in the Haut-Médoc and all but five are divided among the four communities overlooking the Gironde estuary, Mar-

Pauillac is one of the six communities in Médoc with a right to their own appellation. *"Les Forts de Latour" is a trademark. The wine is made at Château Latour, in part with grapes from vines less than ten years old, considered unsuitable for Château Latour, and in part from vats that have been rejected for use in* "le grand vin." *Though the wine may not be Château Latour, neither is its price; it is consistently of very high quality and is generally considered to be the equal of many a classed growth.*

GRAND CRU CLASSÉ EN 1855

CHÂTEAU GRAND-PUY-LACOSTE

SAINT GUIRONS

Pauillac

APPELLATION PAUILLAC CONTROLÉE

1981

MIS EN BOUTEILLE AU CHÂTEAU

75 cl

Société du Château Grand-Puy-Lacoste, Propriétaire à Pauillac(Gironde)
PRODUCE OF FRANCE

Classed as a fifth growth in 1855, Grand-Puy-Lacoste today is the equal of many third growths.

gaux (the farthest south, gathering together several neighboring communities into its *appellation*), Saint-Julien, Pauillac, and Saint-Estèphe.

It is customary to describe the wines of Saint-Estèphe as tough and earthy, with less finesse than the others, those of Pauillac as the fullest and most concentrated, Saint-Julien as lean and elegant, and Margaux as softer than the others, with greater delicacy. The classed growths of Graves, all gathered into a few communities just to the south of Bordeaux, are granted the same adjectives as the Saint-Juliens but are also said to be earthy and austere in youth.

"Graves" means gravel, and the classed growths of Médoc and Graves are all grown on gravelly mounds — hardly hills — on a rockbed of limestone or ferruginous sandstone; they all have a family resemblance, but the wine of a specific chateau often does not correspond to the generalizations applied to its community. The silken elegance, at once austere and seductive, of Châteaux Ducru-Beaucaillou and Léoville-Las Cases may represent the Saint-Julien ideal but all of the community's growths do not share it; if the huge, dense wines of Chateaux Latour and Mouton-Rothschild are bigger-than-life symbols of Pauillac, then Château Lafite-Rothschild, Pauillac's other first growth (with one foot in the earth of Saint-Estèphe), shares with Château Margaux the reputation of being the least earthbound, the most delicate of clarets, all nuance and finesse. Château Haut-Brion, the Graves first growth, corresponds to none of the Graves explicatives; one of the five first growths, it is the most accessible when young, supple fruit and easy grace veiling a firm frame and belying its powers to age equably. Other red Graves — Domaine de Chevalier and Châteaux Pape-Clément, Haut-Bailly, Bouscaut, or Malartic-Lagravière, for instance — might easily be mistaken for Médocs. A blind tasting, whatever its other virtues, can be a properly humbling experience.

WHITE GRAVES

The two principal white grapes of the Bordelais are very different in character. From sauvignon are drawn fresh, vibrant, sharp, tingling, primary scents and flavors with great immediacy and usually little lasting power. Sémillon, initially, lacks aroma and fresh fruit; its wines, when young, seem rather neutral, flat, and unexciting, but they age well and, after a few years, an eloquent bouquet begins gently to unfold. A traditional white Graves may profit from the spontaneous charm of sauvignon when young while drawing on the more complex gifts of the sémillon grape with the passage of time. Sémillon is especially susceptible to noble rot, a quality perhaps more important in the past, when more sweet wines were made. (A few still come from southern Graves around Langon and the Sauternais.) As the fashion for light, dry white wines becomes more firmly entrenched, the traditional proportions of two-thirds sémillon to one-third sauvi-

Unlike Médoc, Haut-Médoc, and the Médoc community appellations, Graves can be either white or red. Malartic-Lagravière is one of the fourteen classed growths of Graves, all of which receive equal status in the classification. The Malartic white is made from one hundred percent sauvignon (blanc), unusual for the great Graves whites. The red is the classic Médoc-Graves mixture of cabernet-sauvignon, cabernet franc, and merlot, with the first of these predominant.

gnon are progressively being reversed; recent plantations are often one hundred percent sauvignon, vinified in the modern manner to produce crisp and refreshing light-bodied wines that are not meant to age. Some of the classified growths also make their wines in this way.

The most distinguished of Graves whites, famous for finesse and longevity, are Domaine de Chevalier and Château Haut-Brion; following up are Châteaux Malartic-Lagravière, Laville-Haut-Brion, Bouscaut, and Carbonnieux. The wines are as diverse in style as varying proportions of grape varieties and vinification methods might suggest. Sémillon dominates at Laville-Haut-Brion and Bouscaut, sauvignon dominates at Domaine de Chevalier and Carbonnieux, Haut-Brion has equal quantities of each, and Malartic-Lagravière is all sauvignon. Domaine de Chevalier ferments the wine in barrels with a studied proportion of new oak each year, bottling after eighteen months; Haut-Brion ferments in stainless steel and raises the wine in all-new oak for a year. The others usually bottle in the spring following the vintage; Laville-Haut-Brion and Bouscaut ferment in barrels, Malartic-Lagravière and Carbonnieux in stainless-steel vats; Carbonnieux stores the wine in vats with a brief passage in new oak, and the others prefer used barrels to avoid the taste of new oak. The color and flavor of Laville-Haut-Brion suggest that the grapes are picked later there than at the other properties.

SAUTERNES

Here the sémillon grape always dominates, averaging eighty percent. The grapes are harvested by successive pickings, only the berries sufficiently altered by noble rot being removed from the bunches at each passage through the vineyard. (Their state is such that the withered, ashen grapes release a smoky cloud of spores as they are nudged free from the bunch and tumble onto others in the *panier*.) The quantity of juice that can be pressed from them is, on the average, about a quarter of that produced by normally ripened grapes.

After difficult times, modern oenology, aided by increased public interest in luscious wines, has recently permitted a number of properties to make ends meet. For the most part, the wines are lighter than in the past and ready to drink earlier, the concentration of noble rot is less intense, and, although many are lightly chaptalized, they are less sweet; some are fermented in temperature-controlled vats and raised in casks for a year or two, while others never see wood. Legislation permits an injudicious yield of twenty-five hectoliters per hectare and a few properties produce the maximum; serious growers average closer to fifteen, with Château d'Yquem at less than ten.

Château d'Yquem is unique in its uncompromising adherence to tradition and absolute quality; in difficult years, seven or eight pickings may be necessary (the record is eleven) to ensure a sufficient intensity of botrytis and natural grape-sugar content. (Chaptalization is out of the question. The ideal balance derives from a sugar concentration equivalent to about twenty percent potential alcohol, with fermentation arresting at fourteen percent to leave the remaining six percent in the form of residual sugars; a higher concentration of sugars means an equally higher concentration of botrytis, whose inhibiting action on the yeasts will entrain a fermentation arrest at a lower degree of alcohol with higher residual sugar, whereas a lower concentration will result in too high an alcohol content and too little residual sugar unless the fermentation is muted by the addition of sulfur dioxide.) The viscous must is fermented in all-new oak barrels and raised in the same wood for three-and-a-half years before bottling. When there is no botrytis there is no Yquem, and it has not been unusual in other years to eliminate a large proportion of the harvest.

The purist tactics employed at Yquem would rapidly reduce a less prestigious growth to bankruptcy, but in very good years, when noble rot invades the vineyards rapidly and completely, many make beautiful wines without having to chaptalize. Among the traditional growths are Châteaux Suduiraut, Rieussec, Climens, and Coutet (the last two, Barsac). Many others whose recent styles are deliberately on the light side have, in the past, produced sumptuous wines that are now in a state of perfection.

Classic Sauternes from classic vintages evolve slowly and live long, beginning their bottle life a clear lemon yellow and progressing through shades of amber and burnished gold to limpid, dark caramel in century-old wines, a complexity of vibrant, honeyed scents and tastes unfolding in unison with the deepening cast of color. Because the development of noble rot depends often on the quality of the weather after the red grapes are all in, good Sauternes vintages do not necessarily correspond to those for clarets. The 1921 vintage has never been challenged as the greatest of the century for Sauternes, and the '21s continue to astonish

A pre-A.O.C. label; today the "Haut" has been struck out. Loupiac, a luscious, noble-rot wine, is directly across the river from Barsac and Sauternes, on the right bank of the Garonne.

today by their freshness, depth, and intensity. Other pre-war peaks are '28, '29, and '37 and, more recently, '45, '47, '49, '53, '55, '59, '62, '67, '70, '71, '75, '76, '80, '81, '82, and '83.

Cérons, next to Barsac, and, directly across the river, Loupiac, Sainte Croix-du-Mont, and Cadillac also make luscious wines in fine years, lighter and with less depth than Sauternes.

SAINT-EMILIONS AND POMEROLS

The wines (all red) of Saint-Emilion and Pomerol are softer, suppler, faster-maturing — and thought to be more accessible to the uninitiated — than those of Médoc or Graves. Most of the credit goes to the merlot grape, better adapted to the clay soils of these regions, which dominates, often to the exclusion of cabernet-sauvignon. The best Saint-Emilions come from two geologically differ-ent areas. The hillsides around the village of Saint-Emilion, known as the "Côtes," have a topsoil largely of clay reposing on a bed of limestone; some of the better-known Côtes growths are Châteaux Ausone, Beauséjour, Belair, and La Gaffelière. The "Graves" de Saint-Emilion lies on a plateau of gravelly mounds next to Pomerol, the structure of the soil being closer to that of Médoc and Graves; its most distinguished growths are Châteaux Cheval Blanc and Figeac. Here, there is less merlot — Cheval Blanc has two-thirds cabernet franc and one-third merlot, and Figeac has approximately equal quantities of cabernet-sauvi-gnon, cabernet franc, and merlot.

One of eleven premier grand cru classé growths, the vines of Figeac are in a section of Saint-Emilion, bordering on Pomerol, called "les Graves de Saint-Emilion" because of the gravelly composition of the soil, which resembles the soils of Médoc and Graves rather than the more typical clay soils of Saint-Emilion. Whereas the merlot grape dominates elsewhere in Saint-Emilion, Figeac is planted to thirty-five percent cabernet-sauvignon, thirty-five percent cabernet franc, and thirty percent merlot.

Just across the border in Pomerol, Châteaux Pétrus and La Conseillante and Vieux-Château-Certan are among the better-known growths. Pétrus is famous not only for its quality but for being practically pure merlot (about five percent cabernet franc). If its keeping qualities belie the reputation of the grape, the essential tannic support no doubt comes from the age of the vines, a low yield, the retention of a proportion of the stems during fermentation, a long maceration with skins and stems, and the use of all-new oak barrels for each harvest. Vieux-Château-Certan, like Figeac, has a higher percentage of cabernet-sauvignon than most vineyards in Pomerol or Saint-Emilion. There are fewer than twelve hundred acres of vines in Pomerol and individual properties tend to be smaller than elsewhere in the Bordelais, but the general quality of the wines is even and of a high level.

Red wine from the Touraine region of the Loire Valley, Chinon is made from cabernet franc. Clos de la Dioterie is the name of a section of the property.

THE LOIRE VALLEY

From Nantais country, at the mouth of the Loire, comes Muscadet, dry white wine made from the grape of the same name, and a sharper, slight white wine that takes the name of the gros plant grape. On the upper Loire, Sancerre, Pouilly-sur-Loire, and, a bit to the west in the Cher valley, Quincy and Reuilly make dry, flinty whites from sauvignon, also called *"blanc fumé"* because of a characteristically "smoky" scent. Pouilly-sur-Loire lends its name to a little white wine made from the chasselas grape; its sauvignon wine is called Pouilly-Fumé. All of these are perfect aperitif or seafood wines and logical accompaniments to first-course salads or cold hors d'oeuvre.

At the heart of the Loire, in Anjou and the Touraine, white wines of greater complexity are made from the chenin blanc grape, or *"pineau de la Loire,"* which, like sémillon, is particularly susceptible to noble rot in good years. From Anjou's Coteaux du Layon, within which lie the two *appellations* Quarts de Chaume and Bonnezeaux, come France's loveliest sweet wines outside of Sauternes. Directly across the river, on the right bank, the chenin blanc at Savennières is now picked before the invasion of noble rot and is vinified as dry wine (though the scents and a certain softness are nonetheless reminiscent of sweet wines); La Coulée de Serrant is exemplary. Vouvray in Touraine may be either dry or sweet, depending on the grower and the vintage; a certain amount, particularly in poor years, is transformed into sparkling wine by the *méthode champenoise*. Fine years produce long-lived wines; 1921 is the most revered vintage and still in fine shape, 1947 and 1959 are beautiful and easier to come by.

Cabernet franc produces the Loire's most serious red wines; the *appellations* are, in Touraine, Saint-Nicolas-de-Bourgueil, Bourgueil, and Chinon and, in Anjou, Saumur-Champigny. Experts claim to discern in them the odor of violets

Another Loire valley red wine, also made from cabernet franc, Saumur-Champigny is usually lighter-bodied than Chinon, refreshing and lovely to drink when young.

and the flavor of raspberry. Lingering behind their fresh fruit is something herbal, hay-like, delicately acrid, and mouth-watering. They share with the wines of Beaujolais the beauty of youth but they age with more grace and eventually come to resemble certain old Bordeaux.

THE RHONE VALLEY

The northern and southern Côtes-du-Rhône are geographically, geologically, and viticulturally two separate regions. On the undulating plains of the south the dominant grape is grenache, whose principal gift is a high degree of alcohol; clairette dominates in the minuscule production of white wine (with the exception of the fortified, sweet Muscat de Beaumes-de-Venise, which is one hundred percent muscat). Most generic Côtes-du-Rhône and all of the superior Côtes-du-Rhône-Villages *appellation* are from the southern Rhône valley; they are nearly all red, usually supple with a pleasant, undistinguished fruit, easy to drink, and easy on the purse. The other southern Rhône *appellations* are Gigondas (mostly red, some rosé), Lirac (red, rosé, white), Tavel (rosé), Rasteau (sweet, fortified Grenache), and Châteauneuf-du-Pape.

Throughout Provence, Châteauneuf-du-Pape means *grand vin* — the bottle reserved for special occasions. At best, it equals its reputation, but the vast extent of the *appellation* (seventy-five hundred acres) plus widely varying vinification techniques and choices of grape varieties impose an unusual diversity of style and quality. Thirteen grape varieties — red and white — are permitted with no further precision. An authentic Châteaneuf-du-Pape may therefore issue from grenache alone or from any number and proportion of varieties among the thirteen; the others most often planted are cinsault, syrah, mourvèdre, and clairette. A Châteauneuf easily supports the aggression of sharp or strong-smelling cheeses that might annihilate a more subtle wine and it can accompany to perfection the rough and rustic but sumptuous flavors embodied in a *daube;* after eight or ten years, its bouquet often acquires a gamy edge that will exalt the blood-thickened hare stew called *civet de lièvre,* or other marinated-game preparations. A few growers make a small amount of white Châteauneuf-du-Pape, strong, solid wine with a lemony tang that, like its red counterpart, has the muscle and presence to rejoice in the high-spirited seasoning of the Provençal table — the saffron, tomato, garlic, and cayenne of a bouillabaisse.

Although an unfortunate and short-sighted legislative policy has recently extended several of the *appellations* to less-propitious soils, the entirety of the northern Rhône *appellations* still covers less than half the surface allotted to Châteauneuf-du-Pape alone. Outside of a few exceptional Châteauneufs, the great Rhône valley wines, red and white, are from the north and the best come from the narrow, schistose, and granitic terraces of a couple of sheer hillsides. Syrah is the only red grape; the white varieties are viognier, roussanne, and marsanne.

The temperamental, low-yielding viognier is unique to the hillsides of the right bank at the northern extremity of the Côtes-du-Rhône; from it is made the lovely white wine of Condrieu (one small vineyard in the area, Château-Grillet, has been granted its own *appellation*), dry and spicy with soft contours and the sweet scents of peaches and fresh almonds. Roussanne and marsanne are associated in varying proportions in the other white wines: that of Saint-Joseph, despite the different grapes, has much in common with Condrieu, of which the vineyards are an extension to the south; most Saint-Péray is made sparkling by the Champagne process; across the river, Crozes-Hermitage white is coarser and earthier, a good, sturdy choice to accompany garlicky or spicy foods or vinaigrettes, savors that are too aggressive in the presence of more delicate wines. These wines are best drunk young, when their fruit is freshest; by contrast, white Hermitage is a great classic with a firm, steely structure, long-lived but introspective in youth, best drunk after its fourth or fifth year — or much later.

In this region, syrah stamps its red wines with an astonishing personality,

Hermitage is both red and white; the red is made only from syrah, the white from roussane and marsanne. The reds have much in common with Côte Rôtie, on a slightly less violent key. Both the red and the white can pass the fifty-year mark with ease. The oldest wines — both red and white — in the Chave cellars are 1929s, and both are in wonderful condition. The Chave family recently moved into its fifth century as proprietors of these vines.

often rather violent when young; the intermingled scents have distinctly wild associations — the bittersweet of wild berries, a trace of medicinal herbs, licorice and truffle, often a marked odor of venison, and, in the taste, a memory of the sea, iodiney like sea urchins. All have a family resemblance but, as with the whites, there are variations of depth and finesse: Saint-Joseph is lighter-bodied, more supple, best drunk younger than the others, and Crozes-Hermitage, like its white counterpart, is a rustic wine. Côte Rôtie, north of Condrieu (a small proportion of viognier, usually less than ten percent, is often fermented with the red grapes), Cornas, and Hermitage are typically massive, dark, tannic wines that evolve slowly and eventually unveil civilized nuances unsuspected in the wild intensity of the young wines. They deserve to be laid down for eight or ten years, and many will live for decades.

OTHER REGIONS

The southern Côtes-du-Rhône may be the real heart of Provence but, viticulturally, Provence refers to an area south and east of Avignon, stretching from Marseilles to Nice. Five A.O.C. make red, rosé, and white wines from a number of different grapes. Cassis is drunk mostly around Marseilles and Bellet, in the Niçoise region. Palette, just outside of Aix-en-Provence and almost entirely within the domain of Château Simone, produces a good, solid red wine and a fine, old-fashioned white, both of which profit from a few years of aging. Bandol produces delicate, pale rosés, more serious than most, and complex, solidly built red wines whose depth of color and vibrant, spicy fruit owe much to the fifty-percent-minimum presence of the mourvèdre grape. The red Bandol of Domaine Tempier averages seventy percent mourvèdre, with the remainder in cinsault, syrah, and grenache, and it blithely ignores bottle-age predictions; none of the vintages from the fifties or sixties yet shows any sign of decrepitude. No one quite knows why Côtes de Provence was elevated to A.O.C. (some say to soothe feelings that were ruffled when a number of Corsican wines were similarly canonized); the wines do not merit the distinction. One vineyard within the V.D.Q.S. Coteaux d'Aix boundaries, Château Vignelaure, makes an unusual and very good red wine — perhaps the only wine in France of its quality that does not enjoy A.O.C. status — from sixty percent cabernet-sauvignon, the remainder in equal parts of syrah and grenache.

Small *appellations* abound in the southwest. Except for the long-lived, luscious, and rare white wine of Jurançon, at once voluptuous and austere, a dry,

The vines of Bandol climb the hillsides of a natural basin that is surrounded by a semicircle of mountains, forming a microclimate in which the little Mediterranean fishing port of Bandol is the crux of the fan. Legislation, for which the proprietor of Tempier fought for years, now imposes fifty percent of the mourvèdre grape. Tempier averages seventy percent. They also make a pale and elegant rosé to which about thirty percent mourvèdre brings more muscle than one usually expects from a rosé. La Migoua is the name of a portion of the property.

nutty flavor offsetting its sweetness, the reds are generally more satisfying than the whites. The most celebrated is Cahors', whose past reputation was of a harsh, black wine that demanded years to mellow; it is still made mostly from the cot (malbec) grape, but altered vinifications have softened its outlines.

But for an insignificant bit of pale-reddish pinot noir, Alsatian wines are white; they take varietal rather than geographical names. Pinot Blanc and Pinot Gris are usually soft, pleasant wines with little depth. Sylvaner and Edelzwicker (a mixture of varieties) are sharp, clean, refreshing wines when drunk within the year. Riesling is the most versatile of the group and of a nobler caste, equally useful as aperitif, as accompaniment to fish and white meats in creamy sauces, or, as in Alsace, to wash down a charcuterie-laden sauerkraut. Gewürztraminer is the most indiscreet of wines; querulous in the presence of most foods, it has a heady, floral-sweet perfume that can be tamed by a richly scented, ripe, runny Münster cheese.

The yellow wine — *vin jaune* — of the Jura, of which the community *appellation* Château-Chalon is the best known, resembles no other (although it is often likened to fino sherry, which is raised in a similar way). A strong, extraordinarily dry, nutty wine made from a strain of traminer (the same grape responsible for the Alsatian gewürztraminer), known locally as savignin, it is raised in large kegs, neither racked nor topped-up, beneath a protective veil of yeasts that forms on the wine's surface, for a minimum of six years before bottling. During this time, the color gradually deepens to bronze and the wine is strengthened, in part because the loss of water by evaporation is greater than that of alcohol and in part because any remaining traces of residual sugar are slowly fermented out, leaving alcohol in their place. A *vin jaune* may take the same role as a great white Burgundy or Graves but can also replace a red wine with certain foods — richly flavored poultry or game birds, for instance — and will often harmonize with the kind of sweet and savory preparations that repel most wines — duck with cherries, pork with various fruits, or game sauces containing currant jelly.

Mechanics, Aromatics, and Basic Preparations

MECHANICS

SLICING AND CHOPPING

It is good to have a sharpening steel always within reach; each time before using a knife, stroking the blade a few times across the steel should become as automatic as brushing one's teeth to face a new day. The common fear of sharp knives is incomprehensible — a dull knife is far more dangerous, both for the user and for the food.

A slicing knife has a narrow blade that is six to eight inches in length. It is moved freely up and down, its only guide being the knuckles of the hand steadying the object being sliced. A chopping knife (which can also serve perfectly well for slicing) has a deep blade, the point of which forms a fulcrum, remaining always in contact with the work surface, while the depth of the blade prevents

the knuckles of the working hand from rapping against the surface. The blade of a practical chopping knife will be eight to ten inches in length, with a depth of one-and-a-half to two inches.

To slice an awkwardly shaped object — a potato, for instance — first remove a slice from one side to create a flat surface, then turn the object, flat surface down, to make it stable. Whichever knife is used, the object to be sliced is held in place with one's free hand, fingertips turned inward, clawlike, to keep them clear of the knife's blade. The side of the blade, as it moves, rests constantly against the farthest joint of one's middle finger and is guided by it.

Articles to be chopped, say an onion, should be first cut in two to create a flat surface against the chopping board, then each half sliced finely, given a quarter turn, and sliced through again. Thus one has a mass of material already reduced to tiny cubes to start with. To chop it more finely, hold the chopping knife in such a way that the tip of the thumb and the curled knuckle of the forefinger touch the base of the blade, while the fingers of the other hand are held loosely against the top of the blade toward the tip. This creates an easy leverage and one need not press or force the knife.

To chop parsley, do not first tear off the leaves — you will have no control over a loose, weightless flurry of shifting leaves. A branch of parsley separates at one point into three stems, each culminating in leaves, the central stem being longer than the others. Snap the central stem free from the others and form a tight bouquet by pulling all the stems, one after the other, between thumb and forefinger until the compact cluster of leaves prevents them from slipping further. Hold the tight little bundle firmly against the chopping board while slicing through the leaves to form a mass of tiny threads.

TO PEEL AND SEED TOMATOES

With a sharply pointed paring knife, core each tomato, cutting out a cone from the stem end, and slit the skin in the form of a cross on the underside, or flower end. Plunge the tomatoes into boiling water and drain immediately. Grasp one of the skin tips at the heart of the cross between thumb and knife blade and slip off a section of skin, pulling toward the stem end. (Because fruits ripen progressively from flower end to stem end, the skin always clings more firmly at the stem end.) Repeat. Halve each tomato, cutting horizontally to expose cross sections of the seed pockets. Squeeze each half, giving it a firm shake to rid it of the seeds, or, to avoid crushing, force out the seeds from each pocket with the tip of the little finger and give the half a shake.

TO PEEL RAW, SHELLED ALMONDS OR PISTACHIOS; TO BLANCH ALMONDS

Plunge the almonds or pistachios into boiling water for a few seconds, then drain them and spread them onto a strong kitchen towel. Fold the towel over them or place another towel on top and rub vigorously — a large proportion will have come free of their skins. The remaining skins will be loosened and the nuts will slip free when pinched.

The term "blanching" (in other contexts synonymous with parboiling), when applied to almonds, means soaking the peeled almonds in cold water to whiten them.

TO PEEL GARLIC

On a chopping board, cut off the bottom tip of the garlic clove (where it was attached to the head). Place the flat of a knife blade on top of the clove, give it a smack with the heel of your free hand, and lift off the peel. The clove will be slightly crushed; if it should remain unbruised, a lighter tap on the knife blade will still rupture the skin's hold and make it easier to remove.

ARTICHOKE HEARTS AND ARTICHOKE BOTTOMS

When the tough outer leaves are removed from a small, tender artichoke, the dark green surfaces pared, and the inner leaf tips trimmed, what is left describes a heart shape. If the artichoke is so young that the choke has not formed, it is left whole; otherwise, the heart is quartered and the choke cut out. Hearts need no preliminary cooking; whole, quartered, or thinly sliced, butter-stewed or sautéed in olive oil, they garnish scrambled eggs or omelettes, meat stews and panfried or baked fish, or they join other vegetables in various ragouts.

Larger artichokes have a special place in the traditional French kitchen because of the fanciful and decorative uses to which their bottoms are put: as containers, hot or cold, for vegetable combinations or purees, mousses, poached or *mollet* eggs, *foie gras,* and an infinity of little ragouts — assemblages of crayfish tails, diced lobster or prawn tails, wild mushrooms, diced truffle, asparagus tips, sweetbreads, cocks' combs, and kidneys, etc. — usually in *velouté*-based or *demi-glace*–based sauces.

Even for bottoms, tenderness is a desirable quality. Round green globe artichokes grow larger than the elongated violet varieties — they can be quite large and still tender. Indications of age and toughness are dried, brown outer leaves, an indentation in profile at the base of the leaves, and relatively narrow stems in proportion to the size of the artichoke. (A young artichoke has a thick, fleshy stem but the stem does not grow as the artichoke becomes larger.)

The cut flesh of artichokes discolors rapidly in contact with air and in most metallic cooking vessels; it turns black in contact with carbon-steel knife blades, and the blackened surfaces have an acrid taste. Use a sharp stainless-steel paring knife, keep a small bowl of lemon juice for dipping or a half lemon for rubbing the surface to prevent discoloration as you work, and choose stainless steel, enameled ironware, or earthenware for cooking.

Paring artichokes is called "turning" because of the spiral motion involved. To turn an artichoke, either for hearts or for bottoms, first break off the stem at

the base. (The stem of an older artichoke contains fibrous strings that reach into the bottom and that are pulled out when the stem is broken; if the stem is sliced off, the strings remain in the bottom.) One by one, bend the tough outer leaves downward until the fleshy base on the inside of the leaf snaps; pull the leaf free, leaving the fleshy base attached to the artichoke bottom. A dozen or more must be removed — stop when the remaining leaves are pale in color and tender all the way through at the base. To remove the tough tips of the remaining leaves, slice off the upper part of the artichoke — for a heart, remove one-third to one-half of the artichoke, for a bottom about two-thirds or, for an old artichoke, nearly all, the leaves being sliced off near their base, just above the bottom. Holding the artichoke upside down, begin paring at the base, where the stem was torn off. The knife should be held in a more or less stationary position while the artichoke is turned with the other hand, removing a spiral of dark green surface flesh. For a heart, only the bottom is pared, with the remaining tender leaves left untouched; for a bottom, the spiraling continues, removing the extremities of the remaining leaves, so that the final shape resembles a flattened sphere. Any dark green parts remaining should be trimmed off. The chokes are not removed until after cooking.

In professional kitchens, artichoke bottoms are cooked in a *blanc* — a flour and water slurry with some lemon juice added to the cooking liquid — to keep them white. With the following method, they will have a grayish cast, perhaps less attractive to the eye, but the artichoke's flavor is better retained. Plunge the bottoms into salted boiling water to which has been added a sprig of thyme, a bay leaf, and a trickle of olive oil. Cook at a simmer or a light boil, covered, for ten to forty minutes, depending on the quality of the artichokes. They are done when a sharply pointed knife penetrates with a slight resistance — they should remain firm. Unless the bottoms are for immediate use, transfer them to a bowl, cool them in their cooking liquid, and refrigerate them in their cooking liquid, covered, until ready for use. Before using them, carefully remove the chokes, using a teaspoon to pry them loose, and sponge the artichoke bottoms dry with a towel. For cold preparations, they are now ready for use; if they are to be served hot, they should be gently cooked in butter for a further ten or fifteen minutes, which greatly enhances their flavor.

USING A DRUM SIEVE

Drum sieves are made with either metal or nylon screens; fine-meshed nylon produces the smoothest purees and will not alter the taste of certain foods that fear the contact of metal. A plastic pastry scraper, sometimes oval in shape, sometimes in the form of a rectangle with two rounded corners, is the only practical instrument for passing material through the mesh; a pestle is impractical and also risks damaging the sieve. When a particularly fine puree is not necessary, an ordinary bowl-shaped sieve and a wooden pestle will do the work more rapidly; however, the quality of certain purees depends on their fineness. A drum

sieve's most valuable use is for the passage of raw flesh or cooked vegetables that have already been reduced to a paste, a semi-puree, or a coarse puree in a mortar, a food processor, or a vegetable mill.

For loose-textured or semiliquid material, place the sieve on a flat surface, high wall down, with a soup plate underneath to collect the puree. The pastry scraper should be held firmly between the thumb and four fingers, with the fingers reaching almost to the lower edge. It should be held nearly flat (at something less than a forty-five-degree angle) and firmly against the mesh and drawn toward oneself in rhythmic repetition while the drum is turned in a circle with more or less regularity by the other hand. The thicker the material, the less regularly the drum need be turned; finally, when working with a small quantity of stiff substance, it is no longer useful to turn the drum. The stiffer the material, the greater should be the care taken ahead of time to reduce it to a consistent puree, and the smaller should be the quantity worked with at a time.

In passing pounded or processed raw meats, no more than a tablespoonful at a time should be attempted. A plate is no longer necessary; the sieve may be placed directly on a clean work surface. To facilitate cleaning, confine the work to the central area of the mesh without touching the drum with the scraper. To spread out the material that collects on the undersurface of the scraper, draw the scraper flat across the mesh from time to time. After passing each spoonful, scrape the surface of the sieve clean and discard the residue. Clean off the puree clinging to the underside of the sieve and begin again.

SKIMMING

There are three different kinds of skimming, for which, in French cooking terminology, there are three verbs: *écumer* (to scum), *dégraisser* (to degrease), and *dépouiller* (to skin). The first two are generally understood and respected. *Dépouillement* (skinning) is too often misunderstood or merely sidestepped. It is a combined cleansing (or purification) and reduction, essential, in particular, to any stock-based sauce bound by a roux (flour cooked in butter or other fat), but also to unbound stock reductions, as in the preparation of *glace de viande*. On this cleansing depend the digestibility, the clarity of flavor, and the suave texture of a sauce.

A heavy saucepan no larger than necessary to contain the sauce or stock will, because of the liquid's limited surface area and its proximity to the rim of the saucepan, prevent too rapid a reduction and make skimming easier. Bring the liquid to a boil, move the pan partially off the heat — or, if it is a small flame, off center — and adjust the heat to maintain a very light boil at one side only of the liquid's surface. A skin will begin to form on the still surface — on a stock, it will be no more than a veil; on a sauce, it will be quite heavy, collecting and growing thicker at the edge of the saucepan farthest from the heat. Into this skin are drawn fats and fine solids in suspension — in fact, for a sauce, everything that went into the roux must be pulled out again except the binding principle itself. (The silken pellicle that forms on an unbound stock is quite different, with only traces of darker deposit gradually precipitating into it.) The skin must be periodically removed, neither with haste nor too often — the skin needs time to form solidly enough to be easily separated from the sauce (it will not go away but, given plenty of time, will be easier to remove). Keep a bowl and a tablespoon beside the saucepan; with the edge of the spoon, delicately draw the wrinkling skin to the edge of the pan farthest from the heat, gather it onto the tilted spoon against the pan's edge, taking care not to spoon up any sauce, and discard it. With the first couple of skinnings, loose, floating fat may appear on the still surface; carefully remove it. When no more fat is drawn into the skin's structure and the forming skin acquires a smooth, untroubled, satiny surface, the sauce is sufficiently cleansed. (With a reducing stock, one skins infrequently but stops only when the desired reduction is achieved.) This cleansing may require from forty minutes to a couple of hours, and the degree of reduction may vary from about one-third to well over half.

The type of meat stew (*gibelotte, navarin, coq au vin,* etc.) that is made by first coloring meat and aromatics in fat, then sprinkling with flour before moistening with stock, wine, water, etc. and simmering until the meat is tender, is too often only summarily degreased, a good bit of indigestible cooked fat remaining in suspension. Its sauce, strained and left to settle briefly to remove the fat that rises to the surface, is always vastly improved by both the cleansing and the reduction described above. Because the sauce has already cooked with the meat, floury tastes having disappeared, twenty minutes to half an hour of cleansing is usually enough; it is then poured back over the meat and its garnish and simmered briefly before serving.

AROMATICS

Basic methods of cooking do not change; it is the choice of aromatics and the ways in which they are used that distinguish not only national and regional styles but the personalized cuisines of individuals. To illustrate but a few national differences: in Italy, garlic cloves are fried in olive oil until they begin to color and then are discarded before the other elements of a stew or sauce are added, only the waft of garlic flavor in the oil remaining to perfume the dish; the French chop or crush it, sweat it in oil without coloring, to avoid the bitterness of browned garlic, and leave it to disintegrate through slow cooking; the Spanish chop the garlic, fry it until brown, and cook it with other ingredients, infusing into the preparation a more violent flavor. Basil, in Italy, is put to multiple and wonderful uses, often in combination with tomatoes, raw or cooked, particularly in Sicily and southern Italy but also, of course, in the Genovese pesto; in France, although it commonly occurs in seventeenth- and eighteenth-century recipes, basil is now traditionally used only in the south, abundantly and exclusively for the concoction of *soupe au pistou,* an antique heritage from Liguria; in Greece, it is planted to ward off flies but is never used in the kitchen. Oregano, a standby of southern Italy and of Greece, is so foreign to French usage that, although it grows wild, scenting the air throughout southern France, few people recognize it in its natural state and, dried and crumbled, it is identified as *l'herbe à pizza* — "the pizza herb." Dill, one of the commonest herbs in Scandinavian, northern European, and Russian cuisines, associated in particular with fish and crustaceans, was until recently virtually unknown to French cuisine; in the last three or four years, however, it has become very common on the menus of fashionable restaurants — usually in combination with raw salmon. The French who are now aware of its existence still rarely know it by its French name, *aneth,* but call it, instead, *fenouil bâtard* — "bastard fennel."

HERBS

The herbs common to the French kitchen are all contained in *fines herbes* and the *bouquet-garni.*

FINES HERBES AND PERSILLADE

Parsley, chives, chervil, and tarragon are the *fines herbes,* used separately or in combination, chopped, to garnish salads of all sorts, vegetables, and sauced meat or fish preparations, added to omelettes and crepe batters, and so forth. Flat parsley is much finer than the curly variety; it is easy to grow (it is biennial but goes to seed in its second year so must be planted anew each spring) and of recent years has become increasingly common on the market. The Provençal *persillade,* a mixture of chopped parsley and garlic (either chopped or, preferably, pounded to a paste in a mortar) is added to all rapid sautés *à la provençale* (vegetables, mushrooms, frogs' legs, scallops, shrimp, strips of lamb heart, etc.) a minute or so before removing them from the heat and finishing with a squeeze of lemon. It may be incorporated into any number of stuffings and, in alliance with olive oil and a bit of lemon juice, serves as a marinade for various meats and offal to be skewered and grilled *en brochette.* French tarragon (the variety called "Russian tarragon" has no taste) does not mix well with other herbs outside of the *fines herbes* group but is often used alone in the cooking of fish and white meats — sometimes, but less successfully, with beef; infused into a hot preparation, it can be overpowering and should be used with discretion. Chopped fresh herbs should be cleanly cut, minuscule particles that sprinkle freely; to avoid a sticky mess, the herbs must be absolutely dry and the knife sharp.

BOUQUET-GARNI

A *bouquet-garni* is a bundle of aromatics, usually herbs enclosed in a sheath formed by a celery branch and leek, tied up to prevent the contents from cooking apart and dispersing into the dish and to permit its easy removal. The tough but flavorful green parts of leeks, too often discarded, are perfect for this purpose, and instead of celery a small stalk or leaf of lovage, which has a wilder and stronger but similar flavor, may be tucked into the bouquet. The herbs that are always present are European bay leaf, thyme, and parsley; the stems of parsley, the leaves of which have been chopped for other purposes, will do very well or they may be replaced by the root of a parsley plant for its more distinct, parsnip-like savor. The bouquets of Provence often contain, in addition, perennial (also called "winter" or "mountain") savory, known locally as *pebre d'ase* — "ass's pepper"   and, for certain long-cooking stews, a thinly pared strip of dried orange peel (taken from a Seville or bitter orange, when the season permits). Finally, wild fennel is often used in fish *fumets;* it is essential to bouillabaisse and Provençal fish soups, and bouquets of fennel are usually stuffed into the cavities of sea bass and the Mediterranean breams — *dorade, sar,* or *pageot* — before grilling.

The size of a *bouquet-garni* depends as much on the length of cooking time as on the quantity of food in preparation — all of the herbs common to *bouquets* are quite aggressive during the beginning of a cooking process but their flavors are attenuated and refined, individual definitions disappearing in a harmonic ensemble, with long cooking. A *bouquet* the size of a wine cork may serve for a ragout of vegetables or tender meats that need no more than half an hour's cooking, whereas a large fist-sized *bouquet* is essential to the stock pot, *daube,* or *pot-au-feu.*

To tie a *bouquet-garni,* first wind the string tightly round a number of times, up and down the length of the bouquet — a single bracelet of string will not do the job. In the recipes to come, when a *bouquet-garni* is called for with no further precision, it always means thyme, bay leaf, and parsley wrapped with a stalk of celery and leek leaves.

OTHER HERBS

Hyssop, one of the biblical herbs and much used in ancient Roman cookery, is little known today. It is easy to grow and most interesting fresh, its finely chopped leaves, delicately bitter and refreshing, adding liveliness to many a salad or marinated raw fish. The tiny, lacy, labiate flowers of hyssop, clear ultramarine, are ravishing scattered over a salad accented by the yellow of hard-boiled egg yolks, or atop thinly sliced raw salmon or the silver sheen of very fresh filleted fish of the sardine-herring family, the one and the other marinated in a bit of lemon juice and olive oil.

Sage and rosemary are vehement herbs. Sage acquires a musty taste when dried. Its fresh leaves, pressed to the surfaces of oiled pork chops before being grilled over wood embers, or, in the Italian manner, sautéed until slightly crisp in the same pan to be scattered over sautéed calf's liver, seem to me to be its most pertinent functions. The smoke of smoldering rosemary is as delicate as its volatile oils are violent; scattered over the coals a few seconds before removing a steak or chop from the grill, it imparts a flavor that is subtle and exciting. Fresh, supple summits of rosemary branches may also be used to brush oil or a marinade over meats or poultry as they grill, leaving a delicate hint of their presence, or a sharpened rosemary branch with a decorative tuft of leaves remaining at the other end can be used as a skewer for brochettes of meats to be grilled. The flowers of both rosemary and sage can be amusing decorative elements in a salad.

Cultivated marjoram (also called "sweet knotted") is a lovely herb that should nonetheless be used judiciously. The fresh flower buds, just before they open, have a finer and more distinctive fragrance than the leaves. When the herb is finely chopped, its alliance with eggs, scrambled or in omelettes, seems predestined; it can be added to foaming brown butter before it is poured over poached brains, and can advantageously replace the chopped sage that is sometimes added to an Italian egg-and-Parmesan–bound ricotta stuffing for ravioli.

Of lesser interest for the purposes of this book, mint can be attractive with certain vegetable or fruit salads, in particular with a cream and lemon sauce. Fresh coriander (Arab parsley, Chinese parsley, cilantro, *dhania,* etc.), abundantly used in Oriental, Arab, and Mexican cuisines, is repellent in the presence of wine. Burnet and borage seem to me to be devoid of interest except for the beautiful little star-shaped blue flowers of the latter, again useful as a salad *décor*.

HERB MIXTURE

Tastes may differ and individual tastes can change. . . . I was surprised, upon rereading the first edition of *The French Menu Cookbook*, to note that I had recommended the addition of rosemary to an herb mixture — less surprised that I had firmly discouraged the reader from using a blender or food processor to reduce the crumbled herbs to a powder. In fact, I have for many years now prepared my dried herb mixture in the same way: thyme is picked in April as it comes into flower, tied in bundles, not too tightly, with raffia, and hung upside down in the kitchen until it is thoroughly dried, then packed into large paper bags, over which other paper bags are inverted, to protect the herbs from dust, and stored. In July both winter savory, before flowering, and oregano, as it comes into flower, are picked and treated in the same way. (These three all grow wild on the Provençal hillsides.) Cultivated marjoram is picked repeatedly throughout the summer as it comes into flower and treated like the others. In early autumn all of the paper bags are assembled and each herb bundle is rubbed and rolled, with cloth-gloved hands, over a large basin until no more flowers and few leaves remain; a couple of handfuls at a time, the herbs are first reduced to a fine crumble in a food processor, then shaken and rubbed through a sieve into another basin; fragments of branches are discarded and remaining leaves and flowers, insufficiently crumbled to pass through, are returned to the processor with the next batch. The herbs are then stored in sealed jars. Because I prepare them in sufficient quantity to share with friends, I have often been able to compare the staying power of stored herbs with those newly prepared; they hold perfectly for a year or so, but during the second year the green color begins to assume a more grayish tint and the fragrance loses in intensity while nonetheless remaining characteristic, still a far superior product to the little flacons of indefinable, dusty, peppery remains distributed commercially, which, one is tempted to believe, must surely be stored for many years before being loosed on the market.

The proportions of the four herbs are somewhat variable, depending on how much of each I have been able to collect during a season, but they always follow a descending order with thyme in the largest quantity, followed by oregano, marjoram, and savory. The mixture is invaluable for seasoning sausage meats, terrines, and other charcuterie and stuffings of all sorts. In a hastily assembled rustic stew, a healthy pinch, with or without a bay leaf tossed in, can often replace a *bouquet-garni*.

AROMATIC VINEGAR

The original edition of *The French Menu Cookbook* contains a formula for aromatic vinegar in which two crushed garlic cloves, a bay leaf, two tablespoons of crumbled herb mixture, a few sage leaves, a couple of cloves, and a few grains of coriander are added to a quart of hot red-wine vinegar that has been reduced to half over heat; the receptacle is covered and the aromatics left to infuse overnight before the vinegar is strained. This method is valuable in particular for improving commercial vinegars.

I now prefer to use a homemade red-wine vinegar, unaltered by heating, in which aromatics macerate for a month or longer before the vinegar is strained through a thickly muslin-lined funnel into bottles, corked, and laid down to rest; like wine, it improves with aging. The *vinaigrier* is a fifteen-quart oak cask kept at room (kitchen) temperature. At approximately eight-month periods the vinegar is drawn off, down to the level of the spigot, into a ten-quart stoneware jug that has been packed with leftover herb bundles after they have been rubbed for the above herb mixture, a few bay leaves, a head or two of garlic cloves, separated and coarsely crushed, and a sprig each of fresh sage and rosemary. The jug is covered with a plate and forgotten until time for bottling, and the *vinaigrier* is refilled from bottles of red wine, themselves filled from leftover glasses and bottle ends, corked, and stored in readiness. During the time in the keg, as the wine is slowly transformed into vinegar, about one-third of it disappears through evaporation. Of the various other flavored vinegars with which I have experimented, the only one I find particularly exciting is that in which an abundance of elder flowers have macerated; they are first spread out on a sheet or on newspapers to dry for a few days in a room away from direct sunlight, then macerated with the vinegar for a month before it is strained and bottled. This vinegar is especially attractive with meat salads.

SALADS

The indications for salads in these menus are deliberately vague. With the exception of the brittle, watery-fibered lettuce known as "iceberg," any of the commonly available lettuces may be used in salads described as "tossed green" or "mixed green." A salad enlivened with *fines herbes* should be light in flavor; greens with peppery or bitter nuances, such as the various members of the chicory family, are best avoided. Chervil is the most delicate of the *fines herbes* and may be used abundantly, the feathery leaves simply torn from the stems without being chopped.

Peppery and spicy leafy things, often with a refreshing, cleansing edge of bitterness, are particularly welcome following robust, rustic preparations or the rich savors of game. Rocket is one of the most exciting of all and easy to grow from seed. Young dandelions and purslane are both garden pests but lovely salad elements. Watercress or field cress, lamb's lettuce (corn salad, *mâche*), red Verona chicory (*radicchio*), or young spinach and sorrel leaves can all lend exuberance to a salad in this spirit, and a breath of garlic goes well with all these things. Finely chopped hyssop leaves or tender spring shoots of savory and basil leaves, gently torn in pieces (chopping blackens them), are among the herbs most adaptable to these salads, and bright, multicolored, and peppery-tasting nasturtium blossoms and buds scattered across the dark green leaves will explode in beauty.

Any salad must be well dried. Nothing is more repulsive than a bowl of salad dripping in water and vinegar with a few globules of oil floating here and there. A salad basket is useful for drying tougher-leafed greens but fragile lettuce leaves should be carefully dried between towels. Many of the wild or semiwild greens

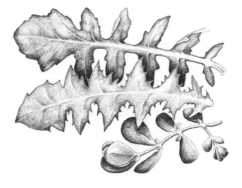

are small-leafed and escape from the whirling salad basket; these, too, must be dried in a towel but may be treated with less care. Many people swear by a salad-drying mechanism containing a perforated drum that is operated by a revolving handle; leaves whirled in this instrument, like those from a salad basket, often require supplementary drying in a towel. Flowers should, of course, never be treated with insecticide; they should be freshly picked and used unwashed, as should garden herbs if they are free of soil or dust.

The quality of a vinaigrette depends on the oil and the vinegar; nothing can replace the fresh, clean, fruity flavor of young virgin olive oil. Depending on the strength of the vinegar, on the elements in a salad, and, to a degree, on personal taste, proportions may vary from three to five parts of oil to one of vinegar. Pungent salads can take a stronger dose of vinegar than delicate lettuces. Unless the bowl is to be rubbed with garlic, seasoning should be limited to salt and pepper. (The common addition of mustard serves to disguise bad vinegar and bad or tasteless oil; it will mask the flavor of good vinegar and annihilate the fruit of good oil.) The easiest and most attractive way to present a salad is to prepare the vinaigrette directly in the salad bowl (not a sticky wooden one), rubbing the bowl first with garlic, if used, then adding the seasoning and vinegar, stirring until the salt has been dissolved (it will refuse to dissolve in the presence of oil), and, finally, adding the oil. The serving fork and spoon may then be crossed in the bowl and the salad leaves arranged on top so that they do not contact the dressing. In this way the salad may be prepared before the meal and presented as such, with herbs and, perhaps, flowers scattered over the surface, then tossed the instant before serving. A moistened tea towel, wrung out, may be laid loosely over to keep it fresh until the service.

Although too eccentric for daily use, fresh walnut or hazelnut oils can occasionally replace all or part of the olive oil in a vinaigrette. Unlike olive oil, they rapidly turn rancid, so it is essential to be certain of one's sources. A pleasant occasional change from vinaigrette is a lemon and cream dressing, made in exactly the same way (but never with garlic); a touch of mustard can be dissolved in the lemon juice before adding cream, and *fines herbes* or chopped fresh dill leaves go well. It is better with tender lettuce than with pungent greens.

AROMATIC VEGETABLES

Primordial among aromatic vegetables are the alliums — onions, shallots, garlic, leeks. Without them we would be helpless in the kitchen. Next in order of importance are carrots, mushrooms, and celery. The two commonest aromatic-vegetable–base preparations in French cuisine are *mirepoix* and *duxelles*.

MIREPOIX

Mirepoix is chopped onion and carrot, supplemented by a bit of chopped celery, crumbled herbs, and, sometimes, chopped parsley, sweated, usually in butter or oil, until tender and rid of the vegetables' humidity. Some cooks prefer to substitute shallots, in part or entirely, for the onions, and some chopped raw ham or *pancetta* is often added.

For the purposes of this book only the term *mirepoix* will be used, but because a number of terms are sometimes used interchangeably and confusingly, in both French- and English-language cookbooks, some definitions may be useful. *"Brunoise"* and *"paysanne"* are not, in themselves, finished preparations but simply indicate the way in which the vegetables are cut up. For a *brunoise,* the vegetables are more or less finely diced; for a *paysanne,* they are sliced or coarsely cut up. A *mirepoix* is made from a *brunoise.* (However, when sweated and diced vegetables are used to garnish a consommé, they are known as *brunoise,* not *mirepoix.*) A *matignon* is prepared in exactly the same way as a *mirepoix,* using sliced vegetables — a *paysanne* — rather than diced. A *mirepoix à la bordelaise* is very finely chopped and always contains parsley. Its name derives from its presence in the traditional preparation of crayfish *à la bordelaise.* (In its simplest expression, crayfish are sautéed over high heat; as they begin to turn red, *mirepoix* and a pinch of cayenne are added and sautéed with them. They are then flamed with Cognac, moistened with white wine, and simmered, covered, for eight or ten minutes. Finally the crayfish are removed and the cooking juices reduced over high heat, buttered off the heat, and poured over the crayfish. Finger bowls are essential.)

Mirepoix is most often used as an aromatic base for braised preparations (meats or vegetables, simmered, covered, in a relatively small amount of liquid — often stock or wine or a combination — that forms the sauce of the finished dish) but sometimes serves also to enrobe pieces of meat or flattened small birds before wrapping them in caul to be roasted or grilled. The degree of fineness to which the vegetables are chopped depends on the use to which the *mirepoix* is put. When used to coat meats, they must be chopped very finely for the mixture to stick together. As a braising base, they are finely chopped for relatively short cooking periods (with sweetbreads, for instance, or certain vegetables that require no more than three-quarters of an hour's braising); with meats that braise for several hours (veal *fricandeau,* beef bourguignon or *à la mode,* braised oxtail), they are quite coarsely chopped. This is important because the sauces are usually strained and a fine *mirepoix,* over a prolonged cooking period, will fall apart into the sauce whereas, during a short cooking period, the *mirepoix* will fail to give all of its flavor to the sauce unless finely chopped.

If used for coating meats, the *mirepoix* is best sweated in butter, which, because it firms up as it cools, makes a more malleable and adherent mixture. If it is used as a braising base, an alternate method to the one that follows consists in sweating the vegetables and herbs in the oven without the addition of fat. The flavor infused into the braising juices is, to my taste, purer, and the final cleansing of the sauce is simplified since there is no fat from the *mirepoix* to be removed by skimming. Choose a heavy, lidded oven casserole or sauté pan large enough so that the ingredients can be spread over the bottom to a depth of no more than approximately half an inch. Put the vegetables, covered, into a moderate oven

(375°F) for about half an hour, checking after twenty minutes to make certain they are not browning; stir them and lower the oven heat if necessary. After half an hour they should begin to caramelize lightly around the edges. Remove the lid and return the casserole to the oven, stirring every two or three minutes, until excess moisture has evaporated — about ten minutes. If the mixture has begun to stick to the bottom, pour in a few drops of white wine and scrape it free with a wooden spoon.

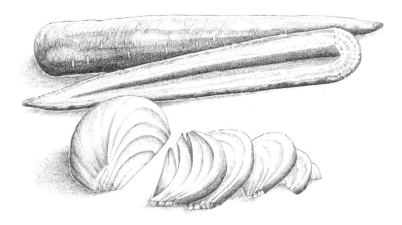

MIREPOIX
2 large carrots (*5 ounces*), peeled, cored, and diced
1 large onion (*5 ounces*), peeled and chopped
1 small rib celery, diced
large pinch herb mixture (*or thyme alone, if preferred*), finely crumbled
½ bay leaf, finely crumbled
small handful chopped parsley
1 ounce unsalted butter
salt

To dice carrots, cut them in half lengthwise, pry out the woody cores with a small knife, and, with a chopping knife, slice each half thinly lengthwise. Flatten these slices out on the work surface and slice through them several times to reduce them to sticks; then, holding them together, slice finely crosswise. For a very fine *mirepoix,* chop through the mass several times. To chop the onion, cut it in two from top to bottom, set a half flat side down, slice it thinly, still lengthwise, then turn the mass of slices around and slice through them. Continue chopping to the desired fineness.

Melt the butter in a heavy sauté pan, add all the ingredients, and cook very gently, stirring at regular intervals, for about half an hour. The vegetables should be cooked but not browned.

DUXELLES

The essential difference between *duxelles* and *mirepoix* is the substitution of mushrooms for carrots, but because the mushrooms need a much shorter cooking time than the onions and, at the same time, throw off an abundant liquid in contact with heat, the mechanics of the two preparations differ. The onions must be first gently softened over low heat but the mushrooms should be added and sautéed over high heat to rid them as rapidly as possible of their moisture. Cultivated mushrooms are commonly used but superior *duxelles* may be made from wild mushrooms and, in particular, with *cèpes* (*Boletus edulis,* Italian *porcini*). For reasons of economy, mushroom stems can be transformed into *duxelles* when the caps are used elsewhere.

Duxelles is sometimes used, like *mirepoix,* as an aromatic braising base but more often as a stuffing, either alone or as one of several ingredients in a forcemeat. It lends aromatic support to innumerable fish gratins, the gratin dish thinly coated with *duxelles,* the raw fish, sliced, filleted, or boned and opened out, placed atop, covered with *duxelles,* sprinkled with white wine and buttered bread crumbs, and baked for a quarter of an hour. A *duxelles* sauce is *duxelles* simmered in white wine, lent body with a bit of pureed tomato, and buttered off the heat. (*Demi-glace* will lend it more consistency in a professional kitchen.)

DUXELLES
 1 large onion (*5 ounces*), finely chopped
 1 ounce unsalted butter
 ½ pound mushrooms, finely chopped (*at the last minute*)
 salt
 handful finely chopped parsley
 suspicion of freshly grated nutmeg
 dash of lemon juice

In a wide sauté pan or large heavy frying pan, sweat the onion over low heat until it is soft and yellowed. Add the mushrooms and turn the heat up. Salt. Stir or toss until the liquid has evaporated and the mixture is fairly stiff. Stir in the parsley, lower the heat, grate in a tiny bit of nutmeg, and, when the mixture begins to stick to the pan, stir in the lemon juice and remove from the heat.

TRUFFLES

Those who have been disappointed upon tasting for the first time a dish containing truffles — or who categorically proclaim truffles to be "overrated" — have never tasted fresh or correctly preserved truffles. It is true that certain varieties of non-commercialized truffle, grayish in color, are of little interest (one exists in North Africa, another in Burgundy), but no one who has ever entered a room containing either a fresh Italian white, or Piedmont, truffle or a fresh black truffle, often designated as Périgord (the same variety, from parts of Italy and Spain, finds its way to France to supplement the productions of Périgord and the Vaucluse), will ever forget the stimulating, pervading intensity and uniqueness of these aromas, so different the one from the other. With overlapping and leeway, the season for fresh white truffles is October to December, and that for black truffles December to March; both are at their best in the latter part of the season, but the prices, extremely variable depending on the year's abundance, reach their height at Christmas.

White truffles are customarily shaved, raw, over a hot preparation — pasta, risotto, scrambled eggs, rapidly sautéed chicken breast or sweetbreads, etc. — at the moment of serving. They are also shaved over salads and, chopped, added to the hot *anchoïade* called *bagna cauda* that serves as a dip for raw vegetables. In Italy the white truffle represents the ultimate gastronomic experience. Such are the vagaries of national habit or prejudice that in France, where the black truffle reigns supreme, white truffles are not available and are practically unknown.

To give their best, black truffles need to be teased — macerated, marinated, steeped, sweated, or left in contact with other ingredients for a certain amount of time. They are rarely used raw (though for most preparations they should only be heated through) but, steeped first in a vinaigrette containing very little vinegar (if the vinegar is not impeccable, substitute a few drops of lemon juice), they are wonderful as a first-course salad in combination with firm-fleshed potatoes, boiled in their skins, peeled, sliced, and tossed with the truffles and vinaigrette while still hot; after the potatoes have cooled, absorbing the truffle flavor, a few leaves of lettuce and lobes of peeled, fresh walnuts may be added. (If the walnut skins cling tightly, dip the shelled nuts first in boiling water for a couple of seconds.)

Black truffles are often wasted in decoration. The most intelligent uses to which they can be put as aromatic support are as additions, chopped, sliced, diced, or juliènned, to sauces (often infused first in a bit of warm Cognac, Madeira, or port to release their perfume), terrine mixtures, and forcemeats or for truffling poultry and meats, occasionally fish, the mixtures assembled, entirely or in part, and the meats truffled as far in advance of cooking as possible to permit a maximum penetration of the truffle's magic.

To truffle poultry, the fragile membranes between skin and flesh are ruptured by prodding with fingertips through the neck opening, loosening the skin from breast and legs; slices of truffle are then tucked into place between flesh and skin and the bird is pulled into shape by trussing. It is best if then refrigerated for a day or so, unwrapped or, at most, loosely wrapped in a tea towel, placed on a grill with air circulating all around, until an hour or two before roasting, braising, or poaching. When the bird is poached, softened outlines of irregular black discs appearing in a polka-dot pattern beneath the translucent skin, it is quaintly termed *en demi-deuil* — "in half-mourning." (One of Alexandre Dumaine's great specialties was truffled chicken steamed in the vapors of a dense stock; the prepared chicken was placed on a plate held just above the stock by a tripod, all in a hermetically sealed earthenware *pot-au-feu*. The juices that collected in the plate were its only sauce, and creamed morels accompanied it.)

Beef fillet or, for smaller animals, boned loin with the tenderloin attached are the most practical cuts of meat for truffling. A beef fillet is partially split and opened out like a book, the opened surfaces repeatedly pierced with the tip of a small knife, pieces of truffle forced into the slits, and the fillet closed up and tied in its original form. Pork is the most interesting possibility for truffled loin, a row of truffle pieces tucked between the loin and the tenderloin, more inserted into knife slits pierced in the loin, and the meat rolled up and tied. Both are held overnight in dishes adapted to their forms, marinated in a bit of white wine and olive oil and covered tightly, removed from the refrigerator a couple of hours before cooking. The beef is wiped dry, rubbed with oil or softened butter, seasoned, and roasted rare, its marinade used to deglaze the roasting pan. The pork is seasoned, half-roasted, excess fat poured off, and basted repeatedly, first with its marinade, then with more white wine as needed (never more than a few spoonfuls of liquid in the pan at a time), until coated in a rich caramel glaze; it is at least as good cold, the following day, as hot from the oven.

Small tender cuts of meat may simply be coated with chopped truffles (made to adhere with pressure from the flat of a knife blade), held on a plate, covered, for an hour or so, arranged in a buttered sauté pan or oven dish, anointed with melted butter and a few drops of Cognac (for game) or white wine, a buttered sheet of parchment paper placed atop, and the covered dish placed in a hot oven for eight to fifteen minutes, depending on the heaviness and conductibility of the dish, the size of the meat cuts, and the degree of doneness required. They may be served as such or their juices can be boiled up with some cream or with a bit of white wine and a dab of reduced stock or *glace de viande* to make a little sauce. Game rejoices in the company of truffles; boned-out hare fillets, shaved free of their skinlike surface membrane, are sublime prepared in this way. Skinned and boned game bird or chicken breasts or fish fillets can receive the same treatment.

Apart from the many terrines and forcemeats of which truffled sausage meat forms the base (two parts of lean pork to one of fat, salt, pepper, allspice, mixed herbs, pureed garlic, a dash of Cognac, and a handful of chopped truffles), Lyons has two sumptuous sausage specialties. For the misleadingly named *pieds de porc farcis,* blanched and rinsed pigs' feet are braised in stock and Madeira, boned, and cut into pieces; the braising liquid is cleansed of all fat while being reduced to a light syrup, part of which, when nearly cool, is mixed into the sausage mixture. On a piece of caul, a heaping spoonful of the mince is flattened into an elongated triangle, a layer of pigs'-feet pieces pressed onto the surface, another layer of mince formed atop, a slice of truffle placed there for the beauty of the thing, and the package enveloped in caul, ready to be grilled. The remaining braising liquid can be served on the side but the sausages do not really need a sauce; more amusing, perhaps, is to accompany them, in the Bordelais manner, by a platter of raw oysters, alternating mouthfuls of hot sausage, cold oysters, and white Graves. For poaching sausages (*cervelas*), diced back fat, truffles, lean loin or leg cut into larger cubes, and peeled, coarsely chopped pistachios lend textural relief to the basic mixture, which is pushed into large beef sausage casings (lacking a *charcutier*'s funnel, a short length of plastic plumbing pipe will serve) to make loosely packed sausages with no air pockets, tied at each end. They are best if kept for several days or a week before cooking, arranged between two tea towels on a pastry grill, and refrigerated. Pricked with a trussing needle on all sides, immersed in a cooled white-wine *court-bouillon,* brought to a simmer, and kept well beneath the boil for three-quarters of an hour, they are served sliced with a bit of *court-bouillon* spooned over, accompanied by little potatoes boiled in their skins; cold, they are lovely sliced thinly.

Truffles can be slipped into many a vegetable gratin or ragout; I like the combination of little onions, unpeeled garlic cloves, quartered artichoke hearts, a *bouquet-garni,* and a scattering of lettuce *chiffonade,* stewed gently with a bit of butter in the vegetables' juices, tightly covered, for a brief hour, a handful of sliced truffles tossed in ten minutes before swirling in more butter off the heat.

Among the more unusual preparations in which the truffle, instead of lending aromatic support, plays the principal role, a truffle stew is memorable: peeled truffles are cut into wedges, sweated with butter, salt, pepper, and a dribble of Cognac in a garlic-rubbed earthenware casserole, tightly covered over a mere suggestion of heat, and a reduction of aromatic red-wine essence and *demi-glace* — to which the pounded puree of truffle peels has been added — swirled into them before spooning the stew into buttered, oven-toasted, and garlic-stroked individual bread cases. Over and over again, a discreet presence of garlic will etch more brightly the truffle's character.

A good, fresh black truffle is heavy, firm, and resilient, neither hard nor spongy. A cross section reveals a rich, blackish-brown color with a lighter, grayish-brown grain; with cooking, it darkens to near-black. In France, truffles are usually sold with their earth clinging and must be thoroughly brushed under running water and dried; for export they are brushed and ready to use. Deep-freezing is the most practical method for preserving them, each double-wrapped and tightly squeezed in aluminum foil, first frozen as rapidly as possible spread out on a grill, then gathered into an airtight container — a tin box, for instance

— to be kept in the freezer. They should not be permitted to thaw before using them; it is possible to cut through them a few minutes after their removal from the freezer. I have kept them for two years with no sign of alteration. The best sterilized truffles are packed into small jars, a small spoonful of Madeira and salt added before sterilizing. If buying commercially preserved truffles, avoid those that are immersed in liquid — they have been boiled in vats of water and packed in tins or jars that are filled with the water before sterilizing. The flavor is lost.

SALT AND PEPPER

Coarse white sea salt is the best seasoner, no doubt because it contains not only sodium chloride but a number of other salts and minerals from the sea. (The gray sea salt sold in health-food and fancy food shops contains such an abundance of foreign material that it throws a heavy, unsightly scum in cooking and is so moist that it cannot be used in a salt mill.)

It is claimed that different individuals have different salt tolerance levels; what is more certain is that palates adjust, through habit or professional deformation, to varying degrees of saltiness. Many professional cooks habitually oversalt (to my taste), whereas amateur cooks more often err in the opposite direction. Some people, intimidated by fashionable medical theory, prefer to eat tasteless food and to impose it on others.

Salt seasons integrally, by penetration, or superficially, by contrast to unsalted foods (crudités) or undersalted foods (poached or steamed meats and fish, for instance, or tossed salads). Freshly ground salt has an odor and a flavor that disappear in integral seasoning but that can bring a fresh spark of excitement to certain deliberately undersalted foods when sprinkled over at the moment of serving. This, however, must be thought of only as a supplementary seasoning; some penetration of salt in a savory preparation is essential to avoid flat bland-ness, to bring out natural flavors, and to lend relief to aromatic supports.

The quantity of salt used depends on whether all of the salt will remain in the finished preparation and, if so, whether the bulk of the preparation will remain essentially the same or be radically reduced during cooking; a sauce or stock, seasoned to taste before being concentrated through evaporation, will be intol-erably salty after reduction. In such cases, very light salting with adjustment of seasoning after cooking is essential. Certain vegetables that are cooked in a few minutes or less in a large quantity of boiling water, which will then be discarded — little green beans, broccoli, tender cauliflower florets, peeled and finely sliced asparagus, tender little green peas or *mange-tout* peas, etc. — require a large handful of salt for only a tiny fraction of it to penetrate the vegetable delicately; "a small pinch" or "lightly salted boiling water" will have no noticeable effect. A vegetable that demands half an hour's cooking in the same quantity of water would be inedible if the same quantity of salt were added. Mixtures that set during cooking — mousselines, stuffings, terrines, puddings, soufflés, etc. — should be tasted before being put to cook. It is common practice to cook a teaspoonful of the mixture, usually by frying or poaching, to taste it; personally, I find it easier to taste the raw mixture and then spit it out. Remember that foods destined to be eaten cold can take more salt (and often a touch of cayenne) than hot foods.

Salt's capacity to draw out liquids, startlingly demonstrated in the salting down of meats or vegetables, has prompted the elaboration of a number of theories concerning roast and grilled meats (roasts should be seared or half-cooked before being seasoned, meats to be grilled should be seasoned only on the side first to be grilled, then seasoned on the other side just before turning — or they should be seasoned only after being removed from the grill, etc.); one need only taste roast or grilled meats that have been seasoned before being put to cook to realize that not only is there no loss of succulence but the salt has penetrated the meat rather than remaining on the surface, improving its flavor.

For pepper, I like to use a mixture — about three parts of black to two of white and something less than one of allspice. Because the allspice berries are of variable size, the larger ones should be coarsely broken up in a mortar.

The stimulating, spicy perfume of good, freshly ground pepper dissipates in cooking, especially in a liquid medium, and the taste turns dull, acrid, unpleasantly bitter. It is difficult to break the habit of automatically peppering most savory foods but well worthwhile imposing a firm rule *never* to add pepper to stews, soups, stocks, sauces, *court-bouillons*, gratins that cook in liquid — in fact, to anything that bubbles — unless it be at the moment of service or, at least in the case of a *poivrade* sauce, only shortly before. Although the fresh scent of the pepper disappears, the aggressive bitterness does not come through in dry heat — roasts, grills, or rapid sautés; pepper is an automatic and valuable addition to most terrines and forcemeats.

WINE IN COOKING

A wine that is not good to drink is useless in the kitchen, but because wines are transformed when boiled or simmered, their original character completely altered, it is foolish to waste a great wine in this context. Robust, richly colored young reds (Côtes-du-Rhône, generic Bordeaux, Bourgogne Passe-tout-grains, Rioja, Zinfandel) or lightly acidic young whites (Bourgogne Aligoté, most Sauvignon wines, Muscadet, Soave) are sensible choices.

Apart from wine's use in marinades or as the principal moistening agent in many long-cooking stews, a flavorful little juice can be prepared in a few seconds' time for any panfried meat by deglazing the pan with a splash of wine (whatever is in your glass or closest to hand): the meat is removed, any excess fat poured off, the wine added over high heat, and the browned meat juices that have solidified on the bottom of the pan scraped free with a wooden spatula to dissolve in the wine, which is then reduced almost completely before being poured over the meat.

An aromatic red-wine essence is made by pouring a bottle or two of red wine

over a *mirepoix,* bringing it slowly to the boil, and simmering gently until the wine is reduced by about three-quarters; the longer the reduction takes, the more flavor is infused into the wine. It is then strained, the solids pressed to extract all liquid. If more is made than needed, it will keep well, sealed in a jar or bottle and refrigerated. A traditional Bordelaise sauce, usually served with grilled beef, is made by reducing and cleansing equal quantities of red-wine essence and brown sauce, sharpening the sauce with a few drops of lemon juice and adding poached, diced bone marrow at the last minute. Some of this essence added to any red-wine *matelote* or to dishes named *en meurette* or *à la bourguignonne* will deepen the color and the flavor of the sauce. It can enrich the red-wine *fumet* in which fish is sometimes poached, the liquid then reduced and mounted with butter (part of which, for full-bodied flavors like salmon, may be replaced by anchovy butter). Some thirty peeled cloves of garlic, first simmered in lightly salted water to cover for fifteen minutes, drained, and simmered for another five or ten minutes in red-wine essence, the garlic cooking water used to deglaze the roasting pan and added to the essence, provide a wonderful little juice and garnish for a pinkly roasted leg of lamb.

Fine wines can be used to advantage when they need not be heated (Champagne in a sorbet, old Madeira added to an aspic jelly after cooling but before it begins to set, fresh fruits macerated in wine) or, as in the instance of a *sabayon* made from Sauternes, in rapid preparations in which the heat is hardly more than a warming, never approaching a boiling temperature. Certain old wines, faded but not broken, are given a brief resurgence of glory, their lost vitality restored, when poured over lightly sugared fresh fruit — claret on strawberries or Sauternes on sliced peaches.

COURT-BOUILLON

With few exceptions, a *court-bouillon* is salted water in which aromatic vegetables and herbs have been boiled, acidulated either with wine or vinegar. It is a poaching liquid for fish or crustaceans, brains, and sausages, occasionally for artichokes.

The basic aromatics are onion, thyme, and bay leaf. To these may be added garlic, leek, carrot, parsley, celery or lovage, a dried chili pepper, and, for many fish and crustaceans, either fennel or dill. To yield their savors rapidly, the vegetables are finely sliced (the garlic may be crushed), and because acidity frustrates the cooking and dispersion of their flavors, it is best to boil the aromatics for a quarter of

an hour in the salted water before adding wine or vinegar, counting another fifteen to thirty minutes' cooking afterward. The proportion of wine to water can vary greatly — half and half is common; for a vinegar *court-bouillon,* three or four tablespoons of vinegar per quart of water is largely enough. If the vegetables are not to be used as garnish, the *court-bouillon* is strained before use. A leftover fish *court-bouillon* can replace part or all of the water for moistening a fish stock.

STOCKS AND RELATED PREPARATIONS

The bewildering jungle of terms and formulas for stock to be found in French cookery books, each with a precise and seemingly complicated series of manipulations, is disheartening until close inspection reveals them all to be the same thing in different degrees of concentration, whether it be achieved by simple reduction or by moistening new stock elements with an already prepared stock, often preceded by repeated light moistenings, reductions, and deglazings with wine or stock. Most cooks deviate from printed formulas, and no one, in any case, in a home kitchen would deliberately set out to fabricate all of these variations on a theme; they happen along the way, by necessity or by accident, and may all be thought of simply as reduced or reinforced stocks. The relevant terms are discussed in the basic veal-stock recipe that follows.

A family *pot-au-feu,* simmered only until the meat is tender, produces a light beef stock, a *poule-au-pot* a light chicken stock. These leftover broths, occasionally supplemented by a hastily assembled bouillon of chopped aromatics and giblets, are the only stocks known to most home kitchens and, on the whole, they serve very well. They can replace part or all of the water for poaching other meats to become richer stocks and they can be concentrated by reduction.

The deep freeze is useful for collecting potential material for the odd stock — lean trimmings from roasts, steaks, or chops, poultry carcasses and giblets (except for livers), including feet (turned rapidly over a flame until blistered on all surfaces, skin and nails pulled off, rinsed) and heads (plumed, singed, beaks cut off, throat washed free of coagulated blood in running water), hutch rabbit carcasses. (If the stock is to be used for game, wild-rabbit, hare, venison, and game-bird remains will improve it; kid, mutton, or lamb should be used only in stocks intended to moisten those particular meats.) Sliced carrots, onions, and leek greens, two or three crushed garlic cloves, thyme, and a bay leaf are scattered in the bottom of a saucepan to keep the meats from sticking and to facilitate skimming; the meats and carcasses, cut or broken into small pieces, go on top with a pinch of salt and cold water to cover generously; it is brought to a boil, skimmed, gently simmered with the lid ajar, and strained after an hour and a half or two. This is a homely stock that will do wonders, often in combination with wine, for homely foods — braised cabbage (with or without an old pheasant or partridge thrown in), braised pork, pigs' ears, feet, or tongues, rustic soups or rough sauces like those in which leftover meats are often warmed up or which can accompany boiled tongue, breaded and grilled tripe or feet, grilled pork chops, etc. The sauce is often fortified with chopped onion, sharpened with vinegar, sometimes with an addition of pureed tomato, or finished with a dab of mustard; if a variety of chopped things — *duxelles,* capers, sour gherkins, parsley — is added before serving, it is called *sauce hachée* — "chopped sauce."

It is possible, under pressure, to make a small emergency stock from lean minced meats mixed with finely chopped aromatics and cold water, brought to a boil with an occasional stir, and simmered undisturbed, lid ajar, for an hour before straining it through muslin or a tea towel.

A bone stock has too little flavor to be useful except as a possible moistening agent for another stock, reinforcing its gelatinous content. Beef bones, in particular, even when combined with meats, only take up valuable space in a stock pot, having hardly begun to release their gelatin when all of the other ingredients' contributions have been exhausted.

BASIC VEAL STOCK

Veal is at once succulent and anonymous. Veal stock could be likened to an unfinished portrait, its background laid in, the essential volumes and harmonies defined, before the details of particular features are imposed on the abstract structure. Its flavor is soft, deep, and voluptuous without being marked by the eccentricity of individual character; it is the perfect vehicle for other flavors, lending body and support without altering or obscuring their primitive qualities. (Chicken is sweeter, beef firmer in flavor; some of each added to a veal stock will give it more complexity with no damage done.)

A good veal stock must be densely flavored and gelatinous, the cuts of meat chosen from hard-working muscles for their gelatinous structure and the bones — veal knuckle is the most valuable — for their readiness to release their gelatin. Both sapid and gelatinous intensity depend on the greatest possible proportion of meat and bones in relation to the quantity of water used to cover them. The meat cuts should be fairly large to permit the complete extraction of their goodness without falling apart and troubling the stock. These conditions impose long cooking, which entails a natural reduction of a couple of quarts by evaporation, and the stock must, therefore, be made in quite large quantity; it is impractical to work with a stockpot of less than a ten-quart volume (and equally impractical to work with one that is too heavy to lift when filled). A pot that is deeper than it is wide will require a smaller amount of liquid to immerse the solid elements and, because of its reduced surface area, will simplify skimming and minimize the loss of liquid by evaporation.

Finally, a good veal stock must be clear, not only to please the eye but for clarity of taste. The gray scum that is removed from the liquid's surface as it approaches the boiling point represents but a small fraction of the solids thrown into suspension, mostly albuminous material drawn from the meats that solidifies in contact with heat. In an undisturbed stockpot, these solids slowly fall out of suspension, gathering thickly on the sides and bottom, adhering more firmly as the cooking progresses, to reveal an absolutely transparent liquid — limpid amber. A round pastry grill placed in the bottom of the pot will prevent meats from sticking and leave the bottom undisturbed for the formation of deposit; the liquid must never boil nor should the contents of the pot be disturbed at any time before straining, at the risk of dislodging the deposits and throwing them back into suspension. (The natural temptation to remove meats while they are still edible should be suppressed; the meat's loss is the stock's gain.) The pot's lid, kept slightly ajar at a determined point, is your control over the precise degree of simmer; beware of guests in the kitchen — with few exceptions, they have a common compulsion to put lids firmly in place. The moment this happens, a rolling boil will be produced and your stock will be dirty.

Game, chicken, or beef stocks can be made either by a healthy addition of those elements to a basic veal stock or by moistening carcasses, parings, or whole joints of the chosen race with veal stock; the presence of veal will always add succulence. A chicken poached in veal stock will produce chicken stock; if the bird has been truffled, the stock will be none the worse for it.

For meat jellies, previously blanched and rinsed pork rinds and calf's foot are added to the stock meats to reinforce the gelatinous content — or a stock can be reduced until a tablespoonful, poured into a metal saucer (for its greater conductivity) and briefly refrigerated, sets to the right firmness.

Beef consommé is stock made only from beef; chicken consommé is made from beef and chicken, game consommé from a variety of furred and feathered game, usually first half-roasted. The proportion of aromatic vegetables is often increased. Consommés should be less gelatinous than a normal stock, never sticky in the mouth; a jellied consommé trembles on the brink of collapse. Clarification emasculates; if prepared with care, neither meat jellies nor consommés need ever be clarified.

The size and shape of your stockpot will determine the quantities of ingredients; the following list is intended only to give a general and pliable notion of proportions. A peeled parsnip, whose flavor resembles that of parsley root, may be added to the list of vegetables. If tap water is heavily chlorinated, some cooks will prefer to substitute a natural-tasting mineral water.

BASIC VEAL STOCK

    4 pounds inexpensive gelatinous cuts of veal (*thick slices of shank, rib tips, neck*)

    1 veal knuckle bone (*hock, heel*), cracked into several pieces

    1 pound beef (*shank or chuck*), in one piece

    1 pound inexpensive chicken parts (*wing tips, necks, backs*)

    2 large onions, peeled, one stuck with 2 or 3 cloves

    3 or 4 large carrots, peeled

    1 whole head of garlic, loose husk removed

    1 large *bouquet-garni* (*page 50*)

    small handful coarse salt (*or less, depending on eventual reduction*)

    water

In the bottom of a heavy stock pot or a large earthenware *pot-au-feu,* place a round, stainless-steel pastry grill of a diameter only slightly less than that of the pot. On top arrange the bones, then the meats, filling the gaps with wing tips and other smaller pieces; the meats should not be packed, but no space should be wasted. The level of the meats should not mount higher than some three inches below the rim of the pot. Pour over water to cover by about one-and-a-half inches — a good one-and-a-half inches should remain between the water's surface and the rim. (As the contents heat, the muscular structures of the meats contract with the grain, swell against the grain, and become firmer. Because of this changing of shape, the pieces displace themselves, those near the surface rising to remain barely immersed; at the same time, the liquid volume expands, the surface level rising; finally, when the vegetables and the *bouquet* are added, it will rise again.)

Whether or not you are using earthenware, it may be necessary to separate the pot from a direct flame by an asbestos mat or other heat disperser to control the simmer when the times comes; heavy copper, in particular, requires so little heat that the lowest attainable direct flame often gives too much. Bring the contents to the boiling point over medium-low heat — they should heat slowly, taking a full hour or longer. As the water heats, a film of gray scum will begin to form on the surface. Don't be in a hurry to remove it — there is a moment just before the boil is reached when the scum quite suddenly rises in a voluminous gray foam. Carefully skim it all off (a moment of inattention will permit the liquid to arrive at a full boil, and the scum will be broken and reabsorbed back into the liquid), add a glass of cold water, and wait for the scum to rise again. Continue skimming in this way, with two or three additions of cold water, until no more than a suggestion of white froth appears on the surface. Add the remaining ingredients, skim once more, place the lid no more than a half-inch ajar, turn the heat very low, and, over a period of twenty minutes or so, adjust it as necessary to arrive at a simmer that is no more than a murmur, the surface only gently broken here and there. Leave it, undisturbed (degreasing serves no purpose), for seven or eight hours, checking only occasionally to confirm the simmer; if, with reduction, it becomes stronger, it can be controlled by moving the lid a fraction of an inch more ajar. Never, at any time, should the lid be slipped into place.

Line a colander (large enough to contain the meats and vegetables) either with a loosely woven cotton cloth or with several layers of muslin rinsed in cold water and wrung out (mainly a precaution against traces of remaining soap or detergent). Place it in a large bowl and pour in most of the stock. Transfer the colander to another bowl and empty the pot into it. If the liquid in the second bowl touches the bottom of the colander, transfer it to the first bowl before leaving the colander to drain. After half an hour, the meats and vegetables can be discarded and all of the stock gathered together. (A full stockpot is heavy and many people prefer to remove most of the solids before straining the stock; it is doubtful that this can be done without troubling the stock to some extent, but in any case it must be done with the greatest of care, removing pieces, one by one, with a perforated spoon, never crushing, stirring, or touching the sides.) Leave the stock to cool until tepid and refrigerate it, uncovered, overnight. The stock will have set to a jelly and the fat can be scraped off the surface with a tablespoon; remaining traces can be removed by pressing paper towels to the jelly's surface and lifting them off with the fat clinging.

The stock may be kept refrigerated on condition that, every two or three days, it be boiled up, held half off the heat with a light boil to the heated side for about a quarter of an hour, and cleansed, the skin that forms on the still surface removed. After two or three of these treatments, the color will have deepened and the stock will set to a much stiffer jelly. This is the best stage at which to freeze it, first chilled, cut into pieces, and wrapped in clinging plastic film, then in foil. A chunk of this, added to many a stew whose principal moistening agent is not stock (*fricassées, daubes, carbonades, boeuf bourguignon, coq au vin,* veal *matelote,* etc.), will lend depth to the flavor and a silken texture to the sauce.

A *glace de viande* is a stock reduced to a thick syrup. It must not be done hurriedly and, as it reduces, it is transferred several times to progressively smaller saucepans, always kept half off the heat and skinned from time to time. When cooled, a *glace de viande* is stiff and rubbery. It will keep indefinitely in a small jar, a bit of plastic wrap pressed to its surface. If it is not used often, mold may form on the surface, but it does not penetrate and may be scraped off. A *glace*'s main use is as a parsimonious last-minute addition, reinforcing body and flavor in deglazing reductions for rapid sautés or other small sauces that contain no binding element.

Logically, *"demi-glace"* should indicate a halfway stage of reduction between a virgin stock and a *glace de viande;* the term is sometimes used in this way, but to most cooks it is an abbreviation for *"sauce demi-glace,"* or brown sauce.

BROWN SAUCE
(*Sauce Espagnole, Sauce Demi-glace*)

Escoffier defines *sauce demi-glace* as an "Espagnole brought to the extreme limit of perfection that it is susceptible of receiving, after a final cleansing (*'dépouille-ment'*)." In today's kitchens, *demi-glace* and *espagnole* are the same thing except that the latter (like "brown sauce" or "brown gravy"), thanks to a long history of careless or mendacious execution, has acquired a bad name, with the result that, no matter what the degree of perfection, a brown sauce is now most often called *"demi-glace"* in English and French alike. Whatever its name, it continues to be attacked by some on the grounds that it makes everything taste alike. The only possible answer is that, obviously, it should not be used in everything.

A brown sauce should be lightly bound and, after careful cleansing, almost translucent, with a brilliant sheen, a fluid, velvety texture, and no trace of fat. Because of long cooking, the small amount of flour contained in it is indiscernible, but it remains the gelatin's vital ally; together, they form the suave, underlying structure of the sauce. (There is a movement afoot, fancied by its protagonists to be purist, to cast flour from the kitchen — it has been pronounced an evil presence in all sauces. The *nouvelle demi-glace* is a reduction of stock or braising juices that depends entirely on the liquid's natural gelatin for its body. The degree of reduction necessary to attain this body falls just short of that for a *glace de viande;* the intellectual purity of intent is betrayed by a suffocating concentration of taste and a gluey excess of gelatin.)

Brown sauce is made in exactly the same way as numberless meat stews. The meats and vegetables are browned, either in the oven or on top of the stove, sprinkled with flour, the pan deglazed, its contents moistened to cover and gently braised, and the sauce strained and cleansed. It is possible, for reasons of economy, to shorten the braising process and strain the sauce without pressing the meats so that they can be served up with pasta, in a pilaf, or in a vegetable stew; the sauce will be that much less rich but still respectable. It is important, because of the degree of reduction, that the stock used for moistening be distinctly under-salted; if the stock is light in body, add some blanched and rinsed pork rinds, cut into small pieces, to the meats.

In a large, heavy, shallow roasting pan, scatter a pound or so each of beef and veal, cut into cubes, a few chicken necks and wing tips, a couple of carrots, a leek, and a celery stalk, all sliced the thickness of a finger, a large onion, coarsely chopped, three or four unpeeled garlic cloves, lightly crushed beneath a knife blade, thyme, and a bay leaf. Dribble over a bit of oil and toss with your hands until everything is coated with a film of oil. Bake in a hot oven (400°F) for half an hour or until meats and vegetables are regularly browned, removing the pan several times to stir or dislodge the ingredients with a wooden spatula and taking particular care that fragments of onion around the edge of the pan do not burn. Sprinkle over a handful of flour, turn the meats and vegetables around and over until no more flour shows white, and return the pan to the oven for another ten minutes, stirring things around a couple of times during this interval. Then on top of the stove, over medium heat, pour over a glass or two of white wine, stir and scrape with the wooden spatula to dislodge and dissolve the pan scrapings, and, when the wine has almost completely reduced, transfer the contents of the pan to a large saucepan, wash out the roasting pan with a little more wine, add it to the saucepan, and pour in enough stock to cover the contents generously. Bring it to the boiling point, adjust the heat to a simmer, and, with the lid slightly ajar, leave it to cook for five or six hours, checking to make certain that the solids remain immersed in liquid and, if necessary, adding more stock.

Over a bowl, ladle some of the contents of the pan into a sieve, press the solids thoroughly to extract as much liquid as possible, remove them, and repeat until all the sauce is strained. Leave it to settle for a few minutes and lift off any fat that rises to the surface. The sauce must now be sieved finely to rid it of an abundance of solid material in suspension; the most practical instrument is the minutely perforated, metal, conical sieve called a *chinois*. Choose a heavy saucepan of a size to contain the sauce just barely and pass the sauce into it through the *chinois,* moving a small ladle up and down against the inside surfaces of the sieve until only a firm paste remains in the tip of the cone. Reheat the sauce and, half off the heat, gently reduce it and cleanse it; this will require about an hour but you will know when it is ready. Taste for salt. If the sauce is not intended for immediate use, it should be transferred to a bowl, partially immersed in ice water, and stirred regularly, kept always in movement, until it cools, to prevent a skin from forming on its surface. It may then be refrigerated and, when it solidifies, a plastic film pressed to its surface to protect it from drying out.

GAME SAUCES

A basic game sauce is made in the same way as the brown sauce except that game replaces the other meats, a few juniper berries are included among the aromatics (sometimes also a couple of leaves of fresh sage), and a splash of vinegar replaces part of the wine in the deglazing process. It may be moistened with either veal stock or game stock. Chopped-up neck and trimmings of venison, the upper parts (rib cage, forelegs, neck, and head — long on flavor and short on flesh) of wild rabbits and hare, wing tips and necks of dressed game birds, cut-up old game birds, too tough to roast, leftover legs from roast grouse, rarely served because of their bitter taste, broken-up pheasant carcasses, left after carving, or any remains of boned-out game, the flesh of which has gone into terrines or forcemeats, are sensible choices for the meats.

To transform this into a *poivrade* sauce, ten or fifteen peppercorns, coarsely broken up in a mortar, are thrown in six or seven minutes before serving — the time necessary to infuse their fragrance and heat into the sauce without the flavor's turning bitter — and strained out at the last minute.

Other game sauces are made by adding cream or a small amount of melted currant jelly — or both — at the last minute. To me, these additions seem to destroy the finesse of a sauce that one has spent a good bit of time nursing to perfection. On the other hand, a further reduction in combination with red-wine essence and a final addition of chopped truffles will do the right thing by a rare roast saddle of hare or grilled venison chops.

FISH STOCK
(*Fumet de Poisson*)

The principles of a fish stock are the same as for meat stocks — immersion of carcasses, trimmings, and aromatics in cold liquid, slowly brought to a boil, skimmed, gently simmered, and strained — with the difference that fish releases its savory and gelatinous elements very rapidly and the aromatics must, therefore, be finely cut up to do their work in such a short time. (It has been repeatedly said and written that fish stock should never cook for more than half an hour, lest a bitter taste be drawn from the bones. I prefer, nonetheless, to stretch the cooking by a quarter of an hour, to draw out the maximum flavor, and have never detected bitterness in the stock.)

Delicately flavored white-fleshed fish are best. Members of the herring or mackerel families and other fatty fish — sturgeon or salmon, for instance — are best avoided (unless, which is often the case with salmon, the stock will be used in the preparation of the same fish). Most of the flat fish — sole, brill, plaice, lemon sole, flounder — are good choices as are whiting, hake, haddock, fresh cod, sea bass, any of the sea breams, and monkfish. Heads of larger fish that are usually sold in slices and carcasses of fish that have been filleted are given away to

customers; restaurants often make away with everything unless you ask your fishmonger in advance to save them. The heads of monkfish are particularly valuable (because of their terrifying appearance, monkfish are always sold beheaded, skinned, and cleaned); a wonderful stock can be made with a single monkfish head alone. (The best way to cut up a large fish head is with a cleaver or large, sturdy knife, not by wielding fierce hacks but, holding the blade in place, by delivering a firm blow to the top of the blade with a wooden mallet.) When trimming fillets of ragged edges and blood-stained abdominal areas, the trimmings should go into the stock. Gills should be torn out of the heads and discarded and any bloody parts rinsed.

Carrot and leek are often not added to a fish stock. The presence of fennel is particular to Provence, where it grows wild in abundance, bringing a delicate anisette fragrance to most fish preparations; in spring, the tender shoots and feathery leaves are used, later in the season the tall stalks and budding flower summits; in the autumn, the stalks are collected and broken or bent into bundles that are tied up for winter use. A stock is a good place to dispose of parsley stems, whose leaves have found other uses. If mushroom caps or sliced mushrooms form part of a garnish, their stems can be chopped up to enrich the stock.

Being easily and rapidly prepared, fish stock is rarely made in advance. (Of course, rather than waste trimmings or carcasses that may be at hand, a stock can be made and frozen, but because it never sets firmly, it should be poured, when cooled to room temperature, into plastic freezer bags that have been fitted inside square freezer containers, the bags sealed, with no air left inside, and frozen. They can then be removed from the boxes and stored in the freezer.)

With care, a fish stock will be quite clear, but never sparkling like a carefully attended meat stock. The carcasses throw an abundance of fine, gray sediment that has not time to settle and attach to the sides and bottom of the saucepan; some of it inevitably passes through the strainer. It will, however, settle to the bottom of the bowl and the clear stock, once chilled, can be ladled (and, when approaching the sediment, spooned) into another bowl, the body being sufficiently gelatinous to prevent the sediment's riling. If the stock is to be used immediately, this refinement must be forgotten, nor should the stock be clarified, a slightly troubled fish stock being preferable to loss of flavor.

Few fish give enough gelatin for a stock to set even lightly, though monkfish gives more than most; a fish jelly will require an addition of commercial powdered or leaf gelatin to set and, to sparkle, it will have to be clarified (see page 90).

Because of its short cooking time, fish stock is best held at a slightly higher temperature than meat stock (its simmer being still well beneath boiling temperature), with a surface movement somewhere between those of a simmer and a light boil.

When the stock is intended for fish preparations using red wine, white wine is replaced by red in the stock as well, producing a lovely amber tone, the clarifying power of the fish bones drawing out of suspension the pigmented tannins.

FISH STOCK

For about two pounds of broken or cut-up fish heads and carcasses, scatter in the bottom of a saucepan a carrot, a leek, and a large onion, all finely sliced, two or three unpeeled garlic cloves, lightly crushed, a branch of fennel and a handful of parsley (or parsley stems), coarsely cut up, a couple of sprigs of thyme, a bay leaf, and, if available, some chopped mushroom stems. Place the fish pieces on top, pour in cold water to just beneath their level, and finish moistening with enough white wine to immerse the contents of the saucepan generously. Salt lightly, bring to the boiling point, skim, and adjust the heat to maintain a pronounced simmer, lid ajar, for thirty to forty-five minutes. Strain, either through a sieve lined with several thicknesses of moistened and wrung-out muslin or, preferably, to keep the draining solids out of contact with the liquid, through a tight-meshed nylon drum sieve, overturned and fitted inside the rim of the bowl. Leave to drain for fifteen minutes or so before discarding the contents of the sieve.

VELOUTE

Velouté is fish, chicken, or veal stock bound by a flour and butter *roux,* cleansed, and reduced. Its relation to fish and white meats is the same as that of a brown sauce to game and red meats and, in it, flour plays the same restricted but essential role. *Velouté* is the base for an endless variety of creamy or clear-colored sauces, classic or of your own device, imbued often with other essences such as the cooking liquids of mushrooms, mussels, or other bivalves, often strengthened also with poaching or braising reductions or with a fragment of *glace de viande*. It can be finished with cream, bound with egg yolks (when a spark of lemon juice is also added) or with the pureed corals of sea urchins; it can be flavored and colored by the addition of vegetable purees (tomato, red pepper, sorrel, spinach, green peas, carrot) or by an infusion of saffron; it is usually buttered at the last minute, sometimes with a flavored butter (anchovy, shrimp, crayfish, shallot, *fines herbes,* etc.). Among the classic *velouté*-based sauces are *suprême* (chicken *velouté,* cream, butter), *ivoire* (*suprême* plus *glace de viande*), *albuféra* (chicken *velouté, glace de viande,* red-pepper butter), *aurore* (any *velouté,* tomato puree, butter), *poulette* (veal or chicken *velouté,* egg yolks, butter), *vin blanc* (fish *velouté,* egg yolks, butter), *normande* (*vin blanc* plus cream).

White *chaud-froid,* the sauce in which white meats, usually poultry, are dipped, then chilled, before the decorated and firmed *chaud-froid* surface is coated with jelly, is a reduction of *velouté* with progressive additions of stiff meat jelly and cream, finished with cream. (Brown *chaud-froid,* used with game birds, is made from brown game sauce without cream.) A stiffer-than-usual *velouté* often serves as a soufflé, mousse, or forcemeat base.

It is a mistake to impose unalterable measures on a preparation of this sort. The important things to remember are that the sauce should not be thick; it will acquire more body with reduction, but should remain fluid; the consistency will be further altered by the final additions of cream, egg yolks, purees, butters, etc. While cooking, it can be thinned down by the addition of more stock or lent more body by further reduction (but not by the addition of more *roux,* the long cooking being essential to the disappearance of the floury taste and texture).

For the preparation of the *roux,* the flour and the butter should be approximately equal in weight — which means twice the volume of flour to that of butter. The weight of butter can, in fact, be slightly less than that of flour; there should be no more than enough to absorb the flour — an excess of butter means only that much more to be removed from the sauce as it reduces, for no cooked butter should remain in the sauce.

As a general guide to proportions, count four to six tablespoons of flour and one to one and a half ounces of butter per quart of liquid.

Choose a heavy saucepan that will, as nearly as possible, just contain the amount of stock to be used. (Too large a pan presents too much surface area, excessive evaporation causing too rapid a reduction in relation to the quantity of sauce; also, a full pan is much easier to skim.) The stock should be liquid — melted but not hot.

Melt the butter over low heat, stir in the flour, and cook, stirring a couple of times, for several seconds — less than a minute — without permitting the flour to color. Whisking at the same time, pour in the stock all at once; increase the heat and continue whisking until the boil is reached. Pull the saucepan partially off the heat and adjust the heat to maintain a very light boil on one side of the liquid's surface. Remove at regular intervals the skin that forms on the still surface. The combined cleansing and reduction may require up to an hour and a half or more. If, when completely cleansed, it requires further reduction, this can be done rapidly over high heat, stirring and scraping the bottom of the saucepan all the while with a wooden spatula to prevent burning. Often, to intensify the flavor and to bring more gelatinous body to a *velouté,* more stock is added after cleansing and reduced over high heat; sometimes, in the case of certain creamed *veloutés,* cream is added progressively during a rapid reduction, as well as at the end.

However the sauce is finished, it should be passed through a fine strainer into a warmed sauceboat or serving bowl to ensure its being absolutely smooth; if it is finished with solid garnish, such as mushrooms or mussels, it should be strained over the garnish in another saucepan before being reheated and finished with its chosen butter off the heat.

White sauce, made with milk and usually finished with cream (sometimes called *béchamel*), is prepared in the same way except that the casein in the milk holds the butter in suspension in the sauce, preventing it from rising to the surface; the sauce may, therefore, not be cleansed but should cook for a good forty-five minutes.

BASIC PREPARATIONS

MOUSSELINE FORCEMEATS

Mousseline forcemeat is a puree of raw flesh bound with egg white, sieved, and mounted with cream. When set by gentle heat, it could be likened to a firm and creamy-textured soufflé. It is made from fish (pike, sole, flounder, whiting, monkfish, salmon, trout, lobster, scallops), chicken, veal, game birds, hare, wild rabbit. When made from a bland flesh — chicken breast or whiting, for instance — it often serves as a vehicle for other flavors or as a mechanical, cohesive support, binding layers of other elements together or containing them within its walls.

Sea-urchin corals or a few drops of saffron infusion, added to the flesh before sieving, can color and flavor a mousseline; spinach, blanched, refreshed, thoroughly squeezed, and reduced to a stiff puree, or garnishes of *duxelles,* chopped pistachios or truffles, green peppercorns, diced precooked crustaceans or fish firmed up in butter, ham or pickled tongue, or blanched vegetables — peas, little green beans cut finely, diced carrots — can be stirred in after the cream is added.

In the form of *quenelles* or poached in molds, mousseline is often served on its own with an accompanying sauce. As a forcemeat, it may be used to stuff whole birds, breasts of chickens or game birds, boned loin of veal, sausage casings, or molds lined with fish fillets, or it may be spread onto fish fillets that are then either folded or rolled into *paupiettes* and poached in *fumet.* As a lining for molds, it not only forms a case for various ragouts or other mixtures that could not otherwise retain their form when unmolded, but often seals firmly in place a surface *décor* (the strips of multicolored, blanched vegetables that adorn an old-fashioned *chartreuse* of braised partridge and cabbage, or the spiraled surface of a macaroni timbale).

Alternating layers of chicken mousseline are used to seal in place layers of differently colored blanched or butter-stewed vegetables — broccoli florets, green beans, strips of carrot, soaked and split dried morels, button mushrooms, sliced artichoke bottoms, asparagus tips — in terrines that reveal decorative patterns when sliced; differently colored fish mousselines may seal alternating layers of fish fillets, shrimp tails, scallops and their corals, etc., to similarly decorative effect.

Tiny *quenelles* to garnish consommés or cream soups are forced from a pastry bag onto the buttered bottom of a sauté pan and boiling water is poured down the side; held over low heat, they are ready a minute or so later when they rise to the surface. Large *quenelles* are formed with two tablespoons, dipped first in cold water; the surface of a heaping spoonful of the mousseline mixture is molded smooth with the other spoon, overturned, then pushed with its tip into the buttered sauté pan. These need to poach for eight to ten minutes, then are drained, arranged in a gratin dish, coated with a creamed *velouté* or other sauce, and heated in the oven until the sauce bubbles and the surface is lightly colored.

Egg white supplements the natural albuminous content of the flesh, binding the mousseline to make it set more firmly. Cream lends smoothness, lightness, finesse. The proportions of egg white and cream to flesh can vary, depending on the use to which the mixture is put; if it is to be simply molded or used as a forcemeat that is contained within something else, a little less egg white and a little more cream may be used for the same amount of flesh, giving a mousseline that is less firm but more delicate; for *quenelles,* or if the mousseline is to provide a supporting wall, requiring the strength to contain other elements, the quantity of egg white can be increased or that of cream reduced — or both; a large charlotte or dome mold will require stronger walls than individual *dariole* molds. Different fleshes produce raw mixtures that are more or less firm; a lobster mousseline, for instance, is too loose in its raw state to be used for *quenelles* or for lining molds.

Any mousseline can be made firmer by incorporating about half the amount of *panade* as that of flesh into the puree before it is sieved. It is made like *chou* paste: to make the right amount for the recipe that follows, count a quarter-cup of water or milk, salt, a half-ounce of butter, a quarter-cup of flour, and the leftover egg yolk. In a small saucepan, bring the salted liquid and the butter to a boil, remove from the heat, add the flour all at once, stir vigorously with a wooden spoon until the mixture pulls itself together, return to the heat, and continue stirring until it forms a shiny mass that no longer sticks to the spoon or the saucepan (with such a small amount, this happens very rapidly — less than half a minute). Remove from the heat, keep stirring and mashing to cool it slightly, and stir in the egg yolk, beating until smooth. Spread the mixture onto a small buttered plate to cool before using.

MOUSSELINE FORCEMEAT (FOR I POUND FORCEMEAT)
½ pound raw flesh, trimmed or scraped free of skin, fat, membranes,
    nervous tissue, tendons, etc.
salt, freshly ground pepper, freshly grated nutmeg, cayenne pepper
1 egg white
1 cup heavy cream

Chop the flesh coarsely and pound it to a puree in a mortar, using a wooden pestle, or reduce it to a puree in a food processor, add seasoning (imperceptible amounts of nutmeg and cayenne) and the egg white, small amounts at a time, pounding or processing after each addition. (If a *panade* is being used, pound or process it in now.) Pass the mixture, a spoonful at a time, through a fine drum sieve (see page 47), pack it into a metal bowl (because of metal's greater conductivity, the puree will chill more rapidly), scrape down the sides, smooth the surface, and press a film of plastic wrap to it to keep it from contact with air. Embed the bowl in cracked ice, contained in a larger bowl, and refrigerate for at least one hour.

Keep the bowl in the ice, draining off water and adding more cracked ice if necessary. Using a wooden spoon, incorporate the cream, a little at a time, covering the mixture again with plastic and refrigerating for another fifteen or twenty minutes after one-third and, again, after two-thirds of the cream has been added. At first the cream will have to be mashed in with the back of the spoon; as more is added, the mixture will become more supple and can be stirred and beaten — the more it is beaten, the better. The last third of the cream may be lightly whipped before being stirred and then beaten in.

RICE

A pilaf differs from boiled rice in that the raw rice is first heated in a trace of fat (which will coat the grains, keeping them separate) before the precise amount of boiling liquid that the rice should absorb is added. The pot is tightly covered and left undisturbed over the lowest of heats until done. As an integral dish to serve as a main course, the rice is cooked in combination with sautéed aromatic vegetables and meats, poultry, or fish as well as herbs and, often, tomatoes and saffron, moistened with stock or water. Other garnishes — parboiled little peas or broad beans, butter-stewed artichoke hearts, sautéed mushrooms, etc. — may be tossed in before serving.

As an accessory to stews or poached white meats or fish whose sauces are

tomatoed or creamed, sometimes bound with egg yolks, an unflavored pilaf provides textural relief and body, while its clean, unassertive taste enhances that of the sauce. It is made from white, long-grained rice. (The flavor of brown rice detracts from the appreciation of the sauce; round-grained Italian rice, whose qualities are essential to a semiliquid *risotto*, is unsuited to a dry pilaf.) The best rices seem never to be those that are commercially packaged; shops specializing in exotic or foreign foods often have a selection of rices in bulk from different parts of the world. For the most part, they need not be rinsed before using but, occasionally, one of a particular origin may have an excessive amount of superficial starch and will give a better result if first rinsed, well drained, and dried on a towel. The easiest way to measure is to count two ladles of water to every ladleful of rice. One-half pound will serve four people.

RICE PILAF
  ½ ounce unsalted butter or 1 tablespoon olive oil
  ½ pound rice
  salt
  2 cups boiling water
  4 tablespoons unsalted butter, cut into small pieces

Warm the butter or oil in a saucepan over low heat, add the rice and a pinch of salt, and stir regularly with a wooden spoon for a couple of minutes or until the grains lose their slightly translucent quality and become milky and opaque. Add the boiling water, cover the pan tightly, and leave the rice to cook at a bare simmer (using an asbestos mat to control the heat, if necessary) for eighteen to twenty-five minutes; the rice is done when the water has been completely absorbed. Mix in the remaining butter, a fork in each hand, separating the grains with the prongs, lifting and tossing delicately rather than stirring, so as not to break or crush the grains.

CREPES

Crepes are unleavened, paper-thin pancakes. When spread with jam or pastry cream — or with various mixtures of finely diced cooked meats or fish, *duxelles,* or truffle, bound with a spoonful or two of some kind of sauce — rolled up, and cut on the bias into diamond shapes, they are called *pannequets.* Sweet *pannequets* are usually sprinkled with confectioners' sugar, savory *pannequets* with melted butter and, sometimes, grated cheese, before being glazed briefly in a hot oven. Spread with similar mixtures and folded, envelope-like, or left flat and ungarnished, they are used to line molds for sweet or savory puddings. Rolled around various stuffings, they replace parboiled sheets of pasta in cannelloni, or they can be filled with soufflé mixtures, one half lightly folded over the top to give the soufflé freedom to swell. Gathered together like a string purse around a little ragout or stuffing and tied with a strand of blanched leek green, they are heated in the oven to garnish roast or braised meats. Rolled up and sliced like noodles, they garnish consommés or can be scattered over salads.

The following recipe should be thought of only as a general guideline; specific measures are of no importance — most important is the consistency, which should be that of fluid cream. Batters that contain relatively little flour in relation to the eggs will make more tender crepes; the substitution of cream for part of the milk will make them even more tender, moist, and delicate, but so fragile that they are difficult to work with, often tearing when being turned. On the other hand, good crepes can be made with water or beer. The addition of sugar to the batter for dessert crepes does not improve them (they will subsequently be sweetened, in any case), but it does make them more likely to stick to the pan. Brandy is not essential but it does improve the flavor, and for savory crepes, finely chopped *fines herbes* is an attractive addition. The batter need not stand before being used.

The bottom of a standard small crepe pan measures five inches; one rarely has use for larger crepes. If the crepe pan is used for melting the butter to go into the batter, it can be lightly wiped with a paper towel and is then ready to use — the batter contains enough butter to prevent the crepes from sticking.

CREPE BATTER
  6 tablespoons flour
  salt
  3 eggs
  1 cup milk (*more, if necessary*)
  1 tablespoon Cognac
  1½ ounces unsalted butter, melted

Sift the dry ingredients into a mixing bowl, make a well in the center, and break in the eggs. Whisk, keeping to the center, until the flour is gradually absorbed into the eggs, adding a bit of milk if necessary, then whisk in about half the milk. Add the Cognac and the melted butter, then whisk in enough additional milk to bring the batter to the consistency of cream. If careless execution has produced a batter that is not absolutely smooth, pour it through a sieve into another bowl.

A small ladle (three-tablespoon capacity) is most practical for pouring; about half a ladleful of batter is the right amount for a small pan. Heat the pan, lightly buttered, over low to medium heat. (After the first two or three crepes, adjust the heat if necessary.) If the pan does not sizzle at contact with the batter, it is not hot enough. Lift the pan from the heat and pour in the batter, at the same time giving the pan a rolling motion, turning it in all directions, so the batter spreads over the entire surface. Return the pan to the heat; after thirty seconds or so, the edges will begin to turn golden and to curl; using a small, elongated spatula (palette knife) or a round-tipped table knife, ease the blade all the way under and flip the crepe over. After about fifteen seconds, slip the crepe out of the pan with your fingertips, place it on a plate, remove the pan from the heat for a few seconds, and pour in more batter. It is essential to remove the pan from the heat for a few seconds each time before pouring a new crepe, for with the heat at the correct intensity for cooking the crepes, the pan rapidly becomes too hot. The batter should be given a stir with the ladle each time before pouring. The crepes should be stacked as they come from the pan and, if they are not to be used immediately, should be covered with plastic wrap to keep them from drying out; if prepared more than a few hours before using them, refrigerate them.

BREAD

The best bread to accompany most foods is the simplest to make; flour, salt, water, and yeast are the ingredients. It will be improved if a sponge is prepared a day or two in advance — a teaspoon of dried yeast granules dissolved in a bowl with a couple of soup ladles of tepid water, enough flour whisked in to form a thickish batter, covered tightly with plastic film, and left at room temperature. If you make bread regularly — two or three times a week — prepare twice the quantity of sponge and use only half of it for the first batch of bread, whisking back into the remaining half enough flour and water to bring it back to the original volume and consistency. If regularly used and replenished with flour and tepid water, the yeast culture will continue to multiply normally without further additions of commercial yeast.

In a large bowl, put about one-and-a-half pounds of unbleached bread flour and a teaspoon, more or less to taste, of salt. A small handful, each, of whole meal and rye flour will act as a seasoning, lending the bread character without sufficiently altering the flavor to render it unsuitable for the table. Pour in the sponge and mix with a fork, adding enough tepid water to bring the mixture to the consistency of a firm but malleable, supple paste. Scrape it out onto a floured work surface, sprinkle a bit of flour over the dough, and begin to knead it, holding it in place with one hand while, with the heel of the other, pushing the mass away from you, folding it back over itself, giving it something less than a quarter of a turn, and repeating the motions, automatically and rhythmically. At first it will seem sticky and unmanageable — sprinkle with more flour as needed — but it will rapidly pull itself together, becoming more resilient; as this happens, exert a bit more force, making certain to push the dough far enough to make it tear before folding and turning. From time to time, pick it up and heave it against the work surface. It should be kneaded for ten to fifteen minutes — better more than less. If the dough hook of an electric mixer is used, it is nonetheless best to finish the dough with a few minutes of hand-kneading. Put the dough into a clean bowl, cover it with a kitchen towel or with plastic wrap, and leave it to rise until doubled in volume — a couple of hours or more at room temperature. (In a warmer place it will rise faster but the bread is better if it takes its time.)

Pull the dough out of the bowl, loosening it from the edges with flicking fingertips. (If more than one loaf is to be made, cut off what is wanted for one and return the rest to the bowl, keeping it covered.) Knead it again, but lightly this time, without holding onto it or tearing it, pushing with the heel of the hand from the center of the mass outward, folding the dough back on itself, turning, pushing, and folding until all the air is forced out and the dough forms a round, smooth ball; cover and leave it to relax for fifteen minutes or so. Treat the remaining dough in the same way. Finally, knead each loaf in the same way again, forming a smooth ball that is placed seam side down on a small board sprinkled with semolina, cornmeal, or other coarse meal (a different board for each loaf). Cover the loaves with a towel and leave them to rise until nearly doubled in volume, probably no more than an hour this time.

If your oven heats only from the bottom rather than by a system of hot-air circulation around the body of the oven, best install a metal plaque in the bottom to diffuse the heat. Put a heavy baking tray in the hot oven (450°F) to heat. The presence of steam is invaluable in that it will prevent the crust from setting so rapidly that it inhibits the continued rising of the loaf when first put in the oven; to this end, place a tray of boiling water in the bottom of the oven and have ready at hand a water-spraying atomizer.

Just before putting the loaf to bake, slash it with a razor blade; this releases tensions, directing the pattern in which the loaf will burst as it expands. (The simplest and one of the most effective patterns is a cross, with one slash from side to side, another from end to end; shallow slits will produce a surface design, deep slashes will give a loaf that opens up into four sections with an abundant crust.) Whatever the pattern, a rapid, assured movement is essential — any hesitation or fiddling around will make a mess. Flour is often sprinkled over the loaf before the surface is slit, the slit sections then opening up to present a contrasting, rougher, and unfloured crust.

Open the oven door, hold the board at a slight tilt over the baking tray, and jerk the board abruptly backward toward yourself; the loaf will slip onto the tray. Spray the inside of the oven and the surface of the loaves with the atomizer and close the door. Twenty minutes later, remove the water tray from the oven and

reduce the heat to 375°F. Check the coloration from time to time — if the loaves are browning too rapidly, turn the oven down more and lay a sheet of foil loosely over them. Smaller loaves may be done in forty-five minutes, larger ones in an hour or something over; pick up a loaf with a towel and rap the bottom with your knuckle — a characteristically hollow sound indicates that it is done. Leave the loaves to cool on a wire rack.

Note: Whatever the shape of the loaf, kneading it into a ball and leaving it covered to relax for a quarter of an hour is the first step in its formation. Certain shapes are difficult to manipulate when risen, and these are best put directly on their baking sheet, first sprinkled with coarse meal, before rising; it may also be preferable to score them before rising. For a fantasy loaf that is mostly crust, the ball can be flattened and rolled out with a rolling pin, long slits cut all the way through with the tip of a knife, stopping just short of the edges, before it is slid onto the baking tray, the slits carefully opened out, and left, covered with a towel, to rise. To prevent elongated loaves from assuming deformed shapes, they can be formed in such a way as to create a network of compartments within the loaf, dispersing tensions as it swells: the ball of dough, seam side up, is flattened, rolled up into a cylinder, flattened again, seam side up, into a long oval, then stretched to twice its length by gently pulling the two ends while giving the dough a flapping movement; the two ends are folded in to meet, the dough is pressed into a neat rectangle and rolled up tightly, in the opposite sense to that in which the ends have been folded, into a cylinder, then rolled back and forth beneath the palms to even the form; by exerting more pressure at the ends, the loaf can be tapered. To make long, narrow loaves, the cylinder will have to be given another rest to reduce the dough's resistance; it is then progressively lengthened by rolling back and forth beneath the palms. All are put to rise seam side down. A *baguette* is scored before rising, the razor blade held nearly horizontal to make shallow, overlapping cuts running the length of the loaf. To vary the design, a loaf's surface can be clipped into with kitchen shears; an *épi* is formed by clipping deeply from above, at a sharp bias and at short intervals, into a long, narrow loaf, laying the partially severed sections alternately to one side and the other of the loaf's axis before leaving it to rise.

ALMOND BISCUITS

Called *tuiles* — "tiles" — because of their warped shape, these are good all-round dessert biscuits and permit one to dispose of leftover egg whites. They may be kept crisp in a tightly closed tin box.

ALMOND BISCUITS
    ½ cup sugar
    3 egg whites
    2 tablespoons flour
    small pinch salt
    2 tablespoons cream
    2 ounces unsalted butter, melted
    2 ounces slivered almonds

Whisk the sugar and egg whites together in a bowl, add the flour and the salt, and continue whisking until well mixed. Incorporate the cream and the melted butter. Stir in the almonds.

Butter a heavy baking sheet, dust it with flour, and give it a smart rap, upside-down, to rid it of excess flour. Distribute the batter on the sheet in teaspoonfuls, leaving enough space between each mound to allow for spreading, and bake in a moderate oven (325°F) for about ten minutes or until they are golden brown around the edges and the center is only slightly yellowed.

They must be removed from the sheet the moment they leave the oven to avoid sticking; if they begin to stick before all are removed, return the sheet to the oven for a few seconds. Scoop each one up with a deft movement of the spatula and press it onto a rolling pin or other cylindrical object to give it its tile-like form. While still hot, the biscuits are soft and pliable, but they turn crisp upon cooling. After a few minutes on the rolling pin, remove the biscuits to a wire rack and leave them until they are completely cooled.

AUTUMN MENUS

Autumn in France means wild mushrooms (in particular, *cèpes* — *Boletus edulis*) and game. From mid-September to just before Christmas (when fancies turn to *foie gras* and truffles), the French open markets far outdo the Dutch still-life painters in their festive display of game. A wild boar or deer is usually the centerpiece, and rows of pheasant, partridge, and woodcock are strung around, punctuated by an occasional splash of wild-duck color. Hare, wild rabbit, garlands and piles of thrush, lark, and "blackbird" (unrelated to the American blackbird) enter into the composition, and, at this season, guinea fowl is often left in its feathers simply to keep it in the spirit of things.

Any bird that has been badly damaged by gunshot, particularly in the intestinal region, should be plumed and cleaned immediately. In other cases, a pheasant will be much improved if hung for about four days (a partridge for three days) in a cool, dry, well-ventilated place. These birds should be plumed, cleaned, and dressed only shortly before being put to use, although, dressed, they may be kept in the refrigerator for a day or so without suffering. Wild duck and quail are at their best when eaten the day after having been killed or, at least, freshly cleaned and dressed immediately and kept refrigerated for only a short time.

Venison should be hung for five days to a week. The hind legs and saddle of young deer are best roasted slightly rare, unmarinated — or, at most, marinated for only a few hours in nothing more than a bit of white wine, olive oil, and a pinch of herbs. The remaining parts may be prepared in identically the same way as *daube à la provençale* (page 278) or *boeuf à la bourguignonne* (page 172).

Two Formal Autumn Dinners

MENU I *(for 6)*

CRAYFISH MOUSSE
[MOUSSE D'ECREVISSES]

A champagne blanc de blancs or a Coteaux Champenois

• • •

RAVIOLI OF CHICKEN BREASTS WITH FINES HERBES
*[PELLMENES DE BLANCS DE VOLAILLE
AUX FINES HERBES]*

*A dry but full-bodied white wine: Alsace (Riesling) or white Burgundy
(Corton-Charlemagne, Clos des Mouches, Puligny-Montrachet, etc.)*

• • •

ROAST LEG OF VENISON WITH POIVRADE SAUCE
[GIGUE DE CHEVREUIL A LA SAUCE POIVRADE]

*A robust red wine: Côtes-du-Rhône (Châteauneuf-du-Pape, Hermitage,
Côte Rôtie) or Burgundy (Nuits-Saint-Georges)*

• • •

SWEET-POTATO PUREE
[PUREE DE PATATES DOUCES]

• • •

ENDIVE AND LAMB'S LETTUCE SALAD
[SALADE D'ENDIVES ET MACHE]

• • •

PONT L'EVEQUE CHEESE
[FROMAGE DE PONT L'EVEQUE]

A finer and older wine than the preceding but in the same spirit

• • •

MOLDED COFFEE CUSTARD
[CREME RENVERSEE AU CAFE]

Quarts de Chaume, a Bonnezeaux, or a sweet Vouvray of respectable age

A roast leg of venison needs a sauce, but may obviously be accompanied by any of a number of very simple sauces (for instance, the roasting pan may simply be washed out with Madeira and the reduction finished with heavy cream). Currant jelly is often added to game sauces.

The juxtaposition of hot and cold, of textures, flavors, and colors, follows a logical pattern, and a rich, "heady" cheese finds its perfect expression here (although many wine lovers prefer, no matter what the circumstances, to nibble at an anonymous cheese in order best to savor the wine). A wine powerful enough not to suffer by comparison with that designed to accompany the venison is, by the same token, able to support a fermented cheese.

The basic preparations for the *poivrade* sauce should be begun the preceding day. The mousse and the dessert may be finished and forgotten on the morning of the chosen day, and the ravioli may be prepared ahead of time. The final preparations, then, consist only in poaching and gratinéing the ravioli, roasting the leg of venison, finishing the sauce, and preparing the sweet-potato puree.

The ravioli, the roast, and the sweet potatoes should all be put into the oven just before the meal begins — that is to say, about twenty minutes before the ravioli are to be served and an hour before the roast. Ordinarily the ravioli should be finished in an oven less hot than that at which the roast should be begun, but that is not too serious — watch it carefully, and when the gratin is perfect, remove it from the oven. If the cream remains in large part unabsorbed, place the dish over a gentle heat on top of the stove for a few minutes. If your oven is not large enough to take both the gratin and the roast, start the former ten minutes earlier — it may be kept in a warm place until ready to serve — and the roast ten minutes later. Encourage your guests to linger over each course — a pleasure, as long as there is no scarcity of wine.

Crayfish Mousse

Mousse d'Ecrevisses

½ ounce unsalted butter
6 tablespoons fine *mirepoix (page 55)*
2 dozen good-sized, lively crayfish
salt, tiny pinch of cayenne pepper
1 cup dry white wine
2 cups fish *fumet (page 72)*, in which ½ ounce gelatin, first softened in a bit
    of cold water, has been dissolved before removing from heat
velouté (page 74) made from half of the gelatinous fish *fumet*
1 cup heavy cream
1 tablespoon chopped tarragon
1 egg white

Melt a small lump of butter in a large sauté pan, add the *mirepoix,* and set over low to medium heat. Add the crayfish, turn the heat to high, add the seasoning, toss and stir the crayfish until they have turned red, add the wine, bring to a boil, lower the heat, and leave to cook, covered, for 7 to 8 minutes. Select the handsomest and most regularly formed of the crayfish — one for each guest — and put them aside. Tear the others in two, carefully remove (and discard) the shells from the tails, and put the tails aside with the whole crayfish. Pound the carapaces (that is to say, the entire upper part of the crustacean, including the pincers), 3 or 4 at a time, in a mortar (or reduce them to a rough puree in a blender, adding a bit of the cooking liquid), then thoroughly work in the butter, pounding and turning the mixture with the pestle. Add this *pommade,* along with the *mirepoix* cooking juices, to the *velouté.* Bring to a boil, mixing and stirring well, remove from the heat, and pass the contents of the saucepan through a food mill or *mouli,* using the medium blade — this will eliminate the coarser debris of the carapaces. Pass this puree, in small quantities at a time, through a fine drum sieve, cleaning the surface well after each passage, discarding the residue, and collecting the puree into a large mixing bowl.

Embed the bowl in cracked ice and stir the puree continuously until it begins to thicken or "set." Whip the cream until it is semifirm but not stiff, then mix it in thoroughly but gently. Pour the mousse into a deep platter or shallow crystal dish large enough to contain the bed of mousse and later the final decoration of tails, crayfish, and jelly without giving a crowded effect. Put the mousse to set in the coldest part of the refrigerator or embed it in ice; do not put it in the freezer.

Combine the remaining *fumet,* the tarragon, and the egg white, beaten stiff, in a saucepan, bring it to a boil, whisking all the time, and, when the boil is reached, lower the heat and simmer for 4 to 5 minutes. Pour into a sieve placed over a bowl and lined with a kitchen towel or other finely textured cloth.

Truss the reserved whole crayfish by pulling the tip of the tail upward in an arc toward the head — gently, without forcing — and, with equal care, easing the pincers back to meet it. Pierce the tail near the base, on each side, with the immobile point of each pincer. Arrange the trussed crayfish on the surface of the solid mousse. Place the additional shelled tails around in a decorative pattern and add something green (parboiled tarragon leaves or small bouquets of chervil) to the composition. Coat everything with the jelly (stirring it, small quantities at a time, in a small bowl embedded in cracked ice, and rapidly spooning it over the *décor* as it begins to thicken), repeating the process a few times on the trussed crayfish, which will require a heavier coating. Chill well. It is both practical and attractive, for the service, to embed the serving dish in cracked ice.

THE CHICKEN RAVIOLI

A particularly happy variation is the substitution of a couple of tablespoons of finely chopped truffle peelings for the *fines herbes,* but possibilities are endless. *Duxelles* (page 58) can also be a useful addition.

Ravioli of Chicken Breasts

Pellmènes de Blancs de Volaille

NOODLE DOUGH
> 2 cups flour
> ½ teaspoon salt (*approximately*)
> 2 whole eggs and 3 yolks

FILLING
> 3 ounces unsalted butter
> 2 good-sized chicken-breast halves (*1 whole breast*)
> salt, freshly ground pepper
> 2 tablespoons finely chopped *fines herbes* (*page 50*)

FINAL PREPARATION
> 1½ ounces unsalted butter
> 1½ ounces freshly grated Parmesan cheese
> 1 cup heavy cream (*approximately*)

THE NOODLE DOUGH

Sift the flour and salt into a large mixing bowl, add the whole eggs and the yolks, and mix together thoroughly. The paste should be fairly firm but malleable. If it does not seem stiff enough, sprinkle in a bit more flour, or if it is too stiff, add a bit of the extra egg white. Knead the paste with the palms of the hands on a lightly floured board, roll it into a ball, wrap it in waxed paper, and leave it to "relax" its elasticity for an hour or so.

THE FILLING

Allow the butter to stand at kitchen temperature for an hour or so to soften. Remove the skin and bones from the chicken breasts, scrape the flesh with a small sharp knife, following the grain and removing all nerve tissue as you proceed. Chop finely until it forms a unified mass of coarse puree. Mix the chicken thoroughly with the butter, the seasoning, and the *fines herbes* and refrigerate until ready for use.

Divide the dough into 4 equal parts and roll out each thinly on a lightly floured board to form an approximately square shape, turning it over regularly and sprinkling with flour if necessary. Imagining the sheet of paste to be lined both horizontally and vertically at 2-inch intervals, place a small teaspoonful of filling in a mound at each intersection. Using a small brush, repeatedly dipped in water, moisten wide swaths in both directions between the mounds of filling, place another sheet of paste on top, and press well all along the moistened areas with the side of the hand so that each bit of filling is completely sealed in. Cut along the center of each sealed line with a wooden pastry wheel. Make certain that each "package" is well sealed on all sides. The ravioli may equally well be made by cutting the sheet of paste into circular or square sections, placing filling in the center of each, moistening the edges, and folding each into a half-circle or triangle. They may be prepared hours ahead of time, in which case they should be kept spread out on a lightly floured towel.

THE FINAL PREPARATION

Drop the ravioli, a few at a time (to avoid their sticking to one another), into a large pot of salted, boiling water. When it returns to a boil, reduce the heat, cover, and let it barely simmer for about 6 minutes. Slowly and carefully pour the contents of the pot into a colander, so that none may be damaged. Pour some hot water over the ravioli to rinse the starch from their surface and leave them to drain.

Butter a large gratin dish or shallow baking dish, sprinkle the bottom with half the grated cheese, arrange the ravioli on top, pour over enough cream so that they are just covered, sprinkle the surface with the remaining cheese, and distribute over the surface ½ ounce of cold, firm butter, cut into thin slices with a small sharp knife. Bake for about 20 minutes in a medium oven or until the cream is about two-thirds absorbed and the surface a golden brown.

THE LEG OF VENISON

If rare or medium-rare meat is looked upon with displeasure, roast venison may as well be discarded from one's repertoire. Well done, it is dry and savorless. The leg should be cut like a leg of lamb, the pelvic bone removed and the leg bone cut just above the lower joint so that a *manche à gigot* may be attached to facilitate the carving at table.

Roast Leg of Venison with Poivrade Sauce

Gigue de Chevreuil à la Sauce Poivrade

1 leg of venison
about 5 ounces fresh pork back fat

MARINADE
   3 tablespoons olive oil
   2 tablespoons white wine
   1 pinch mixed herbs (*page 52*)
   salt, freshly ground pepper
   poivrade sauce (*page 71*)

THE LARDING

The larding needle (hollow, with a very sharp, flexible point, widening toward the other end, which is splayed or hinged to permit the insertion of strips of fat) should be bent into a gentle curve at the needle end. The piece of fat, well chilled to ensure its being as firm as possible, should be cut with a sharp knife into long strips about ⅛ inch wide, and each strip cut into ⅛-inch "sticks." The plump, wide surface of the leg and the two sides (that is to say, the three-quarters of the surface not resting on the bottom of the roasting pan) should be larded.

The only practical way to lard a piece of meat is to seat oneself comfortably and place the article to be larded on a clean towel on one's knees. A *lardon* of fat is inserted into the hollow of the needle and the flesh is transpierced with the grain. To facilitate the task, the *lardons* should be fairly long, but once trimmed each will be about 1½ inches long, the central half of that length being embedded in the flesh and the ends protruding an equal distance on either side. For aesthetic reasons, the leg should be neatly larded in closely placed rows from top to bottom, the odd rows falling into one alignment and the even rows into another.

The formal design of golden-brown protrusions on the surface of the roast forms a presentation as attractive as it is essential to the moistness and flavor of the flesh.

THE MARINADE

Place the larded leg on a platter, sprinkle over it the marinade ingredients, turn it so that all surfaces are well moistened, and cover the meat with plastic wrap. It may be kept like this for several hours — or a day or two, if necessary.

THE FINAL PREPARATION

As nearly as possible, the roasting pan should be of heavy material (cast iron is perfect), shallow, and just big enough to contain the roast.

The roast should be carefully sponged dry with a towel and the dried surface rubbed or patted with oil. (Any other moisture creates a steaming process, which prevents the rapid browning that seals the surface, locking all the juices inside. Oiling, on the other hand, hastens this browning process.)

Count 8 to 10 minutes of actual roasting time per pound plus a 15-minute rest in a warm place. Start the roast in a hot oven (450°F); after 10 minutes, season it with salt and freshly ground pepper and turn the oven down (325°F). After another 15 minutes, begin to baste.

Present the roast unadorned on a heated platter, the sauce and sweet-potato puree served separately. Carve at table.

Sweet-Potato Puree

Purée de Patates Douces

2 pounds sweet potatoes
2 large white potatoes
salt, freshly ground pepper
4 ounces unsalted butter, softened

Bake the white potatoes and sweet potatoes in the oven until they are well done — 45 to 60 minutes, depending on the size and variety. Split them in two, remove the flesh with a spoon, and pass it through a fine sieve into a saucepan, pressing with a wooden pestle. Avoid a turning, "grinding" motion, which lends an elastic, compact quality to the texture. Season to taste and reheat over medium heat, stirring with a wooden spoon. Remove from the heat and add the butter — not all at once, for only enough should be added to bring the puree to the desired creamy, but not runny, consistency.

THE COFFEE CUSTARD

The quality of a poached custard depends on its containing only just enough egg for the form to hold at a tremble, once unmolded, and on its being poached at a temperature just below boiling. (If the water in the *bain-marie* is allowed to boil, the marvelous velvety "suspension" will collapse into a vaguely rubbery article riddled with tiny holes.) Any simple mold will serve. The charlotte is traditional, but the savarin mold may permit a prettier presentation.

Molded Coffee Custard

Crème Renversée au Café

CARAMEL
   ¼ cup sugar
   2 or 3 tablespoons water

CUSTARD
   ½ cup sugar
   tiny pinch of salt
   1 cup milk
   ½ vanilla bean
   2 whole eggs and 3 yolks
   1 cup very strong, hot, freshly made drip coffee
   almond oil (*for mold*)

THE CARAMEL

Bring the sugar and the water to a boil in a small saucepan. Keep the mixture at a light boil, watching it all the time, until it turns a deep honey color. Remove it immediately from the heat and pour it into the mold, turning it rapidly in all directions to coat the bottom and as much of the sides as possible before the caramel solidifies. When it is thoroughly cooled, lightly oil the sides that remain untouched by the caramel.

THE CUSTARD

Combine the sugar, salt, milk, and vanilla bean in a saucepan and bring it to a boil. Remove it from the heat and leave it to infuse for a few minutes. Remove the vanilla bean.

Beat the eggs and yolks together in a bowl, then slowly add the milk and coffee, while continuing to beat. Pass the mixture through a fine sieve into another bowl, allow it to stand for about 5 minutes, and carefully skim off all the foam that has come to the surface. Pour the mixture into the mold and cook it in a *bain-marie* (place the mold in a larger pan, pour in enough nearly-boiling water to immerse the mold by two-thirds, and put it in a low to medium oven) for about 40 minutes or until the center is no longer liquid. A solid mold will require a longer cooking time than a savarin.

Chill the custard. Unmold just before serving, first running the tip of a small knife around the edges.

Two Formal Autumn Dinners

MENU II *(for 4)*

SORREL SOUP
[POTAGE GERMINY]

• • •

FRITTO MISTO (MIXED FRITTERS)
[FRITTO MISTO (BEIGNETS MIXTES)]

A light, dry white wine: Burgundy (Saint-Véran, Mâcon-Viré, Rully, Auxey-Duresses) or Loire Valley (Pouilly-Fumé, Sancerre), Graves, or a California Sauvignon Blanc

• • •

PHEASANT SALMIS
[SALMIS DE FAISAN]

A Médoc or Graves (red), at least 8 to 10 years old

• • •

SAUTEED CEPES (WILD MUSHROOMS) A LA BORDELAISE
[CEPES SAUTES A LA BORDELAISE]

Same wine as the preceding

• • •

ROCKET SALAD WITH NASTURTIUM FLOWERS
[SALADE DE ROQUETTE AUX FLEURS DE CAPUCINES]

• • •

CHEESES
[FROMAGES]

An older Médoc (from Pauillac, for instance) or Graves (Haut-Brion, Domaine de Chevalier, Pape-Clément) from a greater year or a Côte de Nuits grand cru

• • •

ORANGE JELLY
[GELEE A L'ORANGE]

This menu involves no particularly complicated preparation, but the *salmis* must be prepared at the last minute and the final steps require a devoted half-hour.

The *cèpes* will suffer little from being prepared ahead of time and kept warm for a half-hour or so. As for the other courses, the sorrel soup may, but for the final thickening, be prepared in advance, the fritters require only the incorporation of beaten egg whites into the batter, and the actual frying, and the dessert is of necessity prepared hours ahead.

Nasturtiums persist until the first freeze.

Serve the *cèpes* toward the end of the *salmis* service. They marry very well indeed, but the subtlety of each risks being muted by the other's rich presence. One may, by serving in this way, appreciate them together and enjoy them apart.

The presence of mushrooms in two different preparations (they also appear in the *fritto misto*) may seem bizarre, but their similarity is in name only.

Save the leftover egg yolks from the orange jelly (immersed in water to prevent their drying out) for thickening in the soup, and save the unused whites from the soup preparation for the *fritto misto*.

THE SORREL SOUP

With very little cooking, sorrel "melts" almost completely into a puree, and in simpler soups than this one nothing is gained by passing it through a sieve. Its light, refreshing acidity renders it useful in many soups, hot and cold. One sorrel soup, simple in preparation and far less rich, but delicious, is made with water, thickened with potato, and lightly buttered before serving; a finely chopped onion is cooked in butter to which shredded sorrel is added, and when it is reduced to a puree, boiling water and finely sliced potatoes are added and cooked until the latter are partially dissolved.

Sorrel Soup

Potage Germiny

6 ounces sorrel leaves
4 ounces unsalted butter
1 quart consommé (*or veal stock—see page 66*)
¾ cup heavy cream
6 egg yolks
salt
handful of chervil leaves (*stems removed*)

Remove the stems from the sorrel leaves, pulling the stems backward to tear out the fibrous threads in the leaves. Wash the leaves in several waters, drain them well, and gather them into a compact mass on the chopping board, holding them firmly together while cutting or chopping them into coarse shreds (*chiffonade*). Melt 1 ounce of the butter in a heavy saucepan, add the sorrel, and cook over low heat, stirring regularly, until it is reduced almost to a puree (about 15 minutes), then pass it through a fine sieve and return it to the saucepan. Add the stock to the sorrel puree. Mix together, in another receptacle, the cream and the egg yolks. Combine the two mixtures, whisking, and cook over low to medium heat, whisking constantly, until the liquid turns creamy and velvety in consistency. It must absolutely not be allowed to come to a boil. Remove from the heat, taste for seasoning and add salt if necessary, whisk in the remaining butter cut into small pieces, pour the soup into a warmed tureen, and sprinkle it with a handful of chervil leaves.

THE FRITTO MISTO
(Mixed Fritters)

A tomato sauce, served separately, often goes well with *fritto misto,* but in this framework it would not be an attractive preface to the *salmis* sauce. The nuances of the marinating liquid and the fried parsley lend sufficient character to permit these fritters to be served without a sauce.

Fritto Misto (Mixed Fritters)

Fritto Misto (Beignets Mixtes)

1 calf's brain
vinegar *court-bouillon* (*page 64*)
3 medium artichoke hearts, partially cooked, quartered, chokes removed
    (*page 45*) (*small, tender artichokes may be used raw*)
4 ounces small, firm mushrooms, stems trimmed, rapidly rinsed and dried in
    a towel

MARINADE
2 tablespoons olive oil
1 tablespoon chopped *fines herbes* (*page 50*)
salt, freshly ground pepper
juice of ½ lemon

FRYING BATTER
¾ cup flour
salt
2 tablespoons olive oil
about ¾ cup tepid water
2 egg whites

1 quart light olive oil (*preferably*) or other frying oil
1 large handful parsley (*flat-leafed, if available*) bouquets (*short sections of stem
    with leaves attached*)

THE CALF'S BRAIN

Put the brain to soak in cold water. Carefully peel off the fine enveloping membrane, immersing the brain repeatedly in water if the membrane resists. (It sometimes helps to hold it under water while removing particularly adherent sections.) Leave it again to soak in cold water to clear it as nearly as possible of bloodstains.

Slip the brain into the boiling *court-bouillon* and poach it, covered, at a bare simmer, for 20 minutes. Remove it from the liquid and drain it.

Cut the brain into more-or-less cube-shaped pieces measuring approximately ¾ inch across, combine them in a bowl with the artichokes and mushrooms, sprinkle over them the ingredients of the marinade, and mix together all the elements, lifting them with the fingertips and letting them drop back into the bowl. Repeat this two or three times in the course of the marination, always gently, for the brains are fragile. They should be left for about 1 hour.

THE FRYING BATTER

Sift the flour and salt into a bowl, make a well in the center, pour in the oil, and slowly add the water, stirring from the center and moving outward in an enlarging circle as the flour is absorbed. Work the batter no more than is necessary to achieve a smooth mixture, and leave it to relax at kitchen temperature for a good hour to ensure its losing all elasticity. Just before using it, gently fold in the two egg whites, beaten stiff.

Heat the oil until it sizzles at contact with a drop of batter. Do not use a frying basket. Drop several of the elements to be fried into the batter; ladle batter over them with a teaspoon, and drop them from the spoon, one by one, into the hot fat. Avoid cooking more at a time than may freely float without touching one another. Turn the fritters in the fat with the prong tips of a fork, taking care not to pierce the crisp surface, and when they are evenly golden, remove them to a kitchen towel, using a large wire skimming spoon to scoop them up. Keep them warm in a folded towel while frying the remaining batches. It may be necessary to regulate the heat to prevent the oil from becoming too hot.

When the last of the fritters are removed from the oil, drop in the parsley and fry it until crisp (only a few seconds). Drain it on a towel but do not try to "sponge" it, for it will crumble. Serve the fritters enclosed in a folded napkin, the parsley sprinkled on top.

THE PHEASANT SALMIS

A pheasant should be young, hatched in the spring of the same year it is killed. The flesh of the breast will seem tender to the touch and the breastbone flexible; the final and longest wing feather remains pointed. (Older birds may be braised with cabbage or used for stock.) Simply roasted, its breast protected by a leaf of fresh pork fat, young pheasant should be served slightly pink (25 minutes at 450°F; 5 minutes before the end of cooking, remove the leaf of fat, slit the skin between legs and body, and force the legs outward, rupturing the thigh joints) and accompanied by triangles or rounds of crouton spread with *farce gratin* (the pheasant's liver, supplemented by that of a chicken, rapidly sautéed in butter with salt, pepper, and a pinch of herbs, flamed with a spoonful of Cognac and passed through a fine sieve).

A *salmis* is a rare-roasted game bird whose sauce is drawn from the carcass and a reduction of white wine and shallots and tempered with stock. In a professional kitchen a spoonful of meat glaze would lend additional body and succulence to the sauce.

Pheasant Salmis

Salmis de Faisan

1 cup dry white wine
1 tablespoon chopped shallots
velouté (*page 74*) made from 2 cups veal or game-bird stock
1 young pheasant
1 sheet (*barde*) fresh pork fat
1 or 2 large truffles, preferably fresh (*if frozen, slice and add to pheasant pieces before thawing; if sterilized, add truffles' preserving juices to the* velouté)
1 tablespoon Cognac
few tablespoons white wine
2 ounces unsalted butter

Boil the wine and shallots over high heat until only a few spoonfuls of liquid remain. Add it to the *velouté*.

THE PHEASANT

Sprinkle the pheasant inside and out with salt, completely cover the breast with the sheet of pork fat, tie it with kitchen string, and place it in a small skillet or other pan just the size to hold it. Roast it in a very hot oven for 20 minutes. Remove it from the roasting pan and discard the pork fat and any fragments of skin that may be charred. Remove the legs, leaving thighs and drumsticks attached, cut the knuckle from the drumstick bone, and peel off the skin. (Reserve the skin.) Clip the breast and wings loose from the carcass with heavy kitchen shears. Cut the bird in two the length of the breastbone, remove the breastbone, and cut each half in two lengthwise. Remove the skin (reserve it) and any fragments of splintered bone, trim the pieces of pheasant neatly, and place them and the legs in a presentable earthenware or copper *cocotte* just large enough to hold them. Distribute the truffles, sliced fairly thickly, over the surface, grind a bit of pepper over, and sprinkle with the Cognac. Keep the dish covered in a warm place while finishing the sauce.

Pour off the fat from the roasting pan and dissolve the caramelized meat juices in a couple of tablespoons of white wine, stirring, scraping, and reducing over high heat. Chop the reserved skin, trimmings, and carcass coarsely, pound in a mortar, add this and roasting juices to the *velouté*, boil for 8 to 10 minutes, and pass the contents of the saucepan through a sieve, pressing the solids firmly with a pestle to extract all the juices. Bring the sauce back to a boil and simmer with the heat to one side of the saucepan, skimming regularly (see page 48), for about 10 minutes or until the sauce is reduced by about a third. Pass it through a very fine sieve, taste for seasoning, and reheat. Away from the flame, swirl in the butter, cut into small pieces. Pour the sauce over the pheasant and truffles and serve immediately.

Sautéed Cèpes à la Bordelaise

Cèpes Sautés à la Bordelaise

1 pound *cèpes*
¾ cup olive oil
1 tablespoon chopped shallot
1 clove garlic
1 tablespoon fine semi-fresh bread crumbs
2 tablespoons chopped parsley
½ lemon
salt, freshly ground pepper

Choose small, firm mushrooms that have not completely opened out. Larger ones should be reserved for grilling. Don't wash them, but wipe each carefully with a damp towel, after having trimmed the stem ends, to remove any adhering earth or sand. Remove the stems, slice each in two lengthwise, and cut out and discard any parts that may be "wormy." Chop about half the stems (the equivalent of a good cupful) fairly fine and put them aside with the shallot and garlic clove. Any heads that are no larger than a small walnut may be left whole; the others should be cut into halves, quarters, or thick slices.

Heat the oil in a large skillet or sauté pan, add the mushrooms and stem pieces, season, and cook them over high heat for about 10 minutes, tossing them or gently stirring them regularly with a wooden spoon. (At the beginning, the mushrooms must not be too crowded in the pan — if it is not large enough, use two pans and additional oil. After all are browned, they may be put together for the finishing processes.) When the mushrooms are lightly browned, turn the heat to low and leave them to cook, covered, for another 5 minutes or so. Turn the heat to high again, add the chopped stems, chopped shallots, and garlic clove, and cook, stirring and tossing, for another 2 or 3 minutes. Drain off as much of the oil as possible. (The large quantity of oil is essential for the first stage in the cooking to be correctly carried out, but must not remain. It may, however, be used again and will lend an attractive flavor to fried potatoes, for instance.) Turn the heat down again, add the bread crumbs and two-thirds of the chopped parsley, stir together, and leave over a low heat, stirring regularly, long enough for the bread crumbs to absorb the remaining oil. Discard the garlic clove. Sprinkle the mushrooms with a few drops of lemon juice, add salt and pepper to taste, and garnish with the remaining chopped parsley.

THE ORANGE JELLY

Commercial jellies have, understandably, formed a block of prejudice against their highly respectable ancestor. Few people today have ever tasted wine or fresh-fruit calf's-foot jellies, limpid, trembling, set in old-fashioned jelly molds with intricate geometric designs and central tubes. Their beauty of presentation rivals their delicacy of flavor.

Orange Jelly

Gelée à l'Orange

2 calf's feet
2½ quarts water
1 cup sugar
juice of 1 orange and 1 lemon, plus several thin strips of the peel of both
2 egg whites
⅔ cup dry white wine
pinch of cinnamon
3½ cups freshly squeezed orange juice

Have the large, upper bone removed from the calf's feet. Soak them in cold water for 2 or 3 hours, then cover them with fresh cold water and parboil them for 10 minutes. Drain and rinse them well, cover with the 5 pints of water, bring to a boil, cover, and allow to simmer very lightly for about 7 hours. Pass the jelly through a sieve and, when it has cooled until firm, remove all traces of fat, first using a spoon, then wiping the surface with a cloth slightly dampened in hot water. About 1 quart of jelly should remain.

Mix the sugar, the juice of 1 orange and 1 lemon, and the peels together in a saucepan, add the jelly, bring to a boil, and leave to cool for 10 minutes. Beat the egg whites with the white wine, add them with the cinnamon to the jelly, bring to a boil, whisking all the time, then simmer for 15 minutes. Line a sieve with a tightly woven towel, pass the jelly through, and leave it until nearly cool.

Let the orange juice settle for half an hour after squeezing, pass it through a fine cloth, stir it into the jelly, pour the mixture into a mold, and chill for at least 4 hours. Unmold just before serving, first dipping the mold for a second in hot water and wiping it dry.

Two Informal Autumn Dinners

MENU I *(for 4)*

BAKED TROUT STUFFED WITH SORREL
[TRUITES A L'OSEILLE AU FOUR]

A young, fruity, dry white wine: Burgundy (Pouilly-Fuissé, Mercurey, Montagny) or Loire Valley (dry Vouvray or Montlouis)

. . .

SAUTEED VEAL KIDNEYS WITH MUSHROOMS
[ROGNONS DE VEAU SAUTES AU CHAMPIGNONS]

One of the Beaujolais (Chiroubles, Morgon, Fleurie, Brouilly) from the most recent vintage or a Loire Valley red wine (Chinon, Bourgueil, Saumur-Champigny) a couple of years old — any of these served slightly cool

. . .

RICE PILAF
[PILAF]

. . .

LAMB'S LETTUCE AND BEET SALAD
[SALADE DE MACHE ET BETTERAVES]

. . .

CHEESES
[FROMAGES]

The same wine as the preceding, or a Côte de Beaune (Volnay, Pommard, Chassagne-Montrachet)

. . .

CREPE TURBAN, SABAYON SAUCE
[TURBAN DE CREPES, SAUCE SABAYON]

A Sauternes or a sweet Vouvray

THE BAKED TROUT STUFFED WITH SORREL

Whiting, small sea bass, or any white-fleshed, non-fatty fish of the right size to serve as an individual portion may be prepared in this way. The relative firmness of the trout's flesh lends itself particularly well to this preparation. The fragility of whiting, once cooked, renders the service difficult. A bed of stewed sorrel laid with fish fillets, buttered parchment paper pressed on top, dotted with butter, and baked is another happy possibility.

A mousseline forcemeat of the same or another fish (page 76) or a tomatoed *duxelles* (page 58) are other stuffing possibilities for fish boned and baked in this way. The final addition of cream is, in these instances, unnecessary.

Baked Trout Stuffed with Sorrel

Truites à l'Oseille au Four

4 medium trout
1 pound sorrel
4 ounces unsalted butter
salt, freshly ground pepper
1 small onion, finely chopped
¼ cup dry white wine
parchment paper cut slightly smaller than top of baking dish, buttered
¼ cup heavy cream

Using a small, sharp-pointed knife, slit each trout the length of the back on each side of the spinal column in order to separate the fillets cleanly from the central skeletal structure, taking care not to puncture the skin of the belly. Clip the spinal column at the base of the head and about an inch from the tail, remove it, empty the fish, and tear out the gills. Rinse the fish inside and out and sponge dry with paper towels.

Pull the stems backward from the sorrel leaves and detach them, pulling with them any fibrous veins from the leaves. Wash the leaves in several waters, drain them, shred them coarsely on the chopping board, and stew them gently in half the butter, seasoned with salt, stirring frequently, until they have "melted" to a near puree.

Spread onions over the bottom of an earthenware or enameled cast-iron baking or gratin dish just large enough to hold the fish comfortably. Season the fish, inside and out, and arrange them in the dish, belly down. Place a small piece of butter inside each and stuff the cavities with the sorrel puree. Place a thin slice of butter on top of each, sprinkle white wine over and around the fish, gently press the buttered paper on the surface, and bake in a hot oven for about 15 minutes. Upon removing them from the oven, pour a tablespoon of cream over each and serve immediately in their baking dish.

THE SAUTEED VEAL KIDNEYS WITH MUSHROOMS

Calves' kidneys are less strong in flavor than others and most recipes do not recommend discarding the liquid that is drained from them after the initial cooking. It is, however, this liquid that contains the flavor that many people fear. Prepared in the following manner, kidneys rarely fail to please the wariest of guests.

The following is a recipe "type," and is among the simplest of ways to prepare sautéed kidneys. The many variations depend on different garnishing and flavoring elements, but the process remains identical. In professional kitchens meat glaze usually lends additional body and intensity to the sauce.

Sautéed Veal Kidneys with Mushrooms

Rognons de Veau Sautés aux Champignons

2 fresh (*not frozen*) veal kidneys
2 ounces unsalted butter
salt, freshly ground pepper
½ pound mushrooms, cleaned and thickly sliced
2 gray shallots, finely chopped
2 tablespoons Cognac
⅓ cup dry white wine
1 cup heavy cream

Remove the fat and fine surface membrane from the kidneys and cut each symmetrically in two lengthwise. Remove the core of fat and cut each section crosswise into approximately half-inch slices.

Heat the butter in a heavy skillet or sauté pan (avoid enamelware), add the kidneys, salt, and pepper, and cook over high heat, tossing or stirring regularly with a wooden spoon for 2 or 3 minutes, just until the kidneys turn grayish and are firm and somewhat rubbery to the touch — no more; they must remain pink inside. Remove them immediately to a strainer or colander, leaving their cooking butter in the sauté pan, and allow them to drain while finishing the sauce. The brief contact with heat will cause them to "bleed" and this liquid should be discarded.

Season and toss the mushrooms in the same butter, still over high heat, for a couple of minutes or until their natural liquid has evaporated and they are slightly browned. Remove them and replace them with the chopped shallots. Stir them around for a few seconds, add the Cognac and the wine, and reduce almost completely, stirring and scraping with a wooden spoon to loosen and dissolve all adhering frying matter; then return the mushrooms to the pan and add half of the cream. Reduce, stirring constantly, until the sauce becomes fairly thick, adding a bit more cream if it seems too sparse. Lower the heat and return the kidneys to the sauce, stirring them around for a few seconds to ensure their being thoroughly reheated in the sauce, but under no circumstances allow the sauce to boil again, as this would toughen the kidneys. Remove from the heat and stir in enough additional cream to bring the sauce back to a very lightly thickened consistency. Taste for seasoning and serve at once, accompanied by a pilaf (page 78).

Lamb's Lettuce and Beet Salad

Salade de Mâche et Betteraves

Lamb's lettuce is found at Italian greengrocers in large cities. It is easy to raise and, in temperate climates, may be picked all winter long.

Bake the beets in the oven and when they are cooled, peel them and cut them into thin slices, large dice, or coarse julienne sticks. They should be allowed to macerate for an hour or two before being served and the vinaigrette should, because of the natural sweetness of the beets, be somewhat more salty than usual. The lamb's lettuce requires a very thorough washing and should be carefully dried by being pressed between two towels. It should be tossed with the beets only at the moment of serving.

Crepe Turban, Sabayon Sauce

Turban de Crêpes, Sauce Sabayon

½ ounce unsalted butter
crepes (*page 79*)
jam or jelly, such as apricot, currant, blackcurrant

CUSTARD MIXTURE
½ cup sugar
2½ cups milk
strip of lemon peel
3 whole eggs
3 egg yolks
tiny pinch of salt

sabayon sauce (*recipe follows*)

Generously butter a standard 1-quart (8¼ inches in diameter) savarin mold. Spread the crepes lightly, almost to their edges, with jam or jelly and fold them, top down, bottom up, and sides in, one over the other, to form nearly rectangular shapes; fold the sides somewhat obliquely, to adjust for their spoke-like placement in the mold. Press the folded crepes firmly into the mold, seam sides down, overlapping slightly. Chill the mold to firm up the butter and strengthen the adherence of the crepes.

For the custard, combine the sugar, milk, and lemon peel in a saucepan and bring the mixture to a boil. Remove it from the heat, leave it to infuse for 15 minutes, and discard the lemon peel. Beat the eggs and extra egg yolks together in a large bowl as for an omelet, add salt, then pour in the milk mixture, whisking constantly. Pass the mixture through a fine sieve into another mixing bowl, leave it to stand a minute or so, and carefully skim the foam from the surface. Pour the custard into the mold slowly, so as not to displace the crepes, and place the mold in a *bain-marie* — a larger receptacle into which enough nearly-boiling water is poured to immerse the mold by two-thirds. Cook in a slow oven for approximately 40 minutes, taking care that the water never reaches a boil. The pudding is done when the center of the cream is firm to the touch (or when a needle or small pointed knife, plunged into the center, comes out clean).

Leave it to cool, and unmold it while it is still slightly tepid. (If it is left to chill in the mold, the hardened butter will resist unmolding.) The mold should, however, be left over the unmolded pudding to act as a cover and protect it from the air until the moment of serving. Serve well chilled, masked by several spoonfuls of chilled *sabayon* sauce, the rest served separately in a sauceboat.

THE SABAYON SAUCE

The principle is the same as of the rich, heady Italian *zabaglione,* but with a light white wine replacing the Marsala, a *sabayon* finds a far wider range of application. It may also be prepared with champagne, Sauternes, etc., but if a particularly fine wine is used, it would be an error to add an additional flavor such as lemon or vanilla. With a hot dessert, *sabayon* should be prepared at the last minute and served hot. The flavor of a cold *sabayon* may be attenuated by the addition of a certain amount of whipped cream, if one likes.

Sabayon Sauce

Sauce Sabayon

½ cup sugar
3 egg yolks
⅔ cup dry white wine
3 thin strips of lemon peel, cut crosswise into tiny, threadlike julienne strips

Beat the sugar and egg yolks together in a saucepan (the sauce doubles in quantity, so choose the saucepan accordingly) until creamy. Add the white wine and the julienne of lemon peel and whisk in a *bain-marie* (in this case, the saucepan is immersed in a larger saucepan of nearly-boiling water on top of the stove) over low heat until the sauce is thickened. The water should be kept near the boiling point, but should not boil. Lower the heat, if necessary, or raise it if the process seems to take too long.

Two Informal Autumn Dinners

MENU II *(for 4)*

PIKE DUMPLINGS A LA LYONNAISE
[*QUENELLES DE BROCHET A LA LYONNAISE*]

A rustic, dry white wine: Cassis or Côtes-du-Rhône (Crozes-Hermitage, non-sparkling Saint-Péray)

· · ·

VEAL CUTLETS A LA TAPENADE
[*ESCALOPES DE VEAU A LA TAPENADE*]

A meridional red wine: Palette (Château Simone), Bandol or Côtes-du-Rhône (Côtes-du-Rhône-Villages, Crozes-Hermitage, Saint-Joseph), or one of the lesser Piedmont wines (Dolcetto, Barbera d'Alba)

· · ·

ARTICHOKE PUREE
[*PUREE D'ARTICHAUTS*]

· · ·

CHEESES
[*FROMAGES*]

The same wine as the preceding course, or a wine of similar type but older, an Hermitage, following one of the Côte-du-Rhônes

· · ·

APPLE MOUSSE WITH PEACHES
[*MOUSSE DE POMMES AUX PECHES*]

One of the Bordelais noble-rot wines: Barsac, Loupiac, Sainte Croix-du-Mont

The work may be organized to eliminate all but a few last-minute details: the pike-dumpling mixture may be prepared a day or so ahead and the *quenelles* need only be poached and gratinéed at the last minute; the veal cutlets may be prepared, except for the actual frying, several hours ahead of time; and the artichoke puree may be merely reheated and buttered at the last minute. The dessert, except for the presentation, is automatically prepared in advance.

THE PIKE QUENELLES A LA LYONNAISE

Pike *quenelles* are often made from a simple pike mousseline forcemeat, and are light and elegant in spirit. The hearty, rustic *quenelles* have more body. They may be served in any simple cream or *béchamel* sauce or any fish sauce (*à l'américaine* or *velouté,* for example, containing a garnish of shrimp tails, mushrooms, mussels, scallops, if one likes) that will not separate through contact with heat. After having been poached, these *quenelles* should always be baked in a sauce, during which time they continue to swell.

Note: Fresh haddock, whiting, monkfish, trout, etc., can be used if pike is not available.

Pike Dumplings à la Lyonnaise

Quenelles de Brochet à la Lyonnaise

PANADE FOR QUENELLES
  2 egg yolks
  ⅔ cup milk
  3 heaping tablespoons flour
  salt, freshly ground pepper, freshly grated nutmeg
  1½ ounces unsalted butter, melted

  ½ pound beef suet (*dry, crumbly fat from around the kidney*)
  ½ pound raw pike, bones and skin removed
  salt, freshly ground pepper
  2 egg whites
  1 cup heavy cream
  2 ounces unsalted butter
  freshly grated cheese (*half Parmesan, half Gruyère*)

THE PANADE

Separate the eggs and put the whites aside. Bring the milk to a boil and leave it to cool slightly. Sift the flour into a mixing bowl, add salt, pepper, a tiny bit of nutmeg, and the egg yolks. Begin mixing, working from the center, add the melted butter, then slowly add the milk, stirring constantly until the mixture is completely amalgamated. Whisk it over medium heat until it is thick, spread the paste on a plate, and chill it.

THE QUENELLES

Crumble the suet in your hands, discarding membranous material, and pound it in a mortar, first alone, then with the chilled *panade,* until they form a well-blended paste. Put this mixture aside. Pound the pike until it is reduced to a puree, then pound the two mixtures together, finally working the pestle in a grinding motion to ensure a total amalgamation. Add salt and pepper if necessary, then add the egg whites in small quantities at a time, working the paste until each addition of egg white is thoroughly absorbed. Pass the mixture through a fine drum sieve, a tablespoonful at a time (page 47). Pack it into a bowl and put it to chill in the refrigerator. It may be kept for several days in this state, if desired, the surface protected by plastic wrap. If it is to be used immediately, pack it in a metal bowl and embed it in cracked ice for an hour before using.

To poach the *quenelles,* use a large receptacle wider than it is deep (a roasting pan is perfect for this purpose), well filled with boiling salted water.

Form the *quenelles* on a lightly floured board, using a heaping tablespoonful of mixture for each and rolling them with the palm of the hand into elongated cylinders. Lower the heat so that the water no longer boils and drop the *quenelles* in one by one. Leave them to poach for a few minutes, covered. (If the water threatens to return to a boil, turn off the heat.) The *quenelles* will first sink. When they rise to the surface, they are ready. Gently lift them from the water, one at a time, with a perforated skimming spoon and put them to drain on a towel or absorbent paper. Arrange them fairly closely in a buttered baking dish, leaving enough space for them to swell during the gratin process. Pour in the cream, distribute the butter in several thin slices over the surface, and sprinkle with the grated cheese. Bake in a medium oven (350°F) for 15 or 20 minutes or until the cream is in large part absorbed and the surface colored golden.

THE VEAL CUTLETS A LA TAPENADE

Tapéno means caper in Provençal, and a *tapenade* is a spread or paste, basically a puree, of capers and black olives whose flavor is heightened by the addition of various other aromatic elements.

Veal Cutlets à la Tapenade

Escalopes de Veau à la Tapenade

4 veal cutlets, cut thin but not flattened
marinade of lemon, dried oregano flowers, olive oil
salt, freshly ground pepper
tapenade (recipe follows)
2 eggs
bread crumbs made of firm-textured, stale, but not dried out white bread,
    grated
olive oil *(for frying)*
stewed tomatoes *(recipe follows)*
1 tablespoon chopped parsley

Trim the cutlets, removing any fat or gristle, sprinkle them on both sides with lemon juice, oregano, and a few drops of olive oil, and leave them to marinate for an hour or so, turning them from time to time.

Season the cutlets on both sides and spread one side of each with the *tapenade*. Put them to chill to render the *tapenade* firmer and easier to handle.

Beat the eggs as for an omelette. Place each cutlet, *tapenade* side up, in the dish of beaten egg, and scoop egg over it with a spoon. Then lift each cutlet carefully to the crumbs, sprinkle crumbs generously over the surface, and pat or press gently with the palm of the hand to ensure their adhering. Remove the cutlets to a chopping board or a piece of waxed paper sprinkled with crumbs and leave them to dry out or "set" slightly before frying.

Heat the olive oil to a depth of about ½ inch (you will need either a very large or two medium-sized frying pans) and cook the cutlets until golden on each side, turning the heat down to medium-low, once the oil is heated. Turn them carefully, without piercing the crust. Drain them on a cloth and transfer them to a heated serving plate, a stewed tomato topped by a pinch of parsley on each. Serve the artichoke puree separately.

TAPENADE

4 salt anchovy fillets, soaked in water and sponged dry with absorbent paper
1 tablespoon capers, rinsed and well drained
¼ pound pitted black olives *(niçoises if available)*
1 teaspoon Cognac
2 tablespoons olive oil

Combine all ingredients in a food processor, or grind the anchovy fillets and capers together in a mortar until they form a paste, add the olives, and pound until the mixture forms a well-unified, coarse puree. Pass it through a sieve, using a pestle, and work in the Cognac and enough oil to form a fairly firm but easily workable paste.

STEWED TOMATOES

4 canned whole peeled tomatoes (*Italian canned "plum" tomatoes are good for this purpose*) or 4 garden tomatoes, peeled and seeded (*page 44*)
1 ounce unsalted butter
1 clove garlic, crushed

When garden-ripened tomatoes are in season, use them, peeled and seeded. If canned tomatoes are used, press them gently to rid them of extra juice and seeds, retaining their form as nearly as possible. Cook the raw tomatoes, seasoned with salt and pepper, over a very low heat with the butter and the crushed garlic clove. Do not cook for too long a period or over too high a heat or they will disintegrate. Canned tomatoes need only be heated through with the butter and garlic. The best are, of course, those that you have canned yourself, peeling and seeding them before canning, covered with pureed tomato and sterilized without any preliminary cooking process.

Artichoke Puree

Purée d'Artichauts

8 large artichoke bottoms, precooked (*page 45*)
about ¼ pound unsalted butter
salt, freshly ground pepper

Stew the artichoke bottoms in half the butter over low heat, using either a stainless-steel or an earthenware dish, the latter protected from the direct flame by an asbestos pad, until very tender. Pass them, along with their cooking butter, through a nylon or stainless-steel sieve (or reduce to a puree in a food processor). Taste for seasoning and reheat the puree rapidly over fairly high heat, stirring and beating it constantly with a wooden spoon to prevent its sticking or burning. Beat in the remaining butter, half of which has been melted and cooked until brown and nutty in odor, the other half fresh, cut into small pieces. The nutty flavor of the brown butter enhances the artichokes' natural flavor. The puree will be fairly thin. For those who prefer more body, a freshly baked, sieved potato may be stirred in.

Apple Mousse with Peaches

Mousse de Pommes aux Pêches

1 pound apples, cored, peeled, and sliced
1 tablespoon water
pinch of cinnamon
2 cups milk
1 vanilla bean
⅔ cup sugar

MERINGUE
2 egg whites
tiny pinch of salt
¾ cup confectioners' sugar

4 egg yolks
½ ounce unflavored gelatin
¾ cup heavy cream
3 home-canned peaches or halved fresh peaches poached in sugar syrup
½ cup good port wine
2 cups stewed apricots, sugared to taste

Cook the apples with the tablespoon of water and the cinnamon in a saucepan over medium heat, stirring from time to time, until tender but not cooked into a complete puree. Pass them through a sieve and put them aside.

Boil the milk with the vanilla bean and the sugar. Remove it from the heat and leave it to infuse for 15 to 20 minutes.

For the meringue, add the pinch of salt to the egg whites and beat them until stiff. Sift the confectioners' sugar over them and mix thoroughly but without violence.

Remove the vanilla bean and reheat the milk, regulating the heat to a bare simmer. Drop teaspoonfuls of meringue into the milk, poaching only a few at a time, for they swell and should not be crowded. After a couple of minutes, carefully turn them over in the simmering milk, leave them to poach another couple of minutes, and remove them to a nylon drum sieve that has been placed over a mixing bowl to collect the milk that drains from them. Repeat the poaching process until all are done, transferring the meringues to a plate as they are drained.

Combine the poaching milk with that collected from draining the meringues. Beat the egg yolks in a saucepan and slowly pour in the milk, whisking the while. Cook over medium heat, stirring constantly with a wooden spoon, until the mixture coats the spoon. Add the gelatin, first softened in a bit of cold water and combined with 2 or 3 tablespoons of egg-milk mixture. Continue stirring the custard over heat for a few seconds to permit the gelatin to dissolve completely, but do not allow the custard to come to a boil. Mix the custard and the apple puree together and chill, keeping an eye on it; when the mixture begins to jell, whip the cream until fairly firm, but not stiff, and fold it well into the apple mixture.

Lightly oil a savarin mold with sweet almond oil (or, lacking that, a tasteless vegetable oil), fill it with the mixture, tap the bottom of the mold 2 or 3 times on a table top to settle the contents, and chill, either in the coldest part of the refrigerator or directly in cracked ice, for at least 4 hours.

Put the peaches to macerate in the port wine.

Pass the stewed apricots through a sieve, add the wine in which the peaches have macerated, and taste for sugar. A bit of lemon juice may be a useful addition.

Just before serving, dip the mold for 2 or 3 seconds into hot water and unmold the mousse onto a large, round, chilled platter. Pour some of the apricot sauce in a circle around the mousse, distributing the meringues on top of the ribbon of sauce, fill the central cavity of the mousse with the macerated peaches, mask them with a few tablespoonfuls of sauce, and serve the rest of the sauce in a sauceboat.

A Festive Autumn Meal for Two

THE MENU

CUCUMBER SALAD, CREAM SAUCE
[CONCOMBRES FRAIS A LA CREME]

*If a light, white wine or champagne was drunk as aperitif, continue it, or
serve the following wine*

• • •

BAKED LOBSTER GARIN
[HOMARD AU FOUR, FAÇON GARIN]

*A white Côte de Beaune (Corton-Charlemagne, or one of the more
distinguished Meursault growths (Perrières, Genevrières, Charmes) or one
of the unusual pinot blancs from the Côte de Nuits (Nuits-Saint-Georges,
la Perrière or Morey-Saint-Denis, Monts-Luisants)*

• • •

BRAISED AND ROAST PARTRIDGE WITH CABBAGE
[PERDRIX AUX CHOUX]

*A robust, young red Burgundy (Fixin, Pernand-Vergelesses, Santenay) or
a fairly young Pomerol (Vieux-Château-Certan, La Conseillante)*

• • •

CHEESES
[FROMAGES]

*The same as the preceding or an older Côte de Nuits (one of the Gevrey-
Chambertin or Vosne-Romanée growths), or, following a Pomerol, an older
Saint-Emilion*

• • •

FRESH FIGS WITH RASPBERRY CREAM
[FIGUES A LA CREME FRAMBOISEE]

A sweet Anjou (Coteaux du Layon, Quarts de Chaume) or a Sauternes

When faced with the problem of composing a menu for two, one is nearly always tempted to fall back on a simple hors d'oeuvre and a *grillade*, there being few *cuisiné* preparations practicable for a small service. Lobster and partridge both lend themselves by nature to a luxurious concept of eating and, by size, to a meal for two. There is otherwise no reason that this menu may not be conceived for any number of guests.

The cucumber salad does nothing for a wine and, if one were drinking a light white wine or champagne as aperitif, it would be better to continue it during the first course rather than dissipate the pleasure of beginning a carefully chosen great white wine at the moment the lobster is served.

All preparations, with the exception of the actual baking of the lobster, the roasting of the young partridge, and the whipping of the cream for dessert, are automatically finished well before the dinner hour. (The cabbage and old partridge may even be prepared the previous day and gently reheated without suffering.)

The lobster should be put to cook just before going to table and the partridge to roast no earlier than 10 minutes after the lobster has been served — lobster is not a thing to eat hurriedly and it is far better to wait for a roast partridge than to risk making *it* wait.

THE CUCUMBER SALAD IN CREAM SAUCE

Cream sauce is occasionally a pleasant change from a vinaigrette for a green salad and nicely accommodates any number of raw-vegetable hors-d'oeuvre salads. Raw mushrooms, first marinated in lemon juice and seasoning, the cream added later, are delicious. Lemon juice should always replace vinegar when cream is used. With cucumbers, fresh dill may replace the chervil.

Cucumber Salad, Cream Sauce

Concombres Frais à la Crème

2 medium cucumbers
salt
1 lemon
freshly ground pepper
½ cup heavy cream
1 tablespoon chopped chervil

Peel the cucumbers and rinse them (a precaution against an occasional bitter-tasting skin). They may either be split lengthwise, the seeds removed, and sliced thinly, or, for a prettier presentation, cut into approximately 2-inch lengths, seeded with a coring device, and each section cut into rings. Spread them in layers in a soup plate or bowl, generously sprinkling each layer with salt, leave them for an hour or two to rid them of their excess water, and drain them well, pressing firmly.

Mix the lemon juice (starting with the juice of ½ lemon and adding more later, if necessary) and pepper (but not salt) in a bowl and slowly stir in the cream. Mix together with the cucumbers, mound the mixture neatly on the serving plate, and sprinkle with the chervil.

THE BAKED LOBSTER GARIN

The simple but ingenious notion of punching a hole in the carapace through which to enrich the flesh of the lobster with herb butter while it cooks eliminates any risk of its drying out. The juices are all retained. The claws lend themselves imperfectly to this preparation and are poached separately *à la nage*.

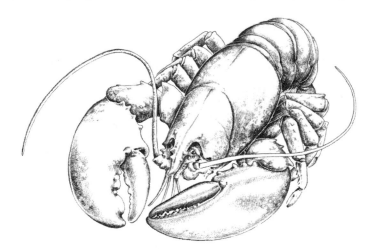

Baked Lobster Garin

Homard au Four, Façon Garin

HERB BUTTER
    ½ cup dry white wine
    2½ tablespoons *pastis (or other anise-flavored liqueur)*
    1 large pinch mixed herbs (*page 52*)
    salt, freshly ground pepper
    ½ pound unsalted butter, softened

ANCHOVY BUTTER
1 salt anchovy, soaked, filleted, rinsed, and dried
½ ounce unsalted butter

3 tablespoons olive oil
white-wine *court-bouillon* (*for the claws*) (*page 64*)
1 lively lobster weighing about 1½ pounds

THE HERB BUTTER

Reduce the white wine, *pastis*, and herbs over high heat until only about 3 table-spoonfuls of liquid remain in the saucepan. Leave the mixture until it is luke-warm, season it with salt and pepper, and whisk it vigorously with the softened butter. (Part of this butter will serve for basting and the remainder will accompany the lobster at table.)

THE ANCHOVY BUTTER

Pound the anchovy fillets to a fine paste in a mortar, then mash in the butter. (Ordinarily, it would be passed through a sieve, but for this preparation, it is not essential.)

The top of a lobster carapace presents the pattern of a cross where the two side shields and the head meet. Before the claws are removed, a sharply pointed, stiff-bladed knife can be pushed down through the shell and the body at the heart of the cross, where the lines meet, severing the central nerve and killing the lobster instantly.

Pour the olive oil into a heavy oval *poêle* or gratin dish of just the size to hold the lobster, and heat it in a very hot oven. Tear off the claws — a simple twist is all that is necessary — and put them into a saucepan with the boiling *court-bouillon* to poach, covered; after they have simmered for 10 minutes, remove the saucepan from the heat, leaving them in the cooking liquid, and put the lobster into its oven-heated dish. Turn it around in the hot oil several times over a period of about 10 minutes, or until it is equally reddened on all sides. Lower the heat of the oven to about 325°F, take out the pan, and, using the handle end of a wooden spoon (for instance), punch a hole in the center (top side) of the lobster shell, which contains the coral and terminates in the head, and insert the anchovy butter and as much of the herb butter as can be forced in. Return it to the oven, and, over a period of 20 minutes, regularly force more herb butter into the hole (4 to 5 tablespoons in all).

Split the lobster in two, discard the gravel sack ("queen") to be found at the head's extremity, and serve accompanied by the rest of the herb butter. Serve the claws after.

BRAISED AND ROAST PARTRIDGE WITH CABBAGE

Braised old partridge *(perdrix)* and cabbage usually is served as is, the bird picked out from its nest of cabbage and presented crowning the mount of cabbage, the garnish of carrots and side pork surrounding it. A sausage is often braised and included in the garnish. (Out of game season, guinea fowl may be treated in the same way.) One must not expect too much of the old partridge, all of whose flavor has gone to enrich the cabbage, but in combination with the young partridge *(perdreau)* roasted slightly rare, just out of the oven, the total experience is perfect.

Should the cabbage-braising liquid remain from a recent *pot-au-feu* (see page 226), it will serve splendidly. While it is unlikely that the home cook will use a concentrated stock made exclusively from partridge carcasses, the result, when this essence serves as the braising liquid, is spectacular.

Braised and Roast Partridge with Cabbage

Perdrix aux Choux

1 medium cabbage (*2 to 2½ pounds*)
½ pound *pancetta (substitute slab bacon, if necessary)*, cut into 2 thick slices
1 old partridge
½ ounce unsalted butter
¼ cup white wine
mirepoix (page 55), prepared from 1 medium carrot, 1 large onion, and more
    herbs than usual
2 carrots, peeled
2 cups veal stock (*page 66*)

ROAST PARTRIDGE
1 young partridge (*hung for 3 or 4 days but not "high"*)
pinch of oregano
½ ounce unsalted butter
1 thin sheet fresh pork back fat

Remove the outer leaves from the cabbage, cut it in two, cut out the core, separate the leaves, and pare the thick ribs from each. Gather the leaves together on a chopping board, and shred them coarsely. Parboil the cabbage in a large quantity of salted water for 10 minutes, drain it in a colander, refreshing it with cold water, and squeeze it thoroughly in your hands to rid it of all excess water.

Cover the slices of *pancetta* with cold water, bring to a boil, simmer for 8 to 10 minutes, and drain.

Cook the old partridge in the butter, in a small skillet or heavy saucepan, for about 15 minutes, turning it regularly, keeping the heat low enough to avoid any smoking. When it is lightly colored on all sides, remove it and wash out the pan with the white wine, scraping loose any frying adherents and reducing the liquid to a tablespoon or two.

Line the bottom of a heavy copper saucepan or an earthenware or enameled cast-iron casserole with half the *mirepoix*, spread a bed of cabbage on top, place the partridge in the middle, a carrot and a slice of *pancetta* to either side, pour over the bit of white-wine reduction from the cooking pan, regularly distribute the remaining *mirepoix,* and add the rest of the cabbage, packing it lightly and smoothing the surface. Heat the stock enough to melt it, pour in enough to rise just above the cabbage's surface, bring to a boil over medium heat, and cook, covered, either over very low heat or in a slow oven, at a bare simmer, for at least 2½ hours in all. After 1 to 1½ hours, the *pancetta* should be thoroughly cooked. Remove it carefully and put it aside. If at this time the quantity of liquid seems excessive, continue the braising with the lid ajar to permit evaporation; if it seems low, add some boiling stock. After 2½ hours, remove the partridge, lift the flesh from the bones (it will be in a condition to fall off), chop it coarsely, and return it to the cabbage. The braising liquid should be almost completely reduced if the cabbage is still quite liquid, continue cooking it for 10 to 15 minutes on top of the stove with the lid off, at a sufficient heat to produce a regular, gentle bubbling, or drain the liquid off into a saucepan, reduce it over high heat, and pour it back over the cabbage. (If it is to be reheated, it may remain slightly liquid — it will arrive at the correct state of reduction through a slow reheating.) Return the *pancetta* a few minutes before serving to heat through. Taste for salt; none should be needed, as the stock, the *mirepoix,* and the pork are all salted and the reduction should do the rest.

THE ROAST PARTRIDGE

Once cleaned and singed, sprinkle salt, pepper, and oregano into the body cavity, insert the butter, salt and pepper the outside, place the sheet of pork fat over the breast, and tie the bird, encircling it 2 or 3 times with kitchen string to keep the slice of fat in place.

It is difficult to give a precise timing or method for roasting partridge — a fresh specimen requires a bit longer than one several days old, and, despite thermostats, ovens differ.

Choose a heavy, shallow roasting pan just large enough to hold the trussed bird (a small frying pan or a tiny gratin dish), start it out in a very hot oven, and, after 5 minutes or so, turn it down to about 350°F. After 10 to 12 minutes in the oven, clip the strings, remove the sheet of fat, and 5 minutes later turn the oven off, leaving the bird in the oven for another 5 or 6 minutes (something over 20 minutes, in all). From the time the slice of fat is removed, it should be basted every couple of minutes. When done, the flesh of the breast should remain slightly rose in color. (A more usual but less satisfactory method consists in roasting the bird unattended in a 400°F oven for 18 minutes.)

Mound the cabbage onto a heated, deep serving platter, split the roast partridge in two, place the halves on the cabbage, and surround them with the slices of side pork, each cut into 4 or 5 sections, and the carrots, cut into thick slices.

Fresh Figs with Raspberry Cream

Figues à la Crème Framboisée

1 pound fresh figs (*tree-ripened and freshly picked, if possible*)
½ pound fresh raspberries
sugar to taste
⅔ cup heavy cream

Peel the figs, leaving them whole (the skin pulls off very easily in strips), arrange them in a serving dish, and chill them well. Pass the raspberries through a nylon (not metal) drum sieve and stir in the sugar. Whip the chilled cream in a chilled bowl until just stiff, mix in the raspberry puree, and pour over the figs.

Four Simple Autumn Menus

*Except for the last menu, which requires no white wine, each of these menus
will be happily served by a thirst-quenching, dry white wine, the younger
the better — Bourgogne Aligoté, Entre-Deux-Mers (Bordeaux),
Muscadet, Gros Plant, Pouilly-sur-Loire, or Quincy (all from the Loire
valley), Swiss Fendant, or, from Italy, Soave (Veneto) or Cortese di Gava
(Piedmont) — and an uncomplicated young red wine, cool, fruity, and
plentiful — Bourgogne Passe-tout-grains, Beaujolais or Côtes-du-Rhône
Primeur, Chinon or Saumur-Champigny (Loire valley), Dolcetto
(Piedmont), or California Zinfandel.*

MENU I *(for 4)*

SALAD OF GRILLED SWEET PEPPERS
[POIVRONS DOUX GRILLES EN SALADE]

• • •

LAMB STEW WITH ARTICHOKE HEARTS
*[RAGOUT D'EPAULE D'AGNEAU AUX COEURS
D'ARTICHAUTS]*

• • •

RICE PILAF
[PILAF DE RIZ]

• • •

WILD SALAD
[SALADE SAUVAGE]

• • •

CHEESES
[FROMAGES]

• • •

PEARS IN RED WINE
[POIRES AU VIN ROUGE]

Grilled Pepper Salad

Poivrons Doux Grillés en Salade

The taste of raw peppers contains no hint of the subtle flavor brought out through grilling. Red, yellow, and green have distinctly different flavors and a mixture of the three is attractive. Choose them large, firm, smooth, heavy, and of regular shape (those tortuously formed cannot be evenly grilled). They are best grilled over hot coals, but may perfectly well be prepared beneath a grill.

The flesh should be semi-cooked. A heat that is too intense will char the skins before the flesh becomes soft; one that is too gentle will dehydrate the flesh before the skins are loosened. Turn the peppers regularly so that all surfaces, including the stem end, are equally grilled. Some surfaces will be charred, others not, and the skins will be blistered. Once grilled, they should be transferred immediately to a plate to avoid any loss of liquid and covered with a damp towel, which has the effect of further loosening the skins.

Remove them, one at a time, to another plate, slip off the skins, pull out and discard the stem ends, and open each pepper out, scooping up all remaining seeds with a teaspoon, draining them in a small sieve so as to lose none of the precious juices.

Prepare a vinaigrette (page 55) by first pounding a small clove of garlic, coarse salt, and freshly ground pepper to a paste in a mortar, dissolving the paste in aromatic vinegar (page 53), and stirring in the peppers' juices before adding the olive oil. Lay the peppers out, in alternating colors, skin sides facing up, on a large platter. Salt anchovies, first soaked, filleted, rinsed, and dried between paper towels, may be laid atop in a criss-cross pattern, and finely sliced spring onions may be scattered around before the abundant vinaigrette is evenly spooned over all surfaces. Chopped flat-leafed parsley, mixed with finely chopped fresh hyssop or savory leaves, can be sprinkled here and there.

THE LAMB STEW WITH ARTICHOKE HEARTS

Although the fat should be removed before cooking, lamb of good quality is naturally covered with a healthy layer of white fat, and the flesh should be a clear, rose-tan color.

The kind of oil used for browning in a preparation of this sort is not terribly important, for although without it onions, meat, sugar, and flour could not be properly colored (all essential to the deep color and rich flavor of the sauce), it will ultimately be skimmed and discarded.

A heavy copper sauté pan is the best utensil; lacking that, one should execute the first steps in a heavy iron skillet and transfer everything to an earthenware or enameled ironware casserole for the longer braising process. The pan should be precisely the right size to hold the pieces of meat placed side by side but barely touching; if it is too large, its surfaces not contacted by the meat will burn while the meat browns; if it is so small that the pieces of meat have to be packed in, they will boil in their juices rather than brown. Moreover, the eventual quality of the sauce depends on the solid elements' being closely arranged in a pan of the right size so that they may be completely submerged in a minimum of liquid.

Lamb Stew with Artichoke Hearts

Ragoût d'Epaule d'Agneau aux Coeurs d'Artichauts

shoulder of lamb, boned
4 to 12 artichokes (*depending on size*) pared and cooked (*page 45*), chokes
    removed
1½ ounces unsalted butter
3 medium onions, coarsely chopped
3 tablespoons olive or other vegetable oil
salt
1 teaspoon sugar
flour
1 scant teaspoon mixed herbs (*page 52*)
2 cloves garlic, crushed and peeled
1 bay leaf
1 cup dry white wine
2 large, firm, well-ripened tomatoes, peeled, seeded (*page 44*), and coarsely
    chopped
water

Cut the shoulder into 8 pieces of approximately equal size, respecting as nearly as possible the natural muscular structure, and remove all surface fat.

Sponge the artichokes dry and leave them whole or cut them into halves or quarters, depending on their size. Stew them gently in butter for 20 to 30 minutes, tossing from time to time or delicately turning them. They should still remain slightly firm. Put them aside.

Cook the onions in the oil over low to medium heat, stirring them regularly, until they are lightly browned. Watch them closely, for they burn easily. Remove them, leaving as much oil as possible in the pan. The slightest fragment of onion that remains in the pan at this point will inevitably burn while the meat is coloring and leave a bitter taste in the sauce. Salt the pieces of meat on all sides and put them to cook in the same fat, turning the heat up somewhat. When they are browned on all sides, lower the heat again, sprinkle with the sugar, and turn the pieces around in the pan from time to time over a period of a couple of minutes until the sugar has had time to caramelize. Hold a lid over the pan, pour off the excess fat, return to the heat, and sprinkle with flour. Turn the pieces over again and, when the flour has lightly browned, return the onions to the pan, sprinkle with the mixed herbs, and add the garlic and the bay leaf. Lift all the elements and turn them around with a wooden spoon until they are well mixed, and pour in the white wine. Turn the heat up, stir and scrape the bottom and sides of the pan well to be certain that all adherent frying matter is loosened and dissolved, reduce somewhat, and add the tomatoes plus just enough boiling water to submerge the meat. Bring to a boil and cook, covered, at a bare simmer, either over very low heat or in a slow oven, for 1½ hours. Skim off the surface fat 2 or 3 times during this period.

Lift out the pieces of meat, discard the bay leaf, and leave the sauce to rest for a few minutes. Skim off all traces of fat that rise to the surface and pass the sauce and onions through a fine sieve into another saucepan. Return the meat to the pan, add the artichoke hearts, and leave, covered, in a warm place.

Bring the sauce to a boil and leave it on the side of a very low heat, skinning it regularly (page 48) for about 30 minutes. It should, at this point, be of a perfect consistency. If it seems a bit liquid, turn the heat up and reduce rapidly, stirring all the while. Taste for salt, pour the sauce over the meat and its garnish, and leave it to simmer, ever so gently, covered, for another 30 minutes. Serve directly from the cooking pot, accompanied by a pilaf (page 78).

Pears in Red Wine

Poires au Vin Rouge

4 or 5 slightly underripe eating pears
1 orange
cinnamon
⅔ cup sugar
1 bottle good red wine

Cut the pears in two lengthwise, core and peel them, and arrange the halves in the bottom of an earthenware or enameled ironware terrine. (If they are to be cooked in the oven, Pyrex or porcelain will do as well.) Wash the orange to remove any hint of insecticide or preservative, and shave a long spiral from the peel, keeping clear of the white, pithy material. Add it to the pears, sprinkle very lightly with cinnamon, add the sugar and the wine, bring to a boil, and leave, covered, to simmer for about 2 hours (with certain hard varieties of cooking pears, one may allow as much as 6 to 8 hours' cooking time) or until they are coated in a thin syrup. Serve them chilled, accompanied by *tuiles* (page 84) or other simple cookies.

Four Simple Autumn Menus

MENU II *(for 4)*

This menu will be happily served by a thirst-quenching, dry white wine, the younger the better — Bourgogne Aligoté, Entre-Deux-Mers (Bordeaux), Muscadet, Gros Plant, Pouilly-sur-Loire, or Quincy (all from the Loire valley), Swiss Fendant, or, from Italy, Soave (Veneto) or Cortese di Gava (Piedmont) — and an uncomplicated young red wine, cool, fruity, and plentiful — Bourgogne Passe-tout-grains, Beaujolais or Côtes-du-Rhône Primeur, Chinon or Saumur-Champigny (Loire valley), Dolcetto (Piedmont), or California Zinfandel.

COMPOSED SALAD
[SALADE COMPOSEE]

• • •

BOILED PIGS' TAILS AND EARS WITH VEGETABLES
[POTEE AUX QUEUES ET OREILLES DE COCHON]

• • •

GOAT CHEESES
[FROMAGES DE CHEVRE]

• • •

PERIGORD PUDDING
[FLAUGNARDE]

THE COMPOSED SALAD

A composed salad may be a combination of any number of things. Lobster, truffles, asparagus tips, chicken breast, crayfish tails, and artichoke hearts often enter into the composition of elegant versions. Depending on its makeup and the menu, it may begin a meal or be the principal course.

Composed Salad

Salade Composée

> 3 small new potatoes of nonmealy variety
> ½ cup dry white wine
> 3 pints mussels, scraped, soaked, and rinsed in salt water
> 1 onion, chopped

SAUCE
> 1 lemon
> 1 teaspoon chopped tender fresh dill (*or a pinch of dried dill weed*)
> scant teaspoon French mustard
> salt, freshly ground pepper
> ½ cup heavy cream (*a few days old, if possible*)

> 1 celery heart, crispened in ice water, if necessary, and sliced thinly, crosswise
> lettuce leaves

Boil the potatoes in their skins, peel them the moment they are drained, slice them into a bowl, pour the white wine over, and leave them to cool.

Put the mussels and chopped onion into a large pot, pour over the wine from the cooled potatoes, cover tightly, and place over high heat, shaking the pot occasionally. Leave them only long enough for all the mussels to open (3 or 4 minutes). Remove them from their shells, put them aside, and allow the cooking liquid to settle for a few minutes. Pour it carefully through a sieve lined with muslin into a small saucepan, leaving all the heavy sediment behind. Reduce the liquid rapidly by half. Taste it — fresh mussels often contain a large quantity of sea water and their cooking liquid is intensely salty — and use it accordingly in the seasoning of the sauce.

SAUCE

Mix together the juice of ½ lemon, the chopped dill, the mustard, and some freshly ground pepper. (If dried dill is used, allow it to macerate for half an hour in the lemon juice.) Stir in the cream and add as much (if any) of the mussels' cooking liquid as the sauce can support without becoming too thin. Taste for salt, lemon, and other seasoning and adjust if necessary.

Mix the celery, the mussels, and the potatoes into the sauce carefully, so as not to damage the potato slices, turn it out onto a platter or shallow bowl lined with lettuce leaves, and sprinkle with chopped fresh dill or *fines herbes*.

BOILED PIGS' TAILS AND EARS WITH VEGETABLES

A *potée* is a mixture of meats and vegetables, boiled, traditionally, in a large earthenware pot. Each province of France has its own. This, although all its components are found in one or another *potée,* is not traditional; it lacks the preserved goose of one, the smoked sausage of another, etc. If ears and tails are available only fresh, sprinkle them generously with coarse salt (put layers of salt and meat in a large bowl or spread out on a platter), cover, and leave for several days. Rinse well before using.

A *potée* for 4 can always feed 6. The unused cooking liquid forms a splendid base for a rough peasant soup.

Boiled Pigs' Tails and Ears with Vegetables

Potée aux Queues et Oreilles de Cochon

1 small cabbage (*preferably green*)
4 medium leeks
4 pigs' tails and 2 ears, salted
½ pound slice of lean bacon, salted or smoked
bouquet-garni (page 50)
1 whole head of garlic, unpeeled
½ pound turnips, peeled
¾ pound carrots, peeled
2 onions, peeled, 1 stuck with 2 cloves
small handful of coarse salt
1 pound fresh white beans, shelled, or 1 cup dried beans, partially cooked
½ pound green beans, cut into short sections

Remove the outer leaves from the cabbage, cut it vertically into quarters, and pare the core, leaving only enough to keep the leaves of each quarter attached. Reassemble the cabbage in a saucepan, cover with salted boiling water, cook, covered, at a slight boil for 15 minutes, and drain.

Remove the tough dark-green parts from the leeks, slit the upper halves, wash them well, and tie them firmly into a bundle, the slit halves folded down. Incorporate the green parts into the *bouquet-garni*.

In a saucepan, cover the tails, the ears, and the slice of bacon with cold water, bring to a boil, leave at a light boil for a couple of minutes, drain, and rinse the meats well in cold water. Place them in the stew pot, cover generously with cold water, bring to the boiling point, skim, and add the *bouquet-garni,* head of garlic, turnips, carrots, onions, and salt. When the liquid returns to the boil, skim once more, cover, leaving the lid slightly ajar, and adjust the heat to maintain a light simmer.

One-half hour later, add the white beans, and gently immerse the cabbage quarters. Return to a boil and leave to simmer as before. When the white beans show signs of softening (after 30 or 40 minutes), add the green beans and the leeks and cook as before for another half-hour or until everything is done.

Discard the onions and the *bouquet-garni,* remove the string from the leeks, split the ears into several sections lengthwise, and cut the bacon into pieces.

Serve in a large deep heated platter, the cabbage quarters placed outside, the meats in the center, and the other vegetables distributed pell-mell around. Pour a couple of ladles of bouillon over the lot.

A pot of mustard, a dish of coarse salt, and a jar of sour gherkins should be at hand. If possible, the accompanying bread should be coarse, heavy, and not too fresh.

THE PERIGORD PUDDING

A Périgourdine specialty, a Périgord pudding *(flaugnarde)* is essentially a dish of baked crepe batter filled with brandy-soaked prunes and raisins. Those accustomed to leavened pastries may, at first contact, find the custardy texture and the somewhat leathery skin bizarre. Its simple honesty rarely fails to seduce.

Périgord Pudding

Flaugnarde

2 ounces dried currants
½ pound prunes *(of the year's production, if possible)*
¼ cup Cognac *(or* eau de vie de prune*)*
½ cup sugar
4 eggs
tiny pinch of salt
½ cup flour
1 cup milk
½ teaspoon vanilla extract
1 ounce unsalted butter

Cover the currants with cold water, bring only just to a boil, remove from the heat, leave the currants to swell for 10 minutes, and drain them. Cut the prunes in two and remove the pits. Combine the prunes and the raisins in a glass jar with a tight-fitting lid, pour the Cognac over, and screw the lid tightly. Shake the jar from time to time, turning it over. After 6 or 7 hours, the liquid will have been completely absorbed.

Beat the sugar, eggs, and salt together in a mixing bowl. Sift in the flour, a little at a time, stirring all the while with a whisk. Stir in the milk, the vanilla extract, and the contents of the jar. (Don't be alarmed by the thinness of the batter.) Liberally butter a gratin dish, ladle in the bulk of the prune-and-raisin batter, and pour the rest of the batter over. Bake in a hot oven (375° to 400°F) for 20 minutes. Serve lukewarm, directly from the baking dish.

Four Simple Autumn Menus

MENU III *(for 4 to 6)*

This menu will be happily served by a thirst-quenching, dry white wine, the younger the better — Bourgogne Aligoté, Entre-Deux-Mers (Bordeaux), Muscadet, Gros Plant, Pouilly-sur-Loire, or Quincy (all from the Loire valley), Swiss Fendant, or, from Italy, Soave (Veneto) or Cortese di Gava (Piedmont) — and an uncomplicated young red wine, cool, fruity, and plentiful — Bourgogne Passe-tout-grains, Beaujolais or Côtes-du-Rhône Primeur, Chinon or Saumur-Champigny (Loire valley), Dolcetto (Piedmont), or California Zinfandel.

FENNEL A LA GRECQUE
[FENOUIL A LA GRECQUE]

• • •

FRENCH MOUSSAKA, WATERCRESS
[MOUSSAKA A LA FRANÇAISE, VERT-PRE]

• • •

FRESH WHITE CHEESES
[FROMAGES FRAIS]

• • •

ORANGE CREAM
[CREME A L'ORANGE]

THE FENNEL A LA GRECQUE

Artichoke hearts, small onions, the whites of leeks cut into 1½-inch lengths, celery hearts split in two, or cauliflower, the florets removed from the stalk, may all be prepared in identically the same way.

Fennel à la Grecque

Fenouil à la Grecque

1½ pounds fennel, outer stalks removed, halved or quartered from top to
    bottom
⅓ cup olive oil
juice of 2 lemons
1 onion, finely sliced into rings
2 cloves garlic, lightly crushed
8 to 10 coriander seeds
1 pinch fennel seeds
bouquet-garni (*page 50*)
salt
chopped parsley

In a saucepan, assemble all the ingredients except the chopped parsley, pour over
boiling water just to cover, and simmer, covered, until the fennel is tender.
Arrange the fennel in a deep serving dish, pour over the contents of the saucepan,
and leave to cool. Serve chilled, sprinkled with chopped parsley.

French Moussaka, Watercress

Moussaka à la Française, Vert-pré

2 pounds eggplant, preferably the small, elongated variety
salt, freshly ground pepper
olive oil
1 pound lean, leftover cooked lamb, chopped
duxelles (*page 58*), prepared with 1 medium onion and ¼ pound mushrooms
1 clove garlic, finely chopped
⅔ cup tomato puree (*not tomato paste*)
healthy pinch of mixed herbs (*page 52*)
large handful of semifresh bread crumbs
1 or 2 eggs
watercress (*for garnish*)

The eggplant will be used to line the mold. Cut them lengthwise into slices the
thickness of a finger. Slices from large eggplants may have to be sectioned into
strips approximately 2 inches wide. Salt and pepper the slices and fry them in
olive oil, over medium heat (in several batches), adding more oil when necessary,
until they are golden on both sides and tender at the stem ends. Drain on paper
towels. Cook the chopped meat, salted, in olive oil over medium heat, stirring
regularly, for about 10 minutes; add the *duxelles* and continue cooking and stir-

ring for a couple of minutes. Add the garlic, tomato puree, and herbs, turn the heat as high as possible, and stir constantly until the mixture is consistent. Stir in the bread crumbs and leave the mixture to cool slightly while preparing the mold.

Use a standard 1½-quart charlotte mold. The pattern created in lining the mold is dictated by the length and shape of the eggplant slices. Taken from long, narrow eggplants, they can be fanned out from the center of the mold, pressed firmly into place, overlapping, to line the bottom and sides, with the large ends overreaching the top. Shorter slices may be only long enough to line the sides, vertically and overlapping, other slices being pressed to the bottom.

Sprinkle the meat mixture with pepper, mix in the egg, and add it to the mold, a spoonful at a time, being careful not to displace any portions of the lining. Tap the bottom of the mold firmly several times against a wooden table surface or on the chopping board to be certain the stuffing is well settled and that no air pockets remain. Press more eggplant strips onto the surface, carefully fold the overlapping ends of the side strips inward, one at a time, and press a buttered or oiled round of parchment paper over the surface.

Place the mold in a larger pan, pour in enough boiling water to immerse it by two-thirds, and poach in a medium oven (350°F) for 40 minutes. Remove the mold from the *bain-marie* and leave it to settle for 7 or 8 minutes before unmolding.

Remove the round of paper, invert a round serving platter over the mold, and, firmly holding a handle of the mold and the edge of the platter between the thumb and fingers of each hand, turn the mold and the platter over together. Wait a few seconds to be certain that the *moussaka* has unmolded and settled onto the platter, then gently lift off the mold. Surround with bouquets of washed and well-dried watercress, the stem ends tucked underneath the edge of the *moussaka*.

Orange Cream

Crème à l'Orange

5 egg yolks
½ cup sugar
1 cup freshly squeezed, strained orange juice
juice of 1 lemon, strained
¼ cup white wine

Beat the egg yolks and sugar together until the yellow color turns pale. Slowly add the liquids, stirring all the while, and cook over low heat in a heavy saucepan, continuing to stir. The mixture will never coat the spoon, and it must not boil. When it assumes something more than a liquid consistency and begins to adhere to the sides of the saucepan, remove it from the heat, immerse the saucepan in cold water, and continue stirring until the cream has completely cooled. Pour it into individual serving dishes, chill thoroughly for several hours at least, and serve accompanied by *tuiles* (page 84) or other simple cookies.

Four Simple Autumn Menus

MENU IV *(for 4)*

This menu will be happily served by an uncomplicated young red wine, cool, fruity, and plentiful — Bourgogne Passe-tout-grains, Beaujolais or Côtes-du-Rhône Primeur, Chinon or Saumur-Champigny (Loire valley), Dolcetto (Piedmont), or California Zinfandel.

GARLIC SOUP
[SOUPE A L'AIL (AIGO-BOUIDO)]

. . .

GRILLED LAMBS' HEARTS AND BABY ZUCCHINI
*[GRILLADE DE COEURS D'AGNEAU ET
PETITES COURGETTES]*

. . .

CHEESES
[FROMAGES]

FRENCH PANCAKE JELLY ROLLS
[PANNEQUETS A LA CONFITURE]

THE GARLIC SOUP

Aïgo-bouido is Provençal for "boiled water." It is believed to be a cure-all. The rustic accompaniment is always dried bread crusts. The simplest version — reserved for those who are seriously ill — is nothing but a couple of cloves of garlic boiled in a quart of water with a branch of thyme and a sage leaf, strained over some olive-oil-soaked crusts of dried bread. A step or two up the ladder, a bay leaf and a few more cloves of garlic are added and the strained liquid is beaten into a mixture of olive oil and egg yolk. (Traditionally, olive oil is cooked in the soup, but its flavor and digestibility both suffer from this treatment.) A rich *aïgo-bouido* (more garlic and egg yolks) is an obligatory course (along with the 13 desserts) in every Provençal Christmas Eve menu. The following recipe is a "super" version, as *aïgo-bouidos* go. For those who fear raw garlic, it cannot be too highly recommended. Whether or not one likes raw garlic, there is no doubt that it is powerful and aggressive in flavor and difficult to digest (although good, they say, for the heart). Cooked garlic is delicate and subdued in flavor, an aid to digestion, and a calmative.

Garlic Soup

Soupe à l'Ail (Aïgo-bouido)

    1 quart water
    1 bay leaf
    2 or 3 sage leaves
    1 sprig of thyme
    10 to 15 cloves garlic, crushed and peeled
    salt

BINDING POMMADE
    1 whole egg and 2 yolks
    1½ ounces freshly grated Parmesan cheese (*or mixed Parmesan and Swiss Gruyère*)
    freshly ground pepper
    ¼ cup olive oil

Bring the water to a boil and add all the ingredients except those of the *pommade*. Cook, covered, at a gentle boil, for 40 minutes, strain through a sieve, discard the herbs, and pass the garlic through into the liquid. Taste for salt.

Combine the egg, yolks, grated cheese, and pepper in a bowl, stir, and then beat with a small whisk until creamy. Slowly pour in the oil, beating all the time, then add, continuing to whisk, a ladleful of the bouillon. Stir the contents of the bowl into the bouillon, transfer it to a saucepan, and whisk it over low to medium heat until it thickens slightly — just enough to be no longer watery. Pour it over a handful of broken-up dried-out crusts of bread in a heated soup tureen and serve immediately.

THE GRILLED LAMBS' HEARTS AND BABY ZUCCHINI

The anonymous veal or beef heart is attractive and delicious either roasted or braised whole with a highly seasoned stuffing, but the quality of the dish depends on the supplementary elements. Lambs' hearts taste like lamb. To avoid becoming tough they must be kept slightly rare.

Small zucchini squash should always be cooked in the simplest and most rapid manner possible, and should never touch boiling water; try them sliced coin-thin, seasoned, and rapidly tossed in very hot olive oil with a couple of cloves of garlic. Discard the garlic cloves and sprinkle with a few drops of lemon juice and some chopped parsley.

Grilled Lambs' Hearts and Baby Zucchini

Grillade de Coeurs d'Agneau et Petites Courgettes

4 lambs' hearts
pinch of mixed herbs (*page 52*)
8 zucchini
olive oil, salt, freshly ground pepper

Slice through the outer wall of each heart from both sides so that it may be unfolded into a more-or-less regular single slice. Sprinkle with the herbs and rub with enough olive oil to coat them thinly, then leave them to marinate for an hour or so. Remove the tips and stem ends from the squash, split them in half, slit the cut surfaces in a criss-cross design with the tip of a small knife, and sprinkle with oil. Neither hearts nor squash should be seasoned until just before putting them to grill. One should have a fairly vivid bed of hot coals, and the grill should be preheated.

Count 4 to 5 minutes' cooking time for the hearts (once turned, they are done when rose-tinted droplets appear on the surface) and about 10 minutes at a less intense heat for the zucchini. These may be begun, placed face down, at the heart of the grill and, after 3 or 4 minutes, when the face is nicely colored, turned, removed to an area of less intense heat, and replaced by the hearts. The zucchini are done when the flesh offers little resistance to the sharp point of a small knife. Both squash and hearts should be lightly basted with olive oil just after they are turned. Care should be taken that no oil drops onto the hot coals, lending an unpleasant smoky flavor.

THE FRENCH PANCAKE JELLY ROLLS

Crepes are served folded or flat. When rolled, usually cut in two at a bias, the ends trimmed to match, they become *pannequets*.

French Pancake Jelly Rolls

Pannequets à la Confiture

unsalted butter
sugar
12 crepes (*page 79*)
jam or jelly, preferably of an acid fruit — currant, apricot, wild plum,
    raspberry — and not too sweet

Butter a shallow baking dish that will be attractive on the table and sprinkle the bottom with sugar. Butter the crepes lightly, spread each with a teaspoonful of jam or jelly, roll them up and place them side by side in the baking dish. Sprinkle the surface with sugar and put into a hot oven long enough for the sugar on the surface to melt and form a glaze.

W

WINTER MENUS

Two Winter Suppers

MENU I *(for 4)*

CAVIAR
[CAVIAR]

Champagne: a light nonvintage blanc de blancs

• • •

SCRAMBLED EGGS WITH TRUFFLES
[OEUFS BROUILLES AUX TRUFFES]

*Vintage Champagne, fuller-bodied than the preceding, containing a high
proportion of black grapes (Krug, for instance), or one of the great white
Burgundy growths from Puligny or Chassagne — Chevalier-, Bâtard-,
Criots-Bâtard-, or Bienvenues-Bâtard Montrachet*

• • •

LOBSTERS A LA NAGE
[HOMARDS TIEDES A LA NAGE]

The same as the preceding

• • •

SALAD WITH FINES HERBES
[SALADE AUX FINES HERBES]

• • •

PINEAPPLE AND FRANGIPANE FRITTERS
[BEIGNETS D'ANANAS A LA FRANGIPANE]

There is little work involved in this menu. The pineapple should be draped in its frangipane hours earlier and need only be dipped in the batter (which also is prepared ahead of time) at the last minute. The *court-bouillon* for the lobsters may be prepared in advance and they need only be thrown in just before one goes to table. The scrambled eggs represent a few minutes' occupation. That is all. The salad will have been prepared ahead of time and the caviar needs only the care of toasting a few thin slices of bread.

THE CAVIAR

Good caviar is large-grained, pale gray, and translucent. It should be served, the container embedded in cracked ice, accompanied by thin slices of hot toast and cold, unsalted butter.

THE SCRAMBLED EGGS
WITH TRUFFLES

Perfect scrambled eggs are of a voluptuous, creamy, pourable consistency, thickened but uncurdled by a slow and progressive absorption of heat. Correctly prepared, they are one of the great dishes and an ideal vehicle for the presentation of other flavors. Black truffles are steeped with the eggs before cooking, the better to permeate the mass with their sublime scent; most garnishes are added just before removing the eggs from the heat — among the more attractive possibilities are fresh sea-urchin corals; asparagus (stalks peeled, sliced thinly on the bias, parboiled for less than a minute, drained, and, just before adding them to the eggs, sautéed for a few seconds in butter); butter-stewed artichoke hearts (or, for a different effect, raw artichoke hearts, sliced coin-thin and sautéed in olive oil over high heat, keeping them somewhat crisp); wild mushrooms (butter-stewed or sautéed *à la provençale*, depending on the variety); fresh white truffles, shaved paper-thin; pinkly sautéed chicken livers; crayfish or shrimp tails, previously sautéed or poached in *court-bouillon;* a remainder of non-soupy ratatouille can be added to scrambled eggs to good effect.

Although the eggs are prepared in a *bain-marie,* out of direct contact with heat, a heavy saucepan, preferably of copper, which absorbs heat slowly and evenly, will nonetheless give the best results. Up to a certain point, it may be said that the longer the eggs take to arrive at the proper consistency, the smoother and creamier they will be. (It has often been written that, for perfect results, eggs can be scrambled only in small quantities; this is absolutely untrue — 30 or 40 eggs, scrambled for a dozen or more guests, will always come closer to perfection than a small amount prepared for 2 or 3 people, simply because of the much longer time required for the same degree of heat to be absorbed into a large mass of eggs.)

Low metal tripods to be placed in the bottom of a larger saucepan or pot are commonly available; lacking one of these, the saucepan containing the eggs can be set on a biscuit cutter or similar device to prevent its touching the bottom of the larger pan. Do not attempt to substitute a double boiler for a *bain-marie* — the control of heat through immersion in hot, but not boiling, water is much more precise than with steam, which, under pressure of the closed container, is hotter than boiling water.

Scrambled Eggs with Truffles

Oeufs Brouillés aux Truffes

CROUTONS
  3 thick slices stale white bread, crusts removed, cut into cubes
  2 ounces unsalted butter

  at least 3 ounces truffles, preferably fresh
  10 eggs
  4 ounces unsalted butter, diced
  1 garlic clove, peeled
  salt, freshly ground pepper

In a heavy omelette pan, over very low heat, color the bread cubes in butter, tossing regularly, adding more butter as necessary, until they are crisp and golden, but not brown, on all surfaces. Hold them in a warm place while scrambling the eggs; they may be placed again over low heat as the eggs begin to arrive at the right consistency.

Slice the truffles and put them into a mixing bowl. (If they are frozen, slice them before unfreezing, as soon as the knife can force its way through. If they are sterilized, save their preserving juices for another preparation.) Break over the eggs and throw in about half of the diced butter, cover the bowl with a plate, and leave it for half an hour or so. Rub a wooden spoon repeatedly, back and front, with the garlic clove — about half of it should disappear. Butter the saucepan. Add salt and grind pepper over the eggs. Place the tripod or other support in the bottom of the larger pan and measure in enough water to immerse the saucepan by about half when it is placed on the support. Remove the saucepan and heat the water without bringing it to the boiling point.

Beat the eggs lightly with a fork — only enough to break them up — and pour the mixture into the saucepan, immerse it in the hot water, and begin soon to stir slowly with the wooden spoon, back and forth and around in a circle, scraping all surfaces — sides, bottom, and corners — repeatedly. Lower the heat if necessary to keep the water beneath the boil. The thickening process is very slow until nearly the right consistency is achieved; then the eggs begin to thicken very rapidly. The pan may be momentarily removed from the water 2 or 3 times toward the end, while you continue to stir the eggs, to control the thickening. While the eggs are still slightly more liquid than desired, remove the pan from the water, throw in the remaining butter, and continue stirring and scraping the pan's surfaces for another minute; the heat retained in the pan continues to cook the eggs. Serve, preferably, directly from the saucepan onto warm but not hot plates. The croutons may be stirred into the eggs at the moment of serving or presented apart to be scattered over.

Lobsters à la Nage

Homards Tièdes à la Nage

white-wine *court-bouillon* (*page 64*)
2 large or 4 small and lively lobsters
8 ounces unsalted butter, diced

Fifteen minutes before going to table, plunge the live lobsters into the pot of boiling *court-bouillon,* making certain they are as nearly covered with the liquid as possible, bring back to a boil, cover the pot, and lower the heat. Turn the lobsters over in their liquid halfway through the cooking process (15 to 20 minutes in all, depending on the size of the lobsters). Remove them from the heat and leave them, covered, in the *court-bouillon.*

To serve, twist off and crack the claws, but leave them intact. Spread out the body, face down, on the chopping board and, piercing it through the upper part of the carapace with a large knife, split it in two lengthwise. Tear out and discard the gravel sack ("queen") from the upper tip of the head, and arrange the halves, split surface up, surrounded by the claws, on a large serving platter. Remove the parsley from the *court-bouillon* and pour over the lobsters a ladleful of *court-bouillon* containing onion rings and carrot slices. In a small saucepan, bring several tablespoons of the *court-bouillon* to a boil and whisk in the butter, a handful at a time, removing the pan from the heat before all this has been absorbed and continuing to whisk. Serve apart. Lobster crackers, a plate or bowl to receive the shells at the table, and finger bowls should not be forgotten.

Pineapple and Frangipane Fritters

Beignets d'Ananas à la Frangipane

The frangipane and the pineapple should be prepared a few hours ahead of time.

FRANGIPANE
1 cup milk
few drops of vanilla extract
3 tablespoons sugar
5 tablespoons flour
small pinch of salt
1 whole egg and 1 egg yolk
2 dried-out almond macaroons
1 ounce unsalted butter
1 ounce pistachio nuts, peeled (*page 44*) and coarsely chopped

half a fresh pineapple

FRYING BATTER
1 egg
¾ cup flour
pinch of salt
1 teaspoon sugar
⅓ cup warm beer
1 ounce unsalted butter, melted
water

oil for deep frying (*preferably light olive oil*)

THE FRANGIPANE

Bring the milk to a boil with the vanilla and sugar and leave it to cool slightly. Sift the flour and salt into a saucepan, add the whole egg and the yolk, and stir with a wooden spoon, keeping the motion to the center, so that the flour is slowly absorbed into the egg, then slowly add the milk, stirring all the time. Cook over medium heat, continuing to stir vigorously, until the mixture becomes very thick. Remove from the heat, crumble in the macaroons, add the butter and the chopped pistachio nuts, mix well, and leave to cool.

THE PINEAPPLE

Cut the pineapple in slices ⅓ to ½ inch thick; cut each slice in quarters, slice off the rind, and remove the woody core. Butter a plate, spread half the frangipane over the surface, arrange the pineapple sections on top, and cover with the remaining frangipane so that each pineapple section is completely coated. Put to chill until needed.

THE FRYING BATTER

Prepare the batter an hour or so before the meal. It must relax to lose its elasticity; otherwise it refuses to coat properly.

Separate the egg and put the white aside. Add the yolk to the dry ingredients and stir in the beer, adding it at 2 or 3 intervals. Stir only until a regular consistency is achieved. Stir in the melted butter and enough water to bring it to the consistency of fresh thick cream. Leave the batter covered with a plate, at kitchen temperature, until needed. At the last minute, gently fold in the stiffly beaten egg white.

Heat the frying oil; when it sizzles at contact with a drop of batter, it is ready. Do not use a frying basket. Carefully cut loose, one from the other, the frangipane-covered pineapple sections and, one at a time, drop them from a spoon into the batter, lift them out, and drop them into the hot oil. Don't try to fry too many at a time. Delicately turn them over in the oil with the prong of a fork, and when they are golden and crisp on both sides, scoop them out with a large skimming spoon. Drain them on paper towels and transfer them to the folded napkin in which they will be served. When all are fried, sprinkle the surface with confectioners' sugar and serve immediately.

Two Winter Suppers

MENU II *(for 4)*

FOIE GRAS
[FOIE GRAS]

A light Barsac (Sauternes), a noble-rot German Rhine Riesling, an Alsatian late-picked Gewürztraminer, or, if a dry wine is preferred, an old white Hermitage or an old Graves, traditionally vinified (Laville-Haut-Brion, Haut-Brion, Domaine de Chevalier)

• • •

FRESH EGG NOODLES WITH TRUFFLES
[PATES FRAICHES AUX TRUFFES]

A Côte de Beaune red (Pernand-Vergelesses, Auxey-Duresses, Monthélie) or a Pomerol (La Conseillante, Vieux-Château-Certan, Nénin)

• • •

TOSSED GREEN SALAD
[SALADE VERTE]

• • •

CHEESES
[FROMAGES]

Following a Côte de Beaune, one of the great Côte de Nuits (Richebourg, Musigny, Bonnes Mares, Chambertin) or, following a Pomerol, a wine from the Graves region of Saint Emilion (Figeac, Cheval Blanc), older than the preceding wine

• • •

STRIPED BAVARIAN CREAM
[CREME BAVAROISE EN RUBANEE]

THE FOIE GRAS

Foie gras means "fat liver." In France, Périgord geese or "mulard" ducks, a sterile cross between Muscovy *(canard de Barbarie)* males and females of a large white race, are considered to be best suited to the special rearing and force-feeding necessary to the production of *foie gras*. (Good *foie gras* is now produced in America by a method that, although not publicly divulged, the producers claim does not involve force-feeding.) *Foies gras* from Hungary and Israel supplement the production from within France to help appease the French appetite for this delicacy.

Fresh *foie gras,* seasoned with salt and spices, often truffled and sometimes marinated in port or Madeira, poached in rich stock or cooked in a terrine in a *bain-marie,* kept pink throughout, has a melting, sensuous texture and a subtlety of flavor unsuspected by those who know only the tinned product. A fresh *foie gras,* weighing about 2 pounds, can be economically stretched to 15 or 20 servings, while remaining sumptuous, by embedding it in a truffled and Cognac-flavored pork and veal forcemeat in a pork-fat-lined terrine, cooked for an hour in a *bain-marie,* and cooled under weight. Commercialized *"demi-conserve" foie gras* is pinkly cooked and often very good; it must be kept refrigerated. Although a complete sterilization necessitates longer cooking and a consequent loss in quality, whole *foie gras (bloc de foie gras)* at best retains a delicate flavor and a velvet texture. Tins bearing the legend "paté," "purée," or "parfait" are pastes containing a certain amount of pureed *foie gras* trimmings in combination with other bland meat fillers.

Cold *foie gras* should be served thickly sliced, accompanied by freshly made hot thin slices of toast.

Fresh Egg Noodles with Truffles

Pâtes Fraîches aux Truffes

NOODLE PASTE
   1½ cups flour
   salt
   2 whole eggs and 2 yolks
   1 tablespoon olive oil

   ½ pound black truffles
   2 cloves garlic, peeled
   ½ pound unsalted butter
   salt, freshly ground pepper
   1 to 2 tablespoons Cognac

THE NOODLES

Sift the flour and salt into a mixing bowl, make a well in the center, and add the whole eggs, yolks, and olive oil. With a fork, work in the flour, adding a bit more flour or a bit more egg white, if necessary, to bring the paste to a firm but easily malleable consistency. Make a ball of it, roll it on a lightly floured board so that the surface will not be sticky, and knead it well, pushing it out flat with the heel of your hand, gathering it back into a compact mass, and repeating the operation. Roll it into a ball, cover it with a towel, and leave it to relax for an hour or so.

Divide the paste into 3 or 4 equal portions, flatten each with the palm of the hand into a regularly formed patty on the floured board, turning it over so it is evenly coated with flour, and roll it out very thin, turning it over 2 or 3 times during the process and dusting it with flour to ensure its sticking neither to the board nor to the rolling pin. These sheets of dough should be allowed to dry for a while before being cut up. The commonest and most practical home-kitchen method consists in hanging them over broomsticks, the two ends of which are supported by chair backs.

Sprinkle each sheet of dough with fine semolina to prevent the noodles from sticking together. Roll the sheet up loosely from opposite sides so that the rolls touch in the center and, with a large knife, cut through them to form more or less narrow ribbons; slip the knife blade beneath the cut rolls, its back to the median line, and lift up the mass of noodles so that they unfurl to either side of the blade. Drop them loosely to the side and begin again.

Slice the truffles fairly thickly. Rub the bottom and sides of an earthenware *poêlon* or casserole all over and repeatedly with the garlic. Discard any solid fragments that may cling to the interior. Add half the butter and place the earthenware vessel over a very gentle heat, either in hot ashes or over a tiny flame, protected by an asbestos plaque. When the butter begins to melt, add the sliced truffles, sprinkle with salt, pepper generously, regulating the pepper mill to the coarsest grind, and sprinkle a bit of Cognac over. Cover the receptacle as tightly as possible and leave it for about 15 minutes over gentle heat, shaking it a bit from time to time. The butter should not even be allowed to come to a bubble — it is not a cooking process, merely a slow warming that permits the various perfumes to mingle and that of the truffles to expand.

Bring a large pot of salted water to a boil and, after the truffles have been warming in their butter for about 10 minutes, add the noodles to the water, first tossing them in a large sieve to rid them of as much excess flour as possible. Fresh noodles require no more than 2 or 3 minutes' cooking time. Drain well, add them to the truffles, toss the contents together lightly, lifting and turning with wooden forks or spoons, and leave, covered, still over low heat, for a few minutes to allow the noodles to become permeated with the truffles and their juices. Toss the contents a couple of times, holding the lid tightly in place. Just before serving, bind the noodles by tossing them with the remaining butter, cut into small pieces.

Striped Bavarian Cream

Crème Bavaroise en Rubanée

RASPBERRY MIXTURE
  ½ pound frozen raspberries (*fresh, in season*)
  ½ cup sugar
  ½ cup water
  1 tablespoon gelatin

CUSTARD MIXTURE
  1 cup milk
  ½ vanilla bean
  4 egg yolks
  ½ cup sugar
  1 tablespoon gelatin

  2 cups heavy cream
  4 tablespoons sugar
  few drops of almond oil (*for the mold*)

Puree the raspberries through a nylon drum sieve. Bring the sugar and water to a boil, stir in the gelatin, first softened in a bit of cold water, and allow the mixture to cool almost completely before stirring it into the raspberry puree. Put the mixture into the refrigerator while preparing the custard. If the raspberry puree should show signs of beginning to set before the custard is prepared and cooled, remove it from the refrigerator.

Bring the milk and vanilla bean to a boil and leave them to infuse for 10 minutes or so. Stir and beat the egg yolks and the ½ cup sugar in another saucepan until creamy and light yellow in color, remove the vanilla bean from the milk, and slowly pour the milk into the egg mixture, stirring with a wooden spoon the while. Add the gelatin, first softened in a bit of cold water, and continue stirring constantly over low to medium heat, regularly scraping the sides, corners, and bottom of the saucepan, until the mixture thickens enough to coat the spoon. Under no circumstances should the boiling point be approached. Immerse the saucepan halfway in cold water and continue stirring to ensure its cooling evenly. When completely cooled, the gelatin will begin to take action. Whip the cream until firm but not stiff, beat in the 4 tablespoons sugar, and incorporate half the whipped cream into each of the two mixtures, stirring and folding thoroughly but without violence. Oil very lightly the interiors of two decorative quart molds, and carefully, so as to avoid their mixing, pour in the cream and raspberry mixtures in alternating layers. Put to chill for at least 4 hours embedded in cracked ice, or for 5 to 6 hours in the coldest part of the refrigerator — but not in the deep-freeze. Unmold before serving.

An Elaborate Formal Dinner Party

THE MENU *(for 6)*

CREAM OF ARTICHOKE SOUP WITH HAZELNUTS
[CREME D'ARTICHAUTS AUX NOISETTES]

The same wine as that chosen to accompany the fish

. . .

GRILLED FISH WITH SEA-URCHIN PUREE
[POISSONS GRILLES A L'OURSINADE]

*One of the Mâconnais whites (Mâcon-Lugny, -Viré, -Clessé,
or Mâcon-Villages)*

. . .

VEAL SWEETBREADS AND MACARONI TIMBALE
[TIMBALE DE MACARONI AUX RIS DE VEAU]

*A bigger, more complex white Burgundy than the preceding (Corton-
Charlemagne, Beaune Clos des Mouches, Clos Blanc de Vougeot), or a
supple, young red Côte de Beaune (Saint-Romain, Saint-Aubin,
Savigny-les-Beaune)*

. . .

RUM SHERBET
[PUNCH A LA ROMAINE]

. . .

ROAST GUINEA FOWL WITH BACON
[PINTADE ROTIE AU LARD FUME]

*One of the Nuits-Saint-Georges first growths (les Saint-Georges, les Porrets,
les Vaucrains, Clos de la Maréchale, etc.)*

. . .

CHESTNUT PUREE WITH CELERY
[PUREE DE MARRONS AU CELERI]

. . .

• • •

TOSSED GREEN SALAD WITH FINES HERBES
[SALADE VERTE AUX FINES HERBES]

• • •

CHEESES
[FROMAGES]

A Corton or one of the Côte de Nuits grands crus

• • •

BLANC-MANGER
[BLANC-MANGER]

A fine old Sauternes

Most often today, if a series of wines is to be presented with a meal, the menu is simple and two or more wines, similar in type (perhaps the same growth from different vintages, or wines from the same vintage and grape varieties but from different growths or properties in the same general region) are served with each course. The present menu may seem archaic in concept, but the drama of succeeding and interrelated food and wine scents and tastes, contained in a harmonious structure, can be created in no simpler way; to taste a progression of related wines of increasing nuance and complexity, all with the same piece of roast beef, reduces the experience to the level of banal laboratory analysis, robbing the wine of its aura and the table of its art.

The *blanc-manger* should be prepared the preceding day and the sherbet put to freeze early, its meringue added an hour or so before dinner. The *oursinade* and the basic chestnut puree may be prepared, the bird barded, ready for roasting, and the sweetbreads and macaroni timbale assembled and refrigerated, ready to be poached, hours in advance. The final organization of the meal depends mainly on putting things to cook at the right time: the fish, depending on their size, should be put to grill just before or during the service of the soup, the timbale should be put to poach just before the soup service, and the roast should be put in the oven at the end of the fish service.

Cream of Artichoke Soup with Hazelnuts

Crème d'Artichauts aux Noisettes

1 quart thin cream sauce (*béchamel*)(*page 76*)
4 or 5 roasted hazelnuts, crushed
8 good-sized artichoke bottoms, precooked (*page 45*)
2 ounces unsalted butter
milk
salt, freshly ground pepper
¾ cup cream
handful of chervil leaves

Ten minutes before removing the *béchamel* sauce from the heat, add the hazelnuts.

Slice 6 of the artichoke bottoms, leave the other two whole, and stew them all in the butter, stirring occasionally, over low heat, without allowing them to brown, for a good ½ hour. (Use either earthenware or stainless steel — any other metal will discolor artichokes.) Put the 2 whole bottoms aside and stir the rest into the *béchamel*. Pass the mixture through a nylon or stainless-steel sieve. Reheat the puree, bring it to a light, creamy consistency by the addition of boiling milk, taste for salt, grind in the pepper, and stir in the cream. Add the two artichoke bottoms, cut into small cubes, pour into a heated soup tureen, and sprinkle the surface with chervil leaves.

THE GRILLED FISH
WITH SEA-URCHIN PUREE

Sea urchins (*oursins*) are now more commonly used in kitchens outside of France than when this book first appeared. Any fish preparation incorporating a puree of urchin corals into its sauce is called an *oursinade;* with grilled fish, the sauce alone is the *oursinade.* If sea urchins are not available, serve a cruet of fruity olive oil and lemon halves in the guise of sauce.

To open a sea urchin, hold it loosely (to avoid being pricked — or hold it in a folded cloth) in one hand, pierce the orifice with the pointed blade of a pair of scissors, cut outward through the shell, then all the way around, to remove a circular lid. Five tongues of coral lie against the curve of the inside wall, in a star pattern. Give the urchin an abrupt shake to rid it of the water and loose, blackish granular material contained inside, and remove the corals, one by one, with the tip of a teaspoon.

The Mediterranean fish most often accompanied by *oursinade* are red mullet (*rouget*), sea bass (called *loup de mer* in the south of France, *bar* elsewhere), sea bream (*dorade* — there are several varieties), pandora *(pageot),* and *sar* (similar to bream). Red mullets, in particular, must be very fresh and are usually neither scaled nor gutted, each guest scraping the fish free of scales and mashing the liver into the sauce. In Provence, large fish are also often left unscaled — this permits them to be grilled over very hot embers, the charred scales being removed with the skin before serving out sections of the fillets; unscaled, the marinade has less effect.

Because of the fragility of fish's flesh and its tendency to stick to the grill and tear when the fish is being turned, special hinged, double-faced fish grills, made of heavy steel wire, that contain the fish and can themselves be turned, are practical — large and flat to take a dozen or so small fish that can be turned with a single gesture, or long and oval-shaped, to accommodate a single large fish.

Grilled Fish with Sea-Urchin Puree

Poissons Grillés à l'Oursinade

FISH

2 or 3 3-ounce or 1 ½-pound red mullet per person; 2 2-pound fish or 1 large 3-pound sea bass will serve 6

MARINADE

1 to 2 tablespoons *pastis (anisette liquor)*
about ¼ cup olive oil
fresh wild fennel branches and chopped fresh fennel leaves or, out of season, dried fennel branches

OURSINADE

salt, freshly ground pepper
⅔ cup sea-urchin corals (*1 dozen ocean urchins, or 2 to 3 dozen of the smaller Mediterranean variety*), sieved or left whole, as preferred, mixed with:
⅔ cup olive oil

If large fish have been scaled, 2, 3, or 4 shallow gashes may be cut on the diagonal into each side of the fish, permitting a deeper penetration of the marinade and a more regular assimilation of heat during grilling. Sprinkle all of the elements of the marinade over the fish, inside (if they have been gutted) and out, tucking some of the chopped fennel leaves into the slits of fish that have been gashed. Stuff the abdominal cavities of gutted fish with fennel branches. Rub the surfaces gently, turn the fish in their marinade, and cover the dish with plastic wrap; leave it for one or several hours in a cool place or refrigerated, removing the dish from the refrigerator an hour before cooking.

Small red mullets should be grilled over intense heat and require only a couple of minutes on each side — better undercooked than overcooked. For larger fish, a deep bed of coals that has begun to go to ash is best; the larger the fish, the more sustained and the less violent should be the heat. Medium-size fish will require 20 to 30 minutes and a 3-pound fish about 45 minutes, turned several times and basted regularly with the remaining marinade or more olive oil. The sharp point of a small knife or a skewer, inserted at the thickest part of the flesh, just behind the gill, is the only test for doneness, outside of intuition and experience; the flesh, at that point, should be only slightly resistant next to the bone.

Lacking a fireplace, an outdoor fire, or barbecue apparatus, the fish may be cooked beneath an oven grill; large fish will be better baked than grilled, in this case, and all should be regularly basted.

Large fish should be served at table, onto heated plates. The fins and the small bones attached to them are first removed, the fish is split lengthwise along the median line corresponding to the spinal column, and the fillets are slipped loose. When the top fillets have been removed, the skeleton may easily be lifted, leaving the two other fillets free. Serve the *oursinade* separately.

THE VEAL SWEETBREADS AND MACARONI TIMBALE

This kind of preparation is mainly an exercise in mechanics and assemblage. The sheath of spiraled macaroni describes a ravishing beehive; the filling can be any boneless ragout — poultry, meat, game, fish — bound firmly with a minimum of sauce; a mousseline forcemeat of corresponding flavor is essential to hold the structure together when unmolded. Less spectacular, but more practical for a small number of guests, are individual timbales, the macaroni eliminated, buttered *dariole* molds lined with mousseline, filled with a little stew, covered over with mousseline and rounds of buttered parchment paper, and poached in a *bain-marie*. The Auberge de l'Ill, in Alsace, is famous for its little frog timbales, called *mousselines de grenouilles,* the molds lined with truffled fish mousseline, filled with a stew of boned frogs' legs, and accompanied by a frog essence mounted with butter. More rustic, but delicious, are molds lined with saffroned fish mousseline and filled with small-cut squid *à l'américaine,* first drained of the liquid in its sauce, the latter reduced and served to accompany the timbales.

Veal Sweetbreads and Macaroni Timbale

Timbale de Macaroni aux Ris de Veau

2 pounds veal sweetbreads
mirepoix (*page 55*)
¼ cup dry white wine
2 cups rich veal stock (*page 66*)
salt, freshly ground pepper
3 or 4 large black truffles
½ pound long macaroni
1½ ounces unsalted butter (*for the mold*)
1 pound chicken mousseline forcemeat (*page 76*)

Soak the sweetbreads in cold water for a good hour, put them into a large saucepan, cover them well with cold water, bring to a boil, leave to simmer for 10 minutes, drain, and plunge them into a basin of cold water. Peel them, carefully removing all fat and gristly or cartilaginous material and as much of the surface membrane as possible without disturbing the part that holds the many-sectioned sweetbread together.

Spread the *mirepoix* over the bottom of a heavy sauté pan or earthenware casserole of just the right size to hold the sweetbreads placed side by side on this bed. Pour in the white wine and over high heat (using an asbestos pad for protection for earthenware) reduce it almost completely, gently shaking the receptacle from time to time to discourage anything's sticking to the bottom. Add the stock (enough to cover the sweetbreads), bring it to the boiling point, and lower the heat so that, covered, a near simmer is maintained. Count about 30 minutes' braising time from the time the simmer is reached. Remove the sweetbreads from the sauce, slice them, and pass the cooking liquid and *mirepoix* through a fine sieve. If the sauce remains plentiful and liquid, reduce it over high heat for a few minutes, stirring constantly. Taste for seasoning, add pepper and salt if necessary. Pour it over the sweetbreads, leave to cool, and stir in the truffles, thickly sliced.

Cook the macaroni in a large pot of salted, boiling water and, when nearly cooked but still quite firm, remove from the heat and drain. Spread the strands of macaroni out, without touching one another, on a towel. Generously butter a 1-quart dome mold or metal mixing bowl in the form of a half-sphere and, beginning with a strand of macaroni that has been fashioned first into a compact, spiraled circle and pressed into the central point at the bottom of the mold, continue twining the strands of macaroni end to end in a close-fitting spiral until the entire mold is lined in this manner. Put the mold to chill in the refrigerator until the butter is set firmly enough to hold the macaroni in place. Cut the remaining macaroni into short lengths and stir it into the sweetbreads.

Spread three-quarters of the mousseline forcemeat evenly over the entire surface of macaroni lining, fill the mold with the sweetbread mixture, pressing it gently into place so as to leave no air pockets, and spread the remainder of the forcemeat over the surface. Press a round of buttered parchment paper over the surface and put the mold to poach in a *bain-marie* in a slow to moderate oven for 45 minutes. (A round metal biscuit cutter or other object of support should be placed in the bottom of the larger utensil on which the round-bottomed mold may rest. The mold should be immersed by about three-quarters in hot water.) If oven space does not permit, the poaching may equally well be operated on top of the stove in a large covered pot. The heat should be kept very low to prevent the water from returning to a boil.

Remove the mold from the *bain-marie* and allow it to settle for 7 or 8 minutes before unmolding it onto a round, heated platter. The bit of liquid that drains onto the platter should be sponged up with a paper towel. The timbale should be cut into pielike wedges at table; a small spatula or pie knife is useful for serving.

Rum Sherbet

Punch à la Romaine

½ cup sugar
1 cup water
1 strip each, orange and lemon peel
strained juice of 1 orange and 1 lemon
⅔ cup dry white wine

ITALIAN MERINGUE
    1 egg white
    about 1 tablespoon water
    ¼ cup sugar

¼ cup rum

Boil the sugar and water together, add the peels, juice, and wine, leave to infuse until cool, remove the peels, and put to freeze, either in a mechanical freezer or in an ice-cube tray — in the latter case, scrape frozen parts from the sides and bottom of the tray from time to time and stir them into the unfrozen mass.

When it is consistently frozen without being too firm, prepare the meringue. Beat the egg white until stiff. In a small saucepan, add just enough water to the sugar to dissolve it, bring to a boil, and cook until a drop of the syrup, let fall into a cup of cold water, forms a soft ball, malleable in the fingers; then pour it evenly, in a tiny thread, into the egg white, beating all the while, until the syrup is completely absorbed. Turn out the frozen fruit-wine mixture into a chilled mixing bowl, stir and fold in the meringue, and return it to the freezer. Just before serving, stir in the rum. The sherbet should be only semisolid — mushy in consistency.

THE ROAST GUINEA FOWL
WITH BACON

Guinea fowl is smothered instead of bled, emphasizing its kinship to game birds. Its flavor is enhanced by the smoky caress of bacon.

Breast meat cannot be cleanly carved with the interfering presence of the wishbone; this should be removed before trussing, first freed from the flesh with the tip of a small knife and fingertips, severed at the apex where it joins the breast bone, pulled backward, and torn or snipped from its attachment to the shoulder joints.

Roast Guinea Fowl with Bacon

Pintade Rôtie au Lard Fumé

2 small guinea fowl (*the young have a finer flavor*)
salt, freshly ground pepper
large pinch of oregano
1 ounce unsalted butter
enough thin strips of bacon to cover breasts completely
⅓ cup dry white wine

Sprinkle salt, pepper, and oregano in the birds' body cavities, add a lump of butter to each, truss the birds, season the outsides, and press bacon strips, lengthwise, over each breast, tying around a couple of lengths of string to hold them in place.

Place the birds on their sides in a shallow, heavy roasting pan or gratin dish of a size just to hold them. Roast for 40 to 45 minutes, starting at 450°F and turning the oven down after 10 or 15 minutes to 375°F. Turn the birds to the other side after 10 minutes and, 10 minutes later, breasts up. After about half an hour in the oven, remove the bacon slices to permit the breasts to color lightly. Remove the trussing strings, transfer the birds to a heated platter, remove as much fat from the oven dish as possible, add the white wine to the birds' juices, and boil up, scraping and stirring, until the scrapings are dissolved and the wine is reduced by half. Send this juice to table in a heated sauceboat and serve the chestnut puree at the same time.

Chestnut Puree with Celery

Purée de Marrons au Céleri

2 pounds chestnuts
1 quart milk
salt
1 teaspoon sugar
1 celery branch
freshly ground pepper
1 fresh, crisp celery heart, cut into small dice
6 ounces unsalted butter

Slice through the hull of the rounded surface of each chestnut, using a small, sharp knife; the hull is tough and resistant and care should be taken not to cut oneself. Plunge them into a pot of boiling water, and after a few minutes remove them, a few at a time, with a skimming spoon, and remove the hull from each as well as the inner, brownish skin. Holding them in a towel protects one's fingers from the heat, and rubbing with it helps remove the inner skin. Any that are particularly resistant may be returned for a couple of minutes to the hot water.

Bring the milk to a boil, add the chestnuts, salt, sugar, and celery branch, and cook gently, covered, until the chestnuts crush easily when pressed with the back of a spoon. (They may have to cook as long as 1½ hours.)

Drain, saving the milk and discarding the celery branch. Pass the chestnuts through a vegetable mill *(moulinette)*, using the finest blade and adding a bit of milk from time to time to facilitate their passage. Taste for salt, season with pepper, and just before serving, rapidly reheat the puree in a heavy saucepan over fairly high heat, stirring constantly with a wooden spoon and, away from the heat, stir in the crisp celery dice and the butter, cut into small pieces. Don't add all the butter at one time — just enough should be absorbed to permit the puree to be thickly poured. It should not be stiff, and a great quantity of butter is necessary to counteract its naturally dry texture and lend it a rich, velvety quality.

THE BLANC-MANGER

A French *blanc-manger* is a Bavarian cream made of almond milk. Formed in an old-fashioned jelly mold, it is a thing of unusual purity and beauty; accompanied by a great Sauternes, both attain sublime heights.

A food processor may replace the mortar in the preparation of almond milk but, in this case, part of the light cream should be replaced by more water and the remaining stirred in afterward (but before passing the almond milk through the towel); the violence of the processor will turn cream to butter, which will clog the towel instead of passing through in liquid form.

The leftover stiff almond paste can be transformed into a sweet biscuit batter, if desired, with a light sifting of flour, sugar to taste, a pinch of salt, 1 or 2 eggs, some milk or cream, and a bit of melted butter to loosen it up.

Blanc-manger

Blanc-manger

½ pound shelled almonds, peeled and blanched (*page 44*)
3 bitter almonds (*if unavailable, substitute a dash of almond extract*)
¾ cup water
1¼ cup light cream
1½ tablespoons gelatin
⅔ cup sugar
½ cup heavy cream
almond oil

Pound the almonds in a stone mortar, adding a spoonful of water each time the paste becomes too resistant to work easily. When half the quantity of prescribed water has been used, put the rest aside and continue pounding and turning, adding the light cream in small quantities at a time, until it has all been added. This should be done slowly and thoroughly to produce the finest possible puree.

Line a sieve, placed over a mixing bowl, with a strong linen towel, first dipped in cold water and well wrung out. Pour in the almond mixture, gather together the edges of the towel in one hand, and begin twisting. Relax your hold from time to time to mix up the almond paste and then twist again, as tightly as possible, continuing until all the almond milk possible has been wrung from the paste.

Soften the gelatin in a bit of cold water, then add the remaining water, first heated, bring to a boil, and add the sugar. Leave until almost completely cooled, stir it into the almond milk, and place the mixing bowl in a larger container of cracked ice. Stir steadily with a wooden spoon until it begins to take, whip the heavy cream until it is fairly firm but not stiff, fold it into the almond mixture, and pour the mixture into a 1-quart mold that has been lightly oiled with almond oil. Embed the mold in cracked ice, place a plate over the top, and keep it in the refrigerator for at least 4 or 5 hours. Unmold only just before serving, first dipping the mold for a couple of seconds into hot water and wiping it dry.

Two Informal Winter Dinners

MENU I *(for 6)*

GRATIN OF STUFFED CREPES
[GRATIN DE CREPES FOURREES]

A light, young, very dry white wine: Sauvignon-de-Saint-Bris, Crépy (Savoie), Swiss Fendant

• • •

STUFFED CALVES' EARS, BEARNAISE SAUCE
[OREILLES DE VEAU FARCIES, SAUCE BEARNAISE]

A supple, young red wine (2 or 3 years old): Premières Côtes de Bordeaux or one of the outlying regions of the Bordelais — Pécharmant, Côtes de Bergerac

• • •

TOSSED GREEN SALAD
[SALADE VERTE]

• • •

CHEESES
[FROMAGES]

The same as the preceding or a red Graves or one of the bourgeois growths of the Médoc

• • •

MOLDED TAPIOCA PUDDING, APRICOT SAUCE
[PUDDING MOULE AU TAPIOCA, SAUCE AUX ABRICOTS]

THE STUFFED CREPES

Stuffed crepes may contain practically anything and they represent one of the prettiest and most satisfactory means of disposing of leftovers (odds and ends of meats, vegetables, mushrooms, etc., bound with a bit of stiff sauce — tomato, *béchamel, velouté, duxelles*). Various soufflé mixtures (either dessert or entrée) are commonly used also.

The sorrel in this recipe may be replaced by spinach (often allied with brains, particularly in Italian cooking), first parboiled, well drained, finely chopped, and stewed in butter long enough to evaporate excess moisture.

Gratin of Stuffed Crepes

Gratin de Crêpes Fourrées

1 calf's brain
4 ounces unsalted butter
10 ounces sorrel
1 egg
salt, freshly ground pepper, freshly grated nutmeg
12 small crepes with *fines herbes* (*pages 79 and 50*)
freshly grated Parmesan cheese
1 medium can whole tomatoes, stewed in butter (*in season, fresh tomatoes, peeled and seeded before stewing — see page 44*)
chopped parsley

Soak the brain in cold water for an hour or so, carefully remove the membrane, and soak it again briefly in fresh cold water. Stew it gently in a small frying pan or saucepan, with 1 ounce of the butter, for about 20 minutes, shaking the pan from time to time to prevent its sticking, and turning it after 10 minutes. Puree it through a fine sieve.

Wash the sorrel in several waters, tear off the stems, pulling them backward to remove any fibrous material in the leaves, gather them into a tight mass on the chopping board, and shred them finely. Stew them, salted, in 1 ounce of the butter, stirring now and then, until they have melted into a puree (15 or 20 minutes).

Combine the brain, sorrel, and egg, whisking or beating with a wooden spoon, taste for salt, and add pepper to taste and a tiny bit of nutmeg. (The whole brain, sorrel, and egg may be combined in a blender.) Stuff the crepes, folding the sides up and over the stuffing and leaving the ends open; the form will be that of a small omelet. Place them side by side in a buttered shallow baking or gratin dish, folded sides down, sprinkle with grated cheese, regularly distribute the remainder of the butter in fine slivers over the entire surface, and bake in a medium-hot oven for about 15 minutes or until the cheese has formed a light gratin and the stuffing has become resilient to the touch. Place halved tomatoes over the crepes and sprinkle with parsley before serving.

THE STUFFED CALVES' EARS

Lucien Tendret's little book *La Table au Pays de Brillat-Savarin,* written at the end of the last century, although mainly anecdotal, contains a handful of perfunctorily presented recipes, not always workable as they stand, but each, when satisfactorily worked out, a small masterpiece. *L'oreiller de la belle aurore,* a truffled paté of game birds, hare, and white meats in a mosaic bound by alternating forcemeats, has become one of the classics of Lyonnaise *grande cuisine.* Alexandre Dumaine (whose table at the Hôtel de la Côte d'Or, in Saulieu, was, for 30 years, at once simpler and grander — more sumptuous but devoid of all pretension — than present standards permit) drew many of his specialties from this booklet. Alain Chapel's menu, at his celebrated restaurant in Mionnay, outside of Lyons, lists several dishes inspired by Tendret, among them his own adaptation of stuffed calves' ears.

Preliminary cooking preparations should be got out of the way the preceding day so that the chilled, stuffed ears may receive their breading a number of hours before the meal. The fragile surface, through drying slightly, is more easily handled and less liable to be damaged during the frying. Last-minute work consists only in the actual frying, and finishing the sauce.

Stuffed Calves' Ears, Bearnaise Sauce

Oreilles de Veau Farcies, Sauce Béarnaise

6 calves' ears, cut off well into the head
1 lemon
2 cups dry white wine
3 cups rich, gelatinous veal stock (*page 66*)
1 veal sweetbread
4 tablespoons *mirepoix* (*page 55*)
breast and liver of a roasting chicken
2 ounces unsalted butter
2 or 3 black truffles
2 tablespoons flour
2 egg yolks
1 tablespoon cream
5 egg whites (*the extra 3 yolks may be submerged in water to protect them from the air and used later for the bearnaise*)
crumbs made from firm-textured, day-old white bread
salt, freshly ground pepper
2 cups olive oil
bearnaise sauce (*recipe follows*)

THE EARS

Neatly trim the base of the ears, taking care neither to cut too closely to the joining section at the base nor to cut into the "well" at the ear's point of entry into the head. Cover them generously, in a large saucepan, with cold water, bring to a boil, and leave them to simmer for 10 minutes. Plunge them into cold water, drain them, and carefully clean them, rubbing gently with a cloth, scraping here and there to remove any remaining hairs, and cleaning out the canal-like areas in the "well" of the ear with a small stiff brush. Rinse them well, sponge them dry, and rub them inside and out with the cut halves of a lemon. Cut pieces of cloth (an old sheet will do) or double layers of muslin into approximately 8-inch squares, wrap an ear in each, neatly and firmly, taking care to force it gently into its natural position (it will have been warped out of shape during the initial parboiling), and sew the package tightly. Choose a large saucepan or deep sauté pan of just the right size to hold the ears placed side by side and touching, but without being packed in. Pour over them the wine and enough stock to cover them completely, bring to a boil, and cook, covered, at a bare simmer for 3½ hours, adding a bit of boiling stock when necessary to keep the ears submerged. Leave them until they are almost cool in their cooking liquid, then remove them from their cloth envelopes and put them aside.

THE SWEETBREAD

Prepare and braise the sweetbread exactly as described in the veal sweetbreads recipe on page 158, using the ears' cooking liquid, somewhat reduced, as braising liquid. Remove the sweetbread, pass the *mirepoix* and braising liquid through a fine sieve, supplement it with enough of the ears' cooking liquid to make a good cupful, and put it aside.

THE CHICKEN BREAST AND LIVER

Remove the skin and bones from the breast, season it, and cook it in the butter without browning, only until just firm — 2 or 3 minutes on each side. A minute before removing from the heat, add the liver.

THE STUFFING

Remove the chicken breast and liver from pan, leaving the butter, and cut the truffles, chicken breast, liver, and sweetbread into small cubes. Reheat the butter in the chicken's cooking pan, add the cubed meats and truffles, sprinkle with flour, and, after stirring everything around to permit the flour to cook slightly, stir in the cupful of braising liquid. As soon as the mixture is thoroughly thickened, remove it from the heat and stir in the two egg yolks, first mixed with the cream.

When cooled, pack the stuffing into the ears, gently so as not to damage them, but firmly enough to leave no possible air pockets, particularly in the ducts at the base, smooth the surface, mounding it slightly, to the edges and point of each ear, and put them to chill for several hours — or overnight — so that ears and stuffing will be firm enough to be easily workable.

THE BREADING

Sprinkle the surfaces of the ears — but not the surface of the stuffing — with flour. Beat 3 of the egg whites with a pinch of salt until they are stiff, carefully pass each ear in the beaten whites, making certain it is evenly coated, and roll it ever so delicately in the crumbs, first placing it on the bed of crumbs and sprinkling the top surface with crumbs. Finally, sprinkle again any parts to which no crumbs have adhered, lightly patting the surface, but never with pressure. Leave them to dry for 2 or 3 hours in the open air (not in the refrigerator), then beat the remaining egg whites, repeat the breading procedure, and leave the ears on a light bed of crumbs to dry for 7 or 8 hours.

Use either 1 pan large enough to hold the breaded ears comfortably without touching or 2 medium-size pans (in which case the quantity of oil may have to be augmented — the fat should be deep enough for the ears to bathe over halfway, permitting them to become evenly colored on all sides with a single turning). Heat the oil until it is fairly hot, and gently put the ears, stuffed surface down, in the fat. Survey them carefully, turning the heat up and down between medium and low, if necessary, to achieve an even, crisp, golden surface without burning. Turn the ears over carefully with the prong tips of a fork, taking care not to pierce the crust. Drain them on paper towels, enclose them in a folded napkin on a warmed platter, and serve immediately, accompanied separately by the bearnaise sauce.

THE BEARNAISE SAUCE

The sauce, mainly an emulsion of butter in slightly cooked egg yolks, is served tepid. Any attempt to heat it beyond this point will result in its separating. It may be prepared somewhat ahead of time and kept in a *bain-marie* of warm, but not hot, water. It is most often served with grilled meats, but can be useful with poached or grilled fish or grilled poultry.

Bearnaise Sauce

Sauce Béarnaise

½ cup dry white wine
¼ cup wine vinegar (*preferably tarragon-flavored white-wine vinegar*)
2 finely chopped shallots
salt, tiny pinch of cayenne pepper
small handful tarragon and chervil branches and leaves, coarsely chopped
    and crushed
3 egg yolks
½ pound unsalted butter, diced
1 teaspoon each finely chopped tarragon and chervil leaves

Combine the wine, vinegar, shallots, salt, cayenne, and the branches and leaves in a small, heavy saucepan or, better, in a small earthenware casserole protected from the direct heat by an asbestos pad. Boil until only 3 or 4 tablespoons of liquid remain, pass through a fine sieve, pressing the debris, and return the liquid to the saucepan. Add the egg yolks and, over very low heat, using a small whisk, stir in a rapid, circular motion. After a few seconds, add about one-third of the butter, continuing to whisk, and, as the butter is absorbed, add another third, and finally the last third, continuing to whisk until the butter is totally absorbed and the sauce begins to thicken. Remove the saucepan from the heat but continue to stir the sauce, which, because of the heat retained in the saucepan, will continue thickening. Taste for seasoning and stir in the chopped herbs.

THE MOLDED TAPIOCA PUDDING

Similar puddings may be made with rice, semolina, vermicelli, noodles, etc. Rather than serve an accompanying sauce, the mold may be lined with caramelized sugar. Served hot or warm, *sabayon* sauce (page 110) is also a fine accompaniment, and served cold, a fresh raspberry puree is another possibility.

Molded Tapioca Pudding, Apricot Sauce

Pudding Moulé au Tapioca, Sauce aux Abricots

2 cups milk
¼ cup sugar
1 small pinch salt
½ vanilla bean
3 ounces unsalted butter (*plus enough to butter the mold*)
4 ounces tapioca
3 eggs, separated

APRICOT SAUCE
  pureed stewed apricots, flavored with a small glass of Madeira or port wine,
    and sweetened to taste

Combine milk, sugar, salt, vanilla bean, and half the butter in a saucepan, bring to a boil, and slowly pour in the tapioca, stirring the while. Stir over direct heat for a minute, then put the saucepan, covered, into a slow oven for about 20 minutes. Turn the mixture out into a mixing bowl, remove the vanilla bean, stir in the rest of the butter and the yolks of the eggs, gently fold in the stiffly beaten whites, and pour into a generously buttered 1-quart mold, the inside of which has been lightly sprinkled with dry tapioca. Poach in a *bain-marie* in hot, but not boiling, water in a slow to moderate oven for about ½ hour or until the center of the pudding is elastic to the touch. Remove from the hot water and allow the pudding to settle for about 20 minutes before unmolding. If it is to be served chilled, leave the mold over it to protect the surface from the air until just before serving. Coat it with a bit of sauce and send the rest of the sauce to table in a separate dish. If the pudding is to be served hot or warm, the sauce should be heated and a lump of butter may be stirred in when it is removed from the heat.

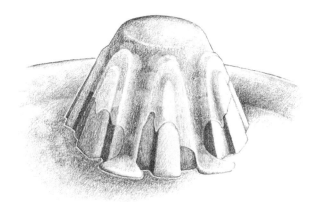

Two Informal Winter Dinners

MENU II *(for 6)*

TERRINE OF SOLE FILLETS
[TERRINE DE FILETS DE SOLE]

*A white Burgundy (Chablis, Pouilly-Fuissé, Mercurey Blanc), or a
California Pinot Blanc*

· · ·

BEEF STEW A LA BOURGUIGNONNE
[SAUTE DE BOEUF A LA BOURGUIGNONNE]

*The same red wine as that used in making the stew or another good but
not great, solid, rustic Burgundy: Passe-tout-grains, Bourgogne, Côte de
Nuits-Villages*

· · ·

STEAMED POTATOES
[POMMES DE TERRE A LA VAPEUR]

· · ·

BELGIAN ENDIVE SALAD
[SALADE D'ENDIVES]

· · ·

CHEESES
[FROMAGES]

The same as the preceding, or an older red wine from the Côte d'Or

· · ·

POACHED MERINGUES IN CUSTARD SAUCE
[OEUFS A LA NEIGE]

Terrine of Sole Fillets

Terrine de Filets de Sole

2 large soles, filleted, fillets soaked in cold water and dried between paper
    towels, skin sides shallowly slashed 3 or 4 times on the bias
fish *fumet,* made from the sole carcasses (*page 72*)
handful fresh white bread crumbs
½ pound sorrel, stemmed, washed, shredded
1 ounce unsalted butter (*plus butter for the mold*)
2 egg yolks
salt, freshly ground pepper
1 pound fish mousseline forcemeat (*page 76*)
1 ounce pistachio nuts, skinned (*page 44*) and coarsely chopped
duxelles (*page 58*), made from 4 ounces mushrooms

In a small saucepan, over high heat, reduce the fish *fumet* to about 4 tablespoons
of syrupy liquid; mash it into the bread crumbs to form a stiff paste.

Stew the sorrel gently in the butter until it is reduced to a near puree and its
liquid has evaporated; leave it to cool for a few minutes, mix it thoroughly with
the bread paste and the egg yolks, and pass the mixture through a fine sieve. Taste
for seasoning, press a sheet of plastic film to the surface, and chill.

Use a long, rectangular 1-quart terrine. Cut a piece of foil or parchment paper,
in width the same as the length of the terrine, and long enough to line the bottom
and two sides and to fold over the surface of the filled terrine. Butter the terrine,
then butter one side of the foil or paper and press it into place, unbuttered side
placed against the buttered bottom and walls of the terrine. Make an even bed in
the bottom of about ⅓ of the fish forcemeat and arrange the sole fillets, slashed
surfaces facing up, on top, slightly overlapping, placed crosswise in a row the
entire length of the terrine, the bottom and two long sides thus lined with the
fillet tips hanging over the edges. Spoon in the sorrel stuffing, even it out, and,
beginning with the last fillet to have been placed, pull the ends of the fillets, one
after the other, inward, one folded over the other so as to form a tube of stuffed
fillets through the central length of the terrine. Add the rest of the forcemeat,
forcing it gently down each side of the roll of fillets, and covering them. Tap the
terrine a couple of times against a wooden surface to settle the contents, fold the
buttered foil or parchment paper over the top, and press it down. Cook in a slow
to moderate oven in a *bain-marie,* the terrine immersed two-thirds of the way up
in hot, but not boiling, water, for about 45 minutes.

Leave the terrine to cool under pressure (a board the dimensions of the
terrine's surface with a weight on top), then put to chill for a day. To unmold,
loosen the paté from the ends of the terrine with the blade of a knife, lift the
body of it loose by pulling up on the parchment-paper or foil flaps that have been

folded over the top, then fold them over the outside walls of the terrine, turn the paté out onto an oval or rectangular platter, and peel off the foil. Surround it with a *chiffonade* of lettuce or other simple *décor*.

Beef Stew à la Bourguignonne

Sauté de Boeuf à la Bourguignonne

3 pounds hind shank and heel of beef without bone, cut into 12 pieces
3 ounces fresh pork back fat, cut into 1-inch-long lardons about ⅓ inch square in cross section
3 cloves garlic, peeled
salt
mixed dried herbs (*page 52*)
2 tablespoons finely chopped parsley
4 tablespoons olive oil
1 bottle robust, deeply colored young red wine
½ pound *pancetta,* in 2 slices, cut crosswise into finger thicknesses, briefly parboiled, rinsed and drained
3 or 4 medium carrots, peeled and cut into short lengths
3 large onions, peeled and coarsely cut up
4 tablespoons flour
4 tablespoons Cognac
bouquet-garni (*page 50*)
1 cup stock (*page 65*)
½ pound small, firm, unopened mushrooms, stems trimmed, rinsed and dried
2 ounces unsalted butter
30 small white garnish onions, peeled
aromatic red-wine essence (*page 63*) (*optional*)

In a mortar, pound a clove of garlic, a pinch of coarse salt, and a large pinch of mixed herbs to a paste, mix in the chopped parsley, and toss well with the small strips of pork fat so that each is well coated with the mixture. With the tip of a small knife, pierce each piece of meat once or twice, with the grain, and force a strip of fat into the slit, making certain that it is well embedded in the flesh. In a mixing bowl, sprinkle the pieces of meat with a pinch of mixed herbs and half of the olive oil, pour over the red wine, and leave it, covered, to marinate for several hours, turning the pieces around in the liquid 2 or 3 times. At the end of this time, pour the meat and its marinade into a colander, collecting the liquid and leaving the meat to drain well.

Add the remaining oil to a large sauté pan and cook the *pancetta* sections over medium heat, stirring and turning, until they are golden and the surfaces lightly crisp. Put them aside, lower the heat, and, in the same oil, cook the carrots and onions, stirring regularly, until they are lightly browned, about 30 minutes. Remove the vegetables to a strainer, taking care that no fragment of onion remains in the pan. Collect the fat that drains from them and return it to the pan, adding more oil if necessary.

Sponge the drained pieces of meat dry in paper toweling, salt them, and, over higher heat, brown them on all sides. Drain off any excess oil, lower the heat, sprinkle over the flour, and turn the pieces of meat 2 or 3 times, over a period of 5 or 6 minutes, until the flour is lightly browned. Return the onions and carrots to the pan, stir everything together, and pour in the Cognac and the reserved marinade, stirring and scraping the bottom and sides of the pan with a wooden spoon or spatula to loosen and dissolve all frying adherents. (If the pan is too full, or if you have had to work with two pans, everything may have to be transferred to an oven casserole at this point.) Tuck in the *bouquet-garni* and the 2 remaining garlic cloves, pour over enough stock to cover, return to the boil, and cook, covered, either in a slow oven or over very low heat (controlled, if necessary, by a heat diffuser), the surface hardly bubbling, for 2½ to 3 hours or until the meat is tender but still slightly firm. Skim off the surface fat 2 or 3 times during this period and gently displace the pieces of meat in their sauce so that nothing sticks to the bottom.

Toss the mushrooms, salted, in half the butter, over high heat for a couple of minutes or until they are lightly colored and their superficial moisture has evaporated. Cook the little onions, seasoned, in the remaining butter, in a pan of a size just to hold them in a single layer, shaking the pan or tossing and turning gently, until they are yellowed and tender, but not browned.

With a slotted spoon, remove the pieces of meat and carrot from the sauce, press the *bouquet-garni* well to extract all liquid, and discard it. Pour the remaining contents of the pan into a fine sieve, stirring and pressing the solid debris with a wooden pestle before discarding it. Return the pieces of meat and carrot to their cooking vessel, scatter over the sautéed *pancetta* pieces, the mushrooms, and the little onions, and keep covered while finishing the sauce.

Leave the sauce undisturbed for a few minutes and remove any fat that rises to the surface; transfer the sauce to a small saucepan, bring it to a boil, and, half off the heat, a light boil maintained to one side, skim it regularly (page 48) for 20 to 30 minutes or until no more fat is collected in the skin that forms on the still surface. If, at this point, the sauce seems too thin, reduce it for a couple of minutes over high heat, stirring constantly. (During this reduction — or at any time during the cooking process — a certain amount of aromatic red-wine essence may be added to deepen both color and flavor; professional cooks often add a spoonful of *glace de viande* also.)

Pour the sauce over the meat and its garnish, slowly reheat, and simmer gently, covered, for 20 to 30 minutes. Lift off any traces of fat thrown off by the garnish, using the tip of a spoon or absorbent paper. Serve in its cooking vessel, accompanied, apart, by freshly steamed potatoes.

Poached Meringues in Custard Sauce

Oeufs à la Neige

THE SAUCE
 1 quart milk
 1 cup sugar
 1 vanilla bean
 10 egg yolks

THE MERINGUE
 4 egg whites
 1 small pinch salt
 1½ cups sifted confectioners' sugar

Bring the milk, sugar, and vanilla bean to a boil in a large sauté pan or other low, wide pan, remove it from the heat, and leave the vanilla bean to infuse while preparing the meringue.

Add a pinch of salt to the egg whites, whisk them until they stand stiffly in peaks, and sift the confectioners' sugar over, folding it in delicately but thoroughly, with the whisk.

Remove the vanilla bean from the milk, bring the milk again to a boil, and regulate the heat so that a bare simmer is maintained. Gently drop heaping teaspoonfuls of the raw meringue into the simmering milk, poaching no more than 5 or 6 at a time, for the meringues swell and should not be crowded. After a couple of minutes, cautiously turn them over and leave to poach a couple of minutes longer. Lift them out with a perforated skimming spoon and slip them onto a nylon drum sieve placed over a mixing bowl. Remove them, once drained, to a large, deep serving platter to make room for the following batches.

When all the meringues have been poached and drained, pass the poaching milk through the drum sieve to join that which has been drained from the meringues. Beat the egg yolks and slowly pour in the milk, whisking at the same time. Pour the mixture into a heavy saucepan and, over low to moderate heat, stir constantly with a wooden spoon, scraping the sides of the saucepan repeatedly, until the sauce is sufficiently thick to coat the spoon. It must not approach the boiling point. Remove the saucepan from the heat immediately, pass the sauce through the drum sieve into another container, and pour it carefully into the serving platter, around, but not over, the meringues. Serve well chilled.

Three Simple Winter Menus

MENU I *(for 6 to 8)*

A light, refreshing white wine, the same that is served as aperitif, could be continued with the celeriac, or a simple and solid red wine may accompany the entire meal — body is more important than nuance. Traditionally, Cahors is associated with cassoulet. Also from the southwest of France, Madiran or Côtes de Buzet or a wine from the southern Côtes-du-Rhône (Gigondas, Lirac), a neighboring region (Côtes du Ventoux, Coteaux du Tricastin), or, from Piedmont, a Nebbiolo d'Alba would serve well.

CELERIAC IN MUSTARD SAUCE
[CELERI-RAVE A LA SAUCE MOUTARDE]

• • •

CASSOULET
[CASSOULET]

• • •

WATERCRESS SALAD
[SALADE CRESSIONIERE]

• • •

FRUIT
[FRUITS]

A *cassoulet* is a meal. It would be an error to precede it with anything but the simplest of *crudités,* or to serve, at the end, more than a fruit or the lightest of fruit-derivative desserts. Not only do the celeriac and the watercress frame the *cassoulet* aesthetically, but their roughage is a distinct aid to digestion.

THE CELERIAC IN MUSTARD SAUCE

Celeriac has come, in recent years, to be more widely used; it is one of the most commonly used vegetables in France — most often served raw in a salad like the following.

Cooked and pureed, its flavor attenuated with one part of potatoes to two of celeriac, plus a certain quantity of onion puree (turnips and garlic may also be added), finished with butter, it is an exquisite accompaniment to a roast, particularly to game.

Celeriac in Mustard Sauce

Céleri-rave à la Sauce Moutarde

1 celeriac (*about 1 pound*), peeled
salt, freshly ground pepper
juice of 1 lemon
1 tablespoon strong Dijon mustard
1 cup heavy cream
chopped parsley

Cut the celeriac into pieces and pass it through the medium blade of the *mouli-juliènne* or special attachment to a food processor (or grate it coarsely). Mix the salt and pepper in the lemon juice, stir in the mustard, and then stir in the cream. Taste for seasoning, mix thoroughly with the celeriac, turn the mixture out onto a serving dish, and sprinkle with parsley.

THE CASSOULET

There are said to be three *cassoulets* (Castelnaudary, Carcassonne, and Toulouse), but their definitions vary too much to be taken seriously and it would be more correct to say that there are as many as there are cooks, and to define a *cassoulet,* in a general way, as a slow-cooked gratin made up of two or more separate preparations, one of which is always a pork and bean stew, the others of which may be chosen among preserved duck or goose, braised lamb, and roast or braised partridge.

Cassoulet

Cassoulet

¼ goose (*breast or leg*) or ½ gosling
healthy pinch of mixed herbs (*page 52*)
coarse salt
goose fat from inside the bird
¼ cup water

BEAN STEW

6 ounces fresh pork rind
½ pound *pancetta*
1 pig's foot
½ pound uncooked garlic sausage (*cervelas*)
2 pounds dried white beans
2 medium carrots, peeled and cut into pieces
1 large onion, stuck with 2 cloves
2 cloves garlic, peeled
bouquet-garni (*page 50*)
salt

LAMB STEW

2 medium onions, peeled and coarsely chopped
2 medium carrots, peeled and cut into short lengths
1 lamb shoulder, all surface fat removed, cut into large pieces but not boned
goose fat
salt
2 tablespoons flour
1 cup dry white wine
3 cloves garlic, peeled
mixed herbs
1-pound can tomatoes (*in season, 3 or 4 fresh tomatoes*)
cooking liquid from beans

2 cloves garlic, peeled without crushing
white bread crumbs

THE GOOSE

Sprinkle the goose with the herbs and salt and leave it overnight. Render the goose fat (melt the pieces of fat with the water over low heat, and when nothing solid is left but the cracklings, strain off the pure fat). Cook the goose gently, immersed in this fat, until tender. Save the fat.

THE BEANS

Cover the pork rind, *pancetta,* and pig's foot with cold water, bring to a boil, simmer for a few minutes, drain, and rinse in cold water. Roll up the pork rind and tie it with a string. Prick the sausage in several places.

Cover the beans generously with cold water in a large, heavy saucepan or earthenware casserole. Bring slowly to a boil, drain them, and return them to the cooking utensil along with the vegetables, garlic, *bouquet-garni,* and pork products. Pour in enough tepid water to cover everything by 2 inches, bring to a boil again, slowly, and adjust the heat so that, covered, the barest simmer is maintained. Do not salt.

The sausage and *pancetta* should be removed and put aside after about 40 minutes. The foot and rind should remain with the beans until they are done — about 2 hours in all. Taste the cooking liquid and salt to taste. Put the rind and pig's foot aside with the sausage and *pancetta*. Discard the onion and *bouquet-garni*.

THE LAMB STEW

Cook the onions and carrots in a couple of tablespoons of goose fat in a heavy sauté pan (just the size to hold the pieces of meat placed side by side) for about 15 minutes, stirring regularly, until lightly browned. Remove the onions and carrots, making certain to leave no fragment of onion behind, and, over high heat, color the pieces of lamb, salted, in the same fat. When they are browned on all sides, sprinkle with flour, turn the pieces over, return the vegetables to the pan, and, when the flour is lightly cooked, add the white wine, garlic, and a sprinkling of herbs. Scrape and stir with a wooden spoon to loosen and dissolve frying adherents and transfer the contents to a heavy casserole. Add the tomatoes and enough of the beans' cooking liquid to cover, and leave, covered, at a bare simmer, either in a slow oven or over very low heat, for 1½ hours, skimming off surface fat 2 or 3 times during this period. Pour the contents of the casserole into a sieve, carefully pick out the pieces of meat and carrot and put them aside, and pass the rest through the sieve. Bring the sauce to a boil, move it to the side of the heat, regulating to a bubble, and skim for 15 minutes (page 48).

Rub the bottom and sides of a large, medium-deep earthenware oven dish with the 2 cloves of garlic until they are completely absorbed. Untie the pork rind, cut it into small rectangles, and distribute them regularly over the bottom of the dish. Cut the goose into two pieces, place them on the bed of rinds, and, after having drained the beans, putting their liquid aside, distribute about ⅓ of the beans over and around the pieces of goose. Split the pig's foot, remove the largest bones, cut each half into 3 or 4 pieces, and arrange them, along with the pieces of lamb and carrot (both those from the lamb stew and those from the beans), evenly over the surface. Cover everything with half of the remaining beans, and distribute the sausage, cut into thick slices, and the *pancetta,* cut into squares, on top, and cover with the remaining beans. Generously sprinkle the entire surface with bread crumbs and, carefully, so as to moisten them without displacing them, pour over, ladle by ladle, the sauce from the lamb stew until the liquid rises just to the surface of the beans. Dust lightly again with bread crumbs, sprinkle several tablespoonfuls of melted goose fat over the surface, and put the dish into a hot oven until it is heated through and the surface begins to bubble. Turn the oven low so that a gentle bubbling is maintained, and, after about 20 minutes, as the liquid reduces, partly by absorption and partly by evaporation, begin to baste the surface, first with the remaining lamb sauce and then, when it is finished, with the beans' cooking liquid. Continue in this way every 20 minutes or so and, when a pretty, golden-crisp gratin has formed on the surface, break it regularly all over with a spoon so that part becomes submerged and the rest is moistened by the sauce. The *cassoulet*, in principle, should remain at least 2 hours in a slow oven, and the gratin should be broken a minimum of 3 times, but if the basting liquids should run short before this time, it is better to stop the gratinéing process than to risk the dish's becoming too dry.

The beans retain their form but at the slightest pressure may be reduced to a creamy puree, and all the elements are coated with a succulent sauce whose body is drawn from the gelatinous rind and pig's foot and whose suaveness is enhanced by the discreet presence of goose fat.

Three Simple Winter Menus

MENU II *(for 4)*

SOUFFLES A LA SUISSESSE
[*SOUFFLES A LA SUISSESSE*]

A light white wine: Burgundy (Mâcon-Viré, Pouilly-Fuissé) or Loire Valley (Pouilly-Fumé, Sancerre) — or a rosé with the entire meal

• • •

SKEWERED LAMBS' KIDNEYS
[*BROCHETTES DE ROGNONS D'AGNEAU*]

Following a white wine, a light-bodied, young, cool red wine: Mâcon, Beaujolais, Côtes-du-Rhône

• • •

SAFFRON RICE WITH TOMATOES
[*RIZ SAFRANE AUX TOMATES*]

• • •

LAMB'S LETTUCE SALAD
[*SALADE DE MACHE*]

• • •

FRESH GOAT CHEESES
[*FROMAGES FRAIS DE CHEVRE*]

The same as the preceding, or a bigger-bodied wine of the same region

• • •

CREPES A LA NORMANDE
[*CREPES A LA NORMANDE*]

Although for most of the simple menus dessert wines have not been recommended, remember that apple desserts — in particular those served tepid or hot — marry especially well with a fine, well-chilled Sauternes

THE SOUFFLES A LA SUISSESSE

The composition of these souffles differs from that of an ordinary cheese souffle only in that the latter would contain one more beaten egg white. The final result, because the *suissesses* are poached in a *bain-marie* and thoroughly cooked — rather than being rapidly puffed up in a hot oven — and then imbibe a large quantity of heavy cream through a further gratin process, in no way resembles a classic souffle, but more nearly brings to mind *quenelles*.

Souffles à la Suissesse

Soufflés à la Suissesse

1 cup milk
6 tablespoons flour
salt, freshly ground pepper, suspicion of freshly grated nutmeg
2 ounces unsalted butter
3½ ounces freshly grated Parmesan cheese
3 egg yolks
2 egg whites
1½ cups heavy cream

Bring the milk to a boil, leave it until lukewarm, and pour it slowly into the flour, stirring to avoid lumping. Season with salt, pepper, and nutmeg and, stirring constantly with a wooden spoon, cook over medium heat until thickened. Leave to cool for several minutes, add half the butter, something over half of the grated cheese, and the 3 egg yolks, and mix thoroughly. Beat the egg whites until they are stiff and fold them in gently but thoroughly.

Butter individual custard molds or porcelain ramekins, spoon them about two-thirds full of the mixture, place them in a large shallow pan, and pour in enough hot, but not boiling, water to immerse them by two-thirds. Poach in a moderate oven for 20 to 25 minutes or until they are firm and spongy to the touch. Leave them to cool slightly and unmold each into your hand, first running the blade of a knife around the edges to loosen it. Arrange them in a buttered gratin dish (of a size just to hold them, placed side by side, but not touching), the bottom of which has been sprinkled with half of the remaining cheese. Pour over enough cream to immerse them by half, sprinkle the rest of the cheese over the surface and bake in a moderate oven for another 20 minutes or until the cream is nearly all absorbed and a light, golden gratin has been formed.

THE SKEWERED LAMBS' KIDNEYS

When skewered with other elements, as here, lamb's heart and liver are often joined to the kidneys. When grilled alone, lambs' kidneys are not cup up but are partially split from the rounded contour toward the core, opened out like books, and skewered, 2 or 3 per person, to hold them open while cooking. Those that are pinkish-beige in color are always more delicately flavored than brownish-red-colored kidneys. Sharpened rosemary branches, with a tuft of leaves left at the far end of each, make attractive skewers.

Skewered Lambs' Kidneys

Brochettes de Rognons d'Agneau

8 lambs' kidneys, each cut crosswise into 3 sections
2 medium sweet onions, quartered, sections separated, or 12 small fresh
    white garden onions, whole
2 sweet peppers, seeded and cut into squares
6 bay leaves, preferably fresh, each cut in 2
mixed herbs (*page 52*)
¼ cup olive oil
2 cloves garlic, peeled
large handful bread crumbs
salt, freshly ground pepper

Combine the kidneys, vegetables, and pieces of bay leaf in a bowl, sprinkle with a couple of pinches of mixed herbs and the olive oil, and toss together. Leave to marinate for an hour or so, tossing or turning from time to time.

Reduce the garlic to a puree in a mortar, add the bread crumbs, and mix well until they are sticky and permeated with garlic.

Alternate 6 pieces of kidney on each skewer with the peppers and onions, season, and roll the skewers in the garlic crumbs, pressing lightly to ensure their being well coated. Grill them over hot coals on a preheated heavy iron grill, turning them 4 times, about every 1½ or 2 minutes, depending on the intensity of the heat, and basting them regularly but lightly with the remaining marinade, until all sides are evenly browned. To be tender, moist, and flavorful, the kidneys must remain pink inside. Arrange them on a bed of rice that has been turned out onto a heated serving platter.

Saffron Rice with Tomatoes

Riz Safrané aux Tomates

1 medium onion, finely chopped
¼ pound unsalted butter
½ pound long-grained rice
pinch (*something less than ¼ teaspoon*) of saffron
salt
2 cups boiling water
1 pound can whole tomatoes (*in season, 3 or 4 medium tomatoes, peeled and seeded — see page 14*)

Use an earthenware or heavy copper utensil with a tight-fitting lid. Cook the onion gently in a little butter for about 10 minutes, until soft and yellowed but not browned. Add the rice, saffron, and salt, stirring from time to time with a wooden spoon, and after a couple of minutes, when the grains have acquired a "milky" tint, pour in the boiling water, stir once, and leave, covered, over low heat so that the barest possible movement may be detected at the water's surface. Remove from the heat after 18 to 20 minutes (some rices require more or less cooking time), and leave to swell and dry out for 5 to 10 minutes.

Meanwhile, drain the tomatoes, cut them in half to remove seeds and liquid, and stew them gently in butter for a few minutes. Just before serving, mix into the rice the tomatoes and the remaining butter, cut into small pieces, delicately and repeatedly lifting the rice with the prongs of a fork so as to loosen the grains from one another without damaging them. Grated cheese may also be added at this time, if desired.

CREPES A LA NORMANDE

If preferred, Calvados may be substituted for Cognac in the preparation of the crepes and a few drops of it dribbled over the rolled crepes before they are sprinkled with sugar.

Crepes à la Normande

Crêpes à la Normande

12 crepes (*page 79*)
3 apples, preferably russets, quartered, peeled, cored, and sliced thin
3½ ounces unsalted butter
½ cup sugar

Sauté the sliced apples in butter over high heat, tossing them regularly, until they are just cooked but firmly retain their shape. Roll a heaped tablespoonful, first sprinkled with a bit of sugar, into each crepe, arrange the crepes in a buttered shallow baking dish, a thin slice of butter on each, sprinkle the surface lightly with sugar, and put the crepes into a hot oven for a few minutes — just long enough to heat them thoroughly and to melt and glaze the sugar lightly.

Three Simple Winter Menus

MENU III *(for 8)*

A Beaujolais (Chiroubles, Brouilly, Saint-Amour, Morgon) from the most recent vintage, served cool, with the entire meal

POACHED EGGS A LA BOURGUIGNONNE
[OEUFS POCHES A LA BOURGUIGNONNE]

· · ·

BEEF TRIPE A LA LYONNAISE
[GRAS-DOUBLE A LA LYONNAISE]

· · ·

COMPOSED SALAD
[SALADE COMPOSEE]

· · ·

CHEESES
[FROMAGES]

· · ·

PINEAPPLE ICE
[GRANITE A L'ANANAS]

THE POACHED EGGS A LA BOURGUIGNONNE

In a professional kitchen the sauce would be prepared in advance, with a *roux* base to thicken it, a spoonful of meat glaze added for extra body and succulence, and lightly buttered at the last moment. Another red-wine *court-bouillon* would then be kept on hand for use as poaching liquid. A *beurre manié* is less satisfactory as a thickening agent but more practical in a home kitchen. The unpleasant floury taste that many people fear in all flour-thickened sauces is present only in a sauce in which the flour has cooked too short a time, but not, mysteriously, in a *beurre manié* – thickened sauce, in which it is subjected to no cooking.

The quantity of wine called for is necessary for poaching the eggs but will make an abundant sauce; before thickening, some may be strained off and saved for another purpose. It is not practical to poach more than four eggs at a time. The shallowness of a sauté pan or an omelette pan will facilitate the adding and removal of the eggs; heavy copper will best hold in the heat; a diameter of 9 inches will contain four eggs and permit of a sufficient depth of liquid.

Poached Eggs à la Bourguignonne

Oeufs Pochés à la Bourguignonne

8 thick slices firm, close-textured white bread, cut to circles with a biscuit
   cutter (*or trimmed with a knife*)
3½ ounces unsalted butter, melted
2 cloves garlic, peeled
aromatic red-wine essence (*page 63*), made from 2 bottles red wine, a slice of
   finely chopped raw ham (*prosciutto*) included in the *mirepoix,* the wine
   reduced by half instead of by three-quarters
salt
8 very fresh eggs
beurre manié: 2 ounces softened unsalted butter and 3 tablespoons flour,
   mashed with a fork into a uniform paste
freshly ground pepper
chopped parsley

Brush the circles of bread on both sides with melted butter, lay them out on a baking sheet, and put them into a moderate oven, turning them over 2 or 3 times, until they are evenly golden and crisp on both surfaces but not dried out. Rub one surface of each lightly with a clove of garlic and place them, garlic sides up, 2 per person, on 4 warmed plates.

Salt the wine reduction to taste. Bring it to a boil, lower the heat, and break in 4 eggs, opening each cracked egg at the liquid's surface so it slips gently in (or, if you prefer, break them first onto four saucers, slipping each rapidly from its saucer into the liquid). Cover tightly, turn off the heat, and leave the eggs to poach for 2 or 3 minutes or until the whites are softly coagulated but the yolks are still liquid. Lift them carefully with a perforated skimming spoon and remove them to a plate, return the liquid to the boil, and repeat. With the tip of a small knife, trim any straggly, unsightly white from around the eggs.

Bring the liquid back to a simmer, whisk in the *beurre manié,* a bit at a time, till the sauce is lightly thickened, then remove from the heat. Place an egg on each round of bread, grind over pepper, and pass the sauce through a fine sieve over the eggs. Sprinkle with parsley.

THE BEEF TRIPE A LA LYONNAISE

Gras-double is beef tripe composed of the four stomachs: blanket tripe (paunch), honeycomb tripe (reticulum), bible tripe (omasum, called "bible-tripe" because it is made up of fine book-like leaves), and reed tripe (abomasum). Outside of France, one must often be satisfied with the first two. Beef tripe is usually sold precooked; bleached tripe, which has no taste, should be avoided. If raw, it should be first well scrubbed, rubbed and rinsed in tepid vinegar water, and simmered for 5 hours or so in a *blanc* (water and flour slurry added to a large pot of water with thyme, bay, onions, salt, and either vinegar or lemon juice).

Often, both the onions and tripe are sautéed in lard, instead of butter and oil, and finished with vinegar instead of lemon.

If an accompaniment is desired, a *paillasson* (potato straw cake, page 265) is perfect, in which case a simple green salad would be more suitable than the composed salad.

Beef Tripe à la Lyonnaise

Gras-double à la Lyonnaise

1 pound sweet onions, halved and sliced
1 ounce unsalted butter
1½ pounds precooked tripe
¼ cup olive oil
salt, freshly ground pepper
juice of ½ lemon

Cook the onions, salted, in the butter, over low heat, stirring and tossing regularly, until they are soft and yellowed, about 15 minutes. Just before removing them from the heat, turn the flame up and toss them until they are lightly browned. Put them aside.

Cut the tripe into bands 3 inches wide, cut each band crosswise into approximately ¼-inch strips, and sponge them dry in paper towels. Heat the olive oil in a large, heavy sauté pan, add the tripe, season with salt and pepper, and cook over high heat, frequently tossing and stirring and scraping the bottom with a wooden spoon, for 8 to 10 minutes or until some of the strips show signs of browning and crisping at the edges. Add the onions, toss everything together for another minute or so, and turn it out onto a heated serving platter. Squeeze the lemon juice into the hot pan, swirl it around, and sprinkle it over the tripe.

THE COMPOSED SALAD

Artichokes, if young and tender, the chokes still undeveloped, are best raw, simply "turned," sliced, and soaked in lemon water, in a salad of this sort. Parboiled fresh, young green beans, precooked salsify, and avocados are other possible ingredients. This salad may either accompany or follow an ungarnished main course.

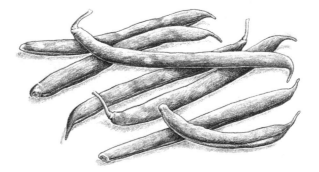

Composed Salad

Salade Composée

3 medium potatoes of a firm, nonmealy variety, boiled in their skins
about ⅓ cup dry white wine (*enough to cover potato slices*)
2 medium artichoke bottoms (*page 45*), sliced
1 celery heart, sliced crosswise
1 heaping tablespoon *fines herbes* (*equal parts of whatever is available: chervil,
    parsley, chives, tarragon*), chopped
vinaigrette (*page 55*)
1 small head lettuce

Peel the potatoes while they are still hot, slice them into a bowl, cover them with the white wine, and leave them to cool. Put the artichoke bottoms and celery, along with the drained potatoes and half the *fines herbes,* to marinate in the vinaigrette. Loosely place the lettuce leaves, washed and gently sponged dry in a towel, on top, sprinkle with the remaining *fines herbes,* and toss only at the moment of serving.

Pineapple Ice

Granité à l'Ananas

1 large ripe pineapple
¾ cup sugar (*or to taste*)
juice of 3 oranges, strained

Remove the top of the pineapple, cutting in at an angle all around, so as to form a lid, and pare the inside of its flesh. Remove all the pulp from the inside of the pineapple. To do this, cut around and about halfway down, close to the skin but being careful not to pierce it, with a long, sharp, pointed knife; then cut all around the core and make spokelike incisions between the two circular cuts. Remove the wedges with the help of a tablespoon and continue scraping around the core until all the pulp has been removed and the shell is empty, except for the upright core. Cut into the base of the core with the point of the knife and break it off as cleanly as possible.

Mash the pulp with a pestle and work it well in a sieve until all the juice possible has been extracted. Mix about 1 cup of the juice with the sugar and boil to form a syrup. When it is cool, mix it with the rest of the pineapple juice and the orange juice, pour the mixture into 2 ice-cube trays, and put them to freeze, along with the pineapple shell and lid. (Lacking a sufficiently large freezing compartment, chill the pineapple separately as well as possible.) After an hour or so, stir the mixture, scraping all solid parts from the sides and bottoms of the trays and mashing it together with the liquid. Repeat this process a couple of times over the course of approximately 3 hours or until, when mixed together, a semifirm but still mushy consistency is achieved; then spoon it into the pineapple shell. It may then be left in the freezing compartment for another hour or so and allowed to become slightly firmer — but if served frozen solid, it loses all its quality.

SPRING MENUS

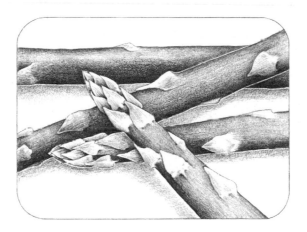

Two Formal Spring Dinners

MENU I *(for 6)*

RAW SHELLFISH PLATTER
[PLATEAU DE COQUILLAGES]

A young, light, very dry white wine: Coteaux Champenois or, from the Loire valley, Muscadet or Sancerre

• • •

TURBAN OF SOLE FILLETS WITH SALMON, SORREL SAUCE
[TURBAN DE FILETS DE SOLE AU SAUMON, SAUCE A L'OSEILLE]

A white wine from the Northern Rhône valley (Condrieu, Château-Grillet, Hermitage)

• • •

ROAST SADDLE OF LAMB WITH HERBS
[SELLE D'AGNEAU ROTIE AUX AROMATES]

A red Graves (Haut-Bailly, Pape-Clément, La Mission-Haut-Brion), a Saint-Julien (Ducru-Beaucaillou, Léoville) or a Saint-Estèphe (Cos d'Estournel, Montrose), from a light and fairly recent year (6 to 8 years)

• • •

GREEN-BEAN PUREE, ARTICHOKE BOTTOMS WITH MUSHROOM PUREE
[PUREE DE HARICOTS VERTS, FONDS D'ARTICHAUTS A LA PUREE DE CHAMPIGNONS]

• • •

CHEESES
[FROMAGES]

One of the great Pauillacs from a bigger and older vintage than the preceding wine

• • •

FROZEN STRAWBERRY MOUSSE WITH RASPBERRY PUREE
[MOUSSE DE FRAISES GLACEE A LA SAUCE MELBA]

The fresh, clean taste of live things from the sea is a welcome opening to any meal and a particularly useful possibility when composing a more or less complex menu in delicate balance, for they add their dimension without placing restrictions on the choice of dishes to follow, and the light, sharp wine that best accompanies them leaves an equally open field in the *suite* of wines.

The turban is highly decorative. The various poached fish-fillet and mousseline preparations count, certainly, among the most delicate in classical cooking, and their lightness and fantasy offset perfectly the sobriety of an unadorned roast. The frozen mousse discourages an accompanying wine, but has no other failings.

Much may be prepared in advance: the mousseline forcemeat, but for the final addition of cream, the *fumet* and the sorrel puree for the fish sauce, the vegetable purees, and the artichoke bottoms. The turban should be put to poach about 20 minutes before going to table and the saddle put to roast at the moment one is seated. The precooked artichoke bottoms may be put to stew in butter when the turban is served. Finishing the fish sauce and reheating the vegetable purees are rapid last-minute chores whose timing requires no forethought.

THE SHELLFISH PLATTER

Oysters, clams, mussels, and sea urchins form the usual composition of a shellfish platter in France. All should be opened just before being served. (See the *oursi-nade* recipe, page 155, for the method of opening sea urchins.) The traditional accompaniments are lemon halves, wine vinegar with chopped shallot, coarsely broken-up (*mignonette*) white peppercorns, fresh unsalted butter, and thin slices of firm, fine-textured rye bread.

Turban of Sole Fillets with Salmon, Sorrel Sauce

Turban de Filets de Sole au Saumon, Sauce à l'Oseille

3 large soles (*about 1 pound each*), filleted carcasses saved
1 pound mousseline forcemeat (*page 76*), made from fresh salmon
1 ounce shelled raw pistachio nuts, skinned (*page 44*) and coarsely chopped
2 cups fish *fumet* (*page 72*), made from the soles' carcasses
½ pound sorrel, stemmed, washed, and shredded
3½ ounces unsalted butter

Incorporate the chopped pistachios into the mousseline forcemeat.

Stew the sorrel in 1 ounce of butter, stirring regularly, for about 15 minutes or until it has melted to a near puree. Pass it through a fine sieve and put it aside.

Soak the fillets in cold water for 10 minutes, lay them, skinned sides facing up, on paper towels, dry the surfaces with more paper towels, and flatten each fillet slightly by pressing against it with the flat side of a large knife blade. Draw a very sharp-bladed knife, 4 or 5 times, on the diagonal, across the surface of each fillet, cutting through the surface membrane to leave very shallow incisions. (Because the membrane shrinks while cooking, it may cause the fillets to buckle if unslit.)

Generously butter a large savarin mold (circular, with rounded bottom and large central tube). Line it with the fillets, pressing each firmly into place (the surfaces sliced free from the carcass next to the mold, the slit skin sides visible), slightly overlapping, with the narrow tip of each hanging over the central tube of the mold and the wider end hanging over the outside. (Slivers may be cut from some of the fillets and a bit of patchwork effected, if necessary.) Spoon in the forcemeat, tap the bottom of the mold firmly against a work surface 2 or 3 times to settle the filling and eliminate any air pockets, fold the fillet tips over the filling to form the turban, and press a buttered round of parchment paper over it, a small hole cut in the center and a few shallow slits cut, spokelike, out from it. (Fold a square of paper, somewhat wider than the diameter of the mold, from corner to corner to form a triangle, fold again, bringing the two folded corners together and, from the twice-folded tip, continue folding, 2 or 3 times, to form increasingly narrow triangles; measure a large radius, holding the narrow tip over the center of the mold, and clip off the excess at the wide end; snip off the end of the narrow tip, unfold once, cut in along the exposed line, and open the paper out.)

Poach in a *bain-marie,* the mold immersed by two-thirds in hot, but not boiling, water, in a slow to medium oven for 40 minutes or until the surface is resilient, firm, and springy to the touch. (The poaching may be conducted over very low heat in a large covered pot with a grill in the bottom if it is not convenient to use the oven.) Remove the mold from the *bain-marie* and leave it to settle for 7 or 8 minutes before unmolding. (The sauce will be finished during this time.) To unmold, remove the buttered paper, place a fine wire rack on top, and turn the rack and mold over together, as if to unmold. This will drain off the troublesome liquids that must otherwise be sponged up with towels from the serving platter. Turn mold and rack together back over and unmold the turban onto a heated round serving platter. Surround it with a ribbon of sauce and send the rest to table separately.

THE SAUCE

Reduce the fish *fumet* in a heavy saucepan over high heat, stirring frequently, by about two-thirds or until it begins to acquire a light syrupy consistency. Add the sorrel puree and continue boiling and stirring for a few seconds until a light but distinct body is achieved. Remove immediately from the heat and whisk in the remaining butter, first cut into small pieces.

THE ROAST SADDLE OF LAMB WITH HERBS

The saddle is the section of back stretching from the haunch to the rib cage. It should be cut just above the haunch so as to include none of the complicated structure of the pelvis, the presence of which makes correct carving impossible. At the rib cage end, however, the last floating ribs may be included in the cut; they are easily boned out — or ask your butcher to do it. Short sections of the side belly, known as aprons, are left attached. Although the fat may be removed before cooking, a healthy layer of firm, dry, white fat is a sign of quality; the flesh should be a clear rose-tan color. It should be sufficiently aged. Specialized butchers will usually have whole animals on hand; small butchers, who receive only one animal at a time, or supermarket butchers often split animals ahead of time and cut the saddle into loin chops. Best order in advance.

Roast Saddle of Lamb with Herbs

Selle d'Agneau Rôtie aux Aromates

1 saddle of lamb, brought to room temperature before roasting
2 cloves garlic, peeled (*page 45*)
mixed herbs (*page 52*)
salt, freshly ground pepper
2 tablespoons olive oil

Remove all the fat; that on the inside, next to the filet mignon and at the underside base of the apron, may easily be pried loose with the fingers. Using a small pointed sharp knife, make an incision through the layer of fat, the entire length of the saddle, following the line of the backbone. First on one side, then on the other, gently force the layer of fat loose from the fillet, using your fingers and, when it resists, the point of the knife, being careful to cut neither into the flesh itself, which is protected by a membrane to which the fat is only lightly attached, nor into the thin membrane that connects the apron to the fillet. Begin, now, at the far tip of the apron and, in the same way, loosen its layer of fat up to the connecting point. Slice through the layer of fat, leaving a thin layer of fat to ensure the apron's remaining attached. Remove the layers of fat and membrane separating the thin layers of flesh in the lower section of the apron.

Rub the garlic cloves repeatedly against the rough surfaces of bone and over the entire surface of the meat. Sprinkle the herbs, salt, and pepper lightly on all surfaces, most sparingly on the underside, and coat with olive oil, rubbing with your hands to ensure an even distribution. Roll the aprons under so that the two rolls touch and rest firmly against the filets mignons.

Place the roast in a heavy, shallow baking dish of just the right size to hold it and count 10 minutes per pound of actual roasting time (25 to 30 minutes in this instance), starting at 450°F and, after 10 minutes, turning it down to 325°F. After roasting, leave it in its roasting pan in a warm but not hot place for 10 to 15 minutes so that the meat may relax. (Most practical is to remove the roast from the oven for a couple of minutes to arrest the cooking, at the same time turning off the oven and leaving the door open so that it may cool slightly before the meat is returned to the warm, closed oven.) The meat will be neither rare nor gray in color, but tender rose throughout. Carve at table.

TO CARVE A SADDLE

The blade of the knife should be longer than the saddle, narrow-bladed and razor sharp. With the back of the fork steadying one side, slice down to the other side of the backbone, following the contours, against the path formed by the vertebrae, nearly separating the loin from the bone, then slice inward, horizontally, removing 5 slices, the 3 center ones of which are regularly formed. Reverse the position of the saddle, pin the carved side with the prongs of the fork, and carve the other loin in the same way. Turn the roast over, slice off the aprons, slice each on the bias into 3 sections, and carve out the filets mignons, or tenderloins, slicing each crosswise into 3 sections. In a service for 6, this produces 1 slice of loin (filet) plus a fragment, 1 section of tenderloin (filet mignon), and 1 section of apron per person. Spoon over the carving juices.

THE GREEN-BEAN PUREE

Instead of rice, dried green flageolet beans, cooked until very tender, may be used (1 part of cooked flageolets to 2 of green beans) to give the necessary body to the puree. The result is more velvety. The rice method is simpler and the flavor more direct.

Green-Bean Puree

Purée de Haricots Verts

2 heaped tablespoons rice
2 pounds fresh, tender green beans
salt, freshly ground pepper, freshly grated nutmeg
¼ pound unsalted butter, cut into small pieces

Parboil the rice for 15 minutes, drain it, and rinse it. Plunge the beans, along with the parboiled rice, into a large pot of salted, rapidly boiling water. Keep at a rapid boil, uncovered, until the beans are tender (a couple of minutes longer than if they were to be served whole). Pour the contents of the saucepan into a colander or large sieve and leave to drain for at least ½ hour, then pass the beans and rice first through a vegetable mill, using a medium blade, then, a couple of table-spoonfuls at a time, through a fine nylon drum sieve (see page 47). Season to taste with salt, pepper, and a tiny bit of nutmeg, smooth out the surface, and put the puree aside, plastic film pressed to the surface, until the last minute.

Heat the puree in a heavy saucepan over high heat, stirring rapidly and constantly with a wooden spoon to prevent sticking or burning. When it is sufficiently heated, remove it from the heat and whip in the butter. Incorporate as much as the beans can absorb without becoming too liquid — the puree, however, should be nearly pourable, not stiff.

THE ARTICHOKE BOTTOMS WITH MUSHROOM PUREE

Artichoke bottoms may be garnished with a variety of purees, among the finest being fresh broad beans, the skins first removed, the beans boiled until tender for 7 or 8 minutes with a branch of fresh savory, then drained, twice sieved, seasoned to taste, reheated, and generously buttered; green peas prepared in the same way, but without the savory, and *soubise* (sliced new onions gently stewed in butter, bound with a bit of thick *béchamel,* and passed through a fine sieve) are also very nice. All are perfect accompaniments to roast or braised lamb, veal, beef, or fowl.

Mushroom purees may remain slightly rough in texture.

Artichoke Bottoms with Mushroom Puree

Fonds d'Artichauts à la Purée de Champignons

6 large artichoke bottoms, precooked and kept somewhat firm (*page 45*)
1 pound firm, unopened mushrooms, trimmed, rinsed, and dried
¼ pound unsalted butter
salt, freshly ground pepper
juice of ½ lemon
chopped parsley

Pass the raw mushrooms through the medium blade of a vegetable mill or puree them in a food processor. Melt 2 ounces of the butter in a heavy saucepan, add the mushroom puree, season, and cook over high heat, stirring constantly with a wooden spoon, until all the vegetable liquid has evaporated. Squeeze in the lemon juice and stew gently, covered, over very low heat, for another 5 minutes.

Melt 1 ounce of butter in a heavy sauté pan of the right dimensions just to contain the artichoke bottoms at their ease. Place them, bottoms down, in the pan, cut 1 ounce of butter into 6 pieces, place a piece in each of the artichoke bottoms, and stew gently, covered, without browning, for about ½ hour, turning them over once or twice.

Remove the artichoke bottoms to a heated serving platter, carefully spoon each full of the mushroom puree, and sprinkle the surface of each with chopped parsley.

THE FROZEN STRAWBERRY MOUSSE WITH RASPBERRY PUREE

A handful of wild strawberries (*fraises des bois*) scattered over the mousse just before serving is an attractive refinement.

Frozen strawberries will not replace fresh, but frozen raspberries, in particular those frozen whole and unsweetened, are excellent.

Frozen Strawberry Mousse with Raspberry Puree

Mousse de Fraises Glacée à la Sauce Melba

¾ cup sugar (*or more, to taste*)
⅓ cup water
1½ pounds fresh, ripe strawberries
1 cup heavy cream

SAUCE

1½ pounds fresh raspberries (*or 2 packages frozen*)
sugar, to taste

Boil the sugar and water together and let cool. Pass the strawberries through a sieve or process them and mix the puree with the syrup. Pour the chilled cream into a cold bowl, whip it until it is semifirm, but not stiff, mix it with the strawberry mixture, and freeze, either in a mechanical ice-cream freezer or in ice trays. If trays are used, scrape the mixture out of the trays into a chilled bowl when half frozen, whip it, and return it to the trays to finish freezing.

Pass the raspberries through a nylon drum sieve, and add sugar to taste. Heap the mousse into a chilled crystal bowl and serve the raspberry sauce separately.

Two Formal Spring Dinners
MENU II *(for 6)*

CRAYFISH SALAD WITH FRESH DILL
[SALADE D'ECREVISSES A L'ANETH]

An uncomplicated white wine with enough muscle to withstand the dill:
Côtes-du-Rhône (Châteauneuf-du-Pape, Crozes-Hermitage), Vernaccia di
San Gimignano from Tuscany, California Chenin Blanc.

. . .

SPRING STEW
[RAGOUT PRINTANIER]

. . .

POACHED CHICKEN MOUSSELINE
[POULARDE POCHEE MOUSSELINE]

A vin jaune *from the Jura (Arbois Vin Jaune or Château Chalon) or a*
lacy, floral red Burgundy from a light and recent year: Volnay
(Champans, Taillepieds, Clos des Ducs) or Chambolle-Musigny (les
Amoureuses, les Charmes)

. . .

CRUSTS WITH FRESH MORELS
[CROUTES AUX MORILLES FRAICHES]

. . .

TOSSED GREEN SALAD, FINES HERBES
[SALADE VERTE AUX FINES HERBES]

. . .

CHEESES
[FROMAGES]

Following a vin jaune, *any old red wine sufficiently robust and distinguished to hold its own by comparison — Côte Rôtie (Côtes-du-Rhône) or Barolo (Piedmont), for instance; following a red Burgundy, one of the great growths from Vosne-Romanée (La Tâche, Richebourg) or a neighboring community, older than the preceding.*

• • •

PINEAPPLE SURPRISE
[ANANAS EN SURPRISE]

All the elements of the crayfish salad may be prepared ahead of time. The vegetables for the stew may be cleaned, peeled, etc., and kept fresh in a damp towel in the refrigerator, the chicken may be boned a day in advance, if one likes, and the forcemeat, but for the final mounting with cream, must be prepared in advance. The crusts may be browned ahead of time.

The chicken should be stuffed and put to poach about 1¼ hours before going to table. The vegetable stew should be put to cook just before the crayfish salad is assembled, and the morels only well after the vegetable stew has been served.

Cream occurs in three different preparations in this menu, but these are so different in nature and the cream in each so different in effect that there is no risk of monotony, and the actual quantity of cream allotted per person throughout the entire meal is not excessive.

Crayfish Salad with Fresh Dill

Salade d'Écrevisses à l'Aneth

white-wine *court-bouillon* (*page 64*), containing several sprigs of dill and a
    small chili pepper
36 large live crayfish, or 5 pounds smaller crayfish
1 heaping tablespoon finely chopped young, tender, feathery dill leaves (*no
    stems*), or chopped *fines herbes* (*page 50*) if fresh dill is not available
salt, freshly ground pepper
juice of 1 lemon
1 cup heavy cream
1 medium head tender-leafed lettuce

The crayfish, because of their quantity, will be cooked in relays. This economizes
on *court-bouillon,* which is that much more flavorful for succeeding batches of
crayfish as well.

Toss a batch of crayfish into the boiling *court-bouillon* (no more than can be
completely immersed), cover the pan, and, when the liquid returns to the boil,
lower the heat and simmer for about 5 minutes. With a wire skimming spoon,
remove the crayfish to a large bowl; proceed in the same way for the others. Pour
the last batch and the *court-bouillon* over the others and leave to cool in the liquid.

Put aside 6 of the largest and most perfectly formed crayfish, keeping them
moist in some of the *court-bouillon.* Tear off the tails of all the others, remove and
discard the tail shells, and put the shelled tails aside, covered with *court-bouillon.*

Pound the carapaces (everything left — heads, claws, legs, coral) several at a
time (depending on the size of the mortar) in a stone mortar (this may be done
in food processors with fixed blades, but not with those whose blades slip loosely
into place), pass each pounded batch through the medium blade of a vegetable
mill, and, once all the juices are thoroughly extracted, discard the dry debris of
shells. When all have been pounded and milled, pass this coarse puree, in small
quantities at a time, through a fine drum sieve (page 47).

Put aside ⅓ of the chopped dill for the *décor* and mix together the remainder
with salt, pepper, and lemon juice, add the cream, mix well, and whisk in the
crayfish puree. Taste for salt and lemon.

Pick over the lettuce, keeping the leaves whole, wash them, and sponge them
dry between two towels. Arrange them on the bottom and around the sides of a
large, deep serving platter, distribute the drained crayfish tails on top, mask the
entire surface with the sauce, place the unshelled crayfish, trussed (pull the tail
slowly upward, in an arc, toward the head, ease each pincer under and backward
to meet it, and pierce the tail shell near the base, on either side, with the stable
prong of each pincer), symmetrically around the border, and sprinkle with the
remaining dill.

Spring Stew

Ragoût Printanier

4 pounds freshly picked young broad beans
6 artichoke hearts or bottoms (*page 45*), quartered, chokes cut out, rubbed
   with lemon, uncooked
30 peeled whole new white onions, each about the size of a small walnut
bouquet-garni (*page 50*), containing a sprig of savory
salt
4 ounces unsalted butter
2 tablespoons water
1 teaspoon chopped fresh tender savory leaves, mixed with an equal amount
   of chopped parsley

Not only must the broad beans be shelled (pods removed), but, with the exception of the tiniest, whose skins remain a bright and tender green, the skin of each bean must be removed. This is a simple but tedious task: tear off a "cap" of skin with a thumbnail and press the other extremity of the bean between thumb and forefinger — the bean will slip out. Once skinned, any whose flesh is not tender and fresh green, but yellowing and pale of color, should be discarded or put aside for a soup.

Use an earthenware casserole or *poêlon* to ensure slow, even cooking and to avoid any metallic contact with the artichokes. Put the artichokes, the onions, and the *bouquet-garni,* lightly salted, to cook, covered, in 1 ounce of butter (separate from direct flame by an asbestos pad), over very low heat, shaking the receptacle from time to time. The vegetables should not color. After 25 to 30 minutes, add the water and the broad beans, sprinkle with salt, and continue to cook, tightly covered, over very low heat, for about 10 minutes, shaking and tossing the receptacle from time to time — avoid stirring so as not to break or crush the vegetables. At this point, the broad beans should remain intact but crush easily beneath the slightest pressure, and no more than a couple of tablespoonfuls of slightly syrupy cooking liquid should remain. Remove from the heat and add the remaining butter cut into small pieces, tossing and swirling the contents until it is absorbed. Serve directly from the cooking utensil, sprinkled with chopped herbs.

THE MOUSSELINE CHICKEN

Given a vague knowledge of anatomy and a smattering of experience, boning out any animal is child's play. Trying to explain the process is far more difficult than its execution, which, having once familiarized oneself with the steps, demands no more than 10 or 15 minutes for fowl. The following method, at once the simplest and the most elegant, is merely a question of turning the flesh and skin of the bird inside out, from throat to tail, removing the bare carcass, and turning it right side out again; in this instance, the bones of the wings and legs are left in place for the sake of presentation. Many may find it easier to feel their way with fingertips and knife tip than to attempt to follow instructions.

Chicken prepared in this way can be accompanied by a creamed *velouté* called *suprême* sauce (page 74) or any of its variations — saffroned, tomatoed, bound with egg yolks, or with finely pureed spinach, broad beans, or green peas and finished with butter (sometimes a crayfish butter). If a *velouté* is served, it should be put to work with a separate batch of chicken stock to have enough time to be properly skimmed and cleansed; some of the rich poaching liquid can then be added to it and rapidly reduced. Rice pilaf or fresh egg noodles are good garnishes to sauced, poached chicken. Chopped truffles, cubes of *foie gras, duxelles,* or tiny raw garden peas, little broad beans, and diced, parboiled spring carrots can replace or supplement the pistachios in the forcemeat. The chicken mousseline is equally good served cold in its jelly.

The cooking vessel should be oval and as nearly as possible of a size just to contain the chicken, completely submerged in a minimum quantity of rich stock.

Poached Chicken Mousseline

Poularde Pochée Mousseline

1 large tender (*4 to 6 months*) roasting chicken
mousseline forcemeat (*page 76*), made from chicken breasts
small handful of fresh, shelled pistachios, skinned (*page 44*), and coarsely
    chopped
1 lemon (*juice*)
veal stock (*page 66*), enriched by the addition of giblets and carcass, etc.,
    resulting from the boning of the chicken and chicken breasts

These instructions are for a bird that has not been gutted or for one, as prepared for the French market, whose intestines have been untwirled through the anus, the skin pierced at no point. The boning process is identical for a bird whose abdomen has been slashed for gutting, but the slash must be sewn up before the bird is stuffed, leaving an unsightly scar, more visible in a poached bird than in one roasted or braised and glazed. If the feet have not been removed, blister the skin over a flame at the same time that the chicken is singed, slip off the blistered skin with paper towels, cut off the extremity of the central toe, and remove the others. Cut through the neck near the base of the head, slit the skin down the back of the neck, carefully pull the skin, and the trachea and esophagus that cling to it, clear of the neck, sever the neck at the first vertebra, cutting halfway through, and twist it off. Pull the trachea, the esophagus, and its attached crop loose from the neck skin and tear them out of the throat.

BONING THE CHICKEN

Use a small, sharp, and sharply pointed paring knife. There are 3 bones attached to each wing joint: one tip of the V-shaped wishbone, the bone corresponding to the clavicle or collarbone, and a bone, the other end of which is free-floating in the flesh of the back, that corresponds to the shoulder blade. Remove, first, the wishbone; making a V-shaped incision with the point of the knife and touching the bone along its entire contour, cut through the tendons or ligaments that connect its pointed end to the tip of the breastbone, force the flesh loose from the 2 prongs with fingertips, and pull it backward, tearing it loose from the wing joints. Remove the clavicles in the reverse sense, first slicing through the tendons connecting them to the wing joints, loosening adhering flesh, and pulling each upward away from the wing joint toward the breast to snap it loose from the breast bone. Sever the attachment of each shoulder blade at the wing joint and, holding it firmly between the thumb and forefinger of the left hand, pull it out of the flesh with the other hand. Force the flesh loose from the breastbone, working along the crest with the point of the knife and forcing that at the sides loose with fingertips. With fingertips, loosen all the way around the rib cage, and finally, at the highest point of the breastbone, cut through the cartilage connecting it to the skin, being careful not to pierce the skin.

With the aid of the knife tip, separate the spinal column from surrounding flesh until about the halfway point in the back. Force the flesh and skin loose from the wide, flat pelvic backbones to either side of the spinal column, being careful to work down into the shallow cavity to each side, forcing with the index fingernail, to separate the cushions of flesh known as oysters, leaving them attached to the body of flesh and skin. Grasp each leg and twist backward from the thigh joint (directly behind each oyster), rupturing its connection to the pelvis, and snip it free from the socket with the knife tip. From mid-back to the tail, the spinal column is directly attached to the skin at the cartilaginous protrusions of each vertebra. Pull the skin away, to each side of the spinal column, at the same time snipping through the cartilaginous vertebrae tips to avoid piercing the skin. Cut through the spinal column at the base of the tail, leaving the last tiny vertebrae in the tail, and lift away the carcass, still forcing with fingertips and knife tip if there is any resistance. Turn the chicken skin side out again. (Sew it up if the abdomen has been slit for gutting.)

Add the pistachios to the mousseline forcemeat. Stuff the chicken through the throat, without forcing (the stuffing swells and the flesh contracts during poaching — loosely stuffed, it will firm up, but firmly stuffed, it will burst), and truss it, using a trussing needle longer than the thickness of the chicken and two 2-foot lengths of kitchen string (note that an unboned bird is trussed in the same way, be it for poaching, roasting, or braising): with the chicken breast down, neck skin folded over the back, run the needle through the upper part of the wing near the shoulder joint, through neck skin and back to pin the skin in place, and back through the other wing near the shoulder joint. Turn the chicken over, breast up. Pull the legs into place so that the knee (folded joint between thigh and drumstick) lies high against the breast; run the needle through legs and body near this joint, pull the bird together gently with the two string ends, and tie a tight double knot. Clip the string ends. Repeat this process, beginning with the bird breast down, then turning it breast up, this time running the needle through the lower part of the wing joints, skin, and back, then through the flesh at the extremity of the drumsticks and the body, pulling, tying, and clipping as before. (If the feet have remained attached, fold them over the breast and tie another length of string loosely around the midsection of the bird to hold them in place.) Rub the bird's surface, all over, with lemon juice. Wrap it tightly in a couple layers of muslin, twisting and tying the ends and clipping off any excess.

Place the bird, breast up, in its cooking utensil, pour over enough stock, melted but not hot, to barely immerse the chicken, bring it to a simmer over medium heat, and cook, covered, at just beneath the simmer, for 2 hours (about 180°F; this is important — it may be useful to keep a check on the temperature with a sugar thermometer). Remove the bird from the stock and drain it on a

rack, to collect the juices, while removing the muslin. Clip the trussing strings beside their knots and, pulling each by its knot, slip the strings out.

Carve the bird at table, either in the traditional way or, wings and legs first removed, cut it into cross-sectional slices. Serve a sauceboat of the cooking liquid separately.

CRUSTS WITH FRESH MORELS

If substituting dried morels, count 2 ounces and soak them for a couple of hours in cold water before proceeding.

Crusts with Fresh Morels

Croûtes aux Morilles Fraîches

6 slices day-old white bread, cut 2 inches thick, crusts removed
4 ounces unsalted butter, melted
1 pound fresh morels
2 ounces unsalted butter
salt, freshly ground white pepper
1 cup heavy cream
1 tablespoon chopped chervil

Hollow out each section of bread, leaving ½-inch-thick walls and bottom: using a small, sharp, pointed knife, cut down, all around the sides, ½ inch in from the edge, without penetrating all the way to the bottom, then, ½ inch from the bottom, pierce one side and cut through the inside crumb in a swivel fashion, the point of entry serving as axis, without widening the slit. The inside section of crumb may then easily be lifted out, any uncut extremities tearing loose without damaging the shell. Brush hollowed-out slices generously, inside and out, with melted butter and put them to color in a slow oven, keeping an eye on them and turning them regularly to ensure their being evenly colored on all sides and no darker than a rich gold at any point. They may, if necessary, be prepared somewhat ahead of time and rewarmed in the oven.

Trim the stem tips of the morels, split each in two, and rinse them rapidly beneath a strong jet of water. Sponge them dry between two towels and in a heavy saucepan over low heat stew them gently in butter, seasoned with salt, for about 10 minutes, regularly tossing and stirring with a wooden spoon. Add about ⅔ of the cream, reduce over high heat, stirring, until it thickens and clings to the mushrooms, remove from the heat, taste for salt, sprinkle with pepper, and stir in the remaining cream. Fill the crusts and serve, a pinch of chopped chervil topping each.

Pineapple Surprise

Ananas en Surprise

1 large, ripe pineapple
½ pound small, ripe strawberries (*or wild strawberries*)
sugar
½ pound fresh (*or frozen*) raspberries, pureed and sweetened to taste

Cut in and downward at an angle around the top of the pineapple to remove a lid, cut out the flesh from the lid, and discard the core. Cut deeply down and circularly around the core in the main body of the pineapple, and as far down as possible without piercing the shell, all the way around, about ⅔ inch from the outside. Cut a series of "spokes" between the two circular incisions and force the sections loose with your fingers, emptying out the remaining flesh with a spoon, crushing it as little as possible. Cut inward all around the base of the core (because of its awkward position, it is not possible to slice it cleanly across), break it off at its base, and discard it. Scrape the inside of the shell clean with a tablespoon and put the lid and the shell to chill. Put aside any mashed pineapple and the juice for another use.

Cut the pineapple flesh into cubes, pick over the strawberries, wash them rapidly, drain them, add them to the pineapple cubes, sprinkle with sugar, and store, covered, in the refrigerator until just before serving. Fill the shell, without packing, with the macerated fruits and pour the raspberry puree over. The pineapple may be served half embedded in cracked ice, which is attractive, ensures its remaining chilled for a second service, and facilitates the service by stabilizing the fruit.

Two Informal Spring Dinners

MENU I *(for 6)*

HORS D'OEUVRE OF RAW VEGETABLES
[*CRUDITES*]

A young, flinty Sauvignon: Loire valley (Pouilly-Fumé, Sancerre, Quincy); Bordeaux (Entre-Deux-Mers) or a California Sauvignon Blanc (also called Fumé-Blanc)

· · ·

SHRIMP QUICHE
[*QUICHE AUX CREVETTES*]

The same wine as the preceding

· · ·

CHICKEN IN RED WINE
[*COQ AU VIN*]

Any good but not extraordinary, fairly young red wine: One of the lesser Bordeaux appellations (Côtes de Blaye, Côtes de Bourg, Canon-Fronsac); Burgundy (Passe-tout-grains or one of the sturdier Beaujolais — Moulin-à-Vent or Chénas); Tuscany (Chianti Classico); California (Cabernet Sauvignon or Merlot)

· · ·

STEAMED POTATOES
[*POMMES DE TERRE A LA VAPEUR*]

· · ·

WILD GREEN SALAD
[*SALADE SAUVAGE*]

· · ·

· · ·

CHEESES
[FROMAGES]

The same as the preceding or a finer and older wine from the same region

· · ·

FLAMRI WITH RASPBERRY SAUCE
[FLAMRI A LA PUREE DE FRAMBOISES]

A noble-rot wine: Bordeaux (Barsac, Cérons, Sainte Croix-du-Mont, Loupiac); Anjou (Coteaux du Layon)

The presentation of this menu is extremely simple, for nearly everything may be prepared in advance: the *coq au vin* must be put to warm, eggs and cream beaten and the quiche put to bake one hour before going to table, and the potatoes put to steam just before the guests are seated — nothing more.

The visual succession is exciting, as it progresses from the tender, natural garden colors of the *crudités* through the delicate pinks and creams of the quiche, masked by a golden gratin, and the rich, bitter-chocolate-colored velvet of the *coq au vin* sauce, thrown into relief by the green of the parsley and the white potatoes, the deep greens of the salad — which, in season, may be enhanced, both in appearance and in taste, by the addition of a handful of brilliantly colored nasturtium flowers — and the pale yellow and cool, transparent red of the *flamri*, recalling, to some extent, the quiche, but with more fantasy and sharper relief. The pale green, ruby, and deep gold of the wines enrich the effect.

The *crudités*, fresh and clean, sharpen the appetite. They do nothing for a wine, but as one's guests' glasses should never be empty, the simplest solution is to serve the same wine that will accompany the quiche. The quiche is delicate in flavor and light in effect. If it were not followed by a rich sauce, it might be accompanied by one, but it stands well without and marries beautifully with a young, fruity white wine.

The high point, culinarily speaking, is the rich and robust main dish, the quality of whose sauce holds the key to the essential success of the meal. It would kill a wine that is elaborate with the nuances of age — therefore, the wine climax follows with the cheeses.

The *flamri* is light. It is refined without being sophisticated, and above all, it is not rich. The sweet wine is so totally different in character from the entire gamut of preceding wines that it, too, refreshes, cleanses, and relaxes a jaded palate.

THE CRUDITES

Crudités can be any combination of fresh, tender, young raw vegetables: tiny, white heads of cauliflower, little radishes, the small, elongated, light green, sweet Italian peppers, hearts of celery, cherry tomatoes, spring onions, bulb fennel, avocados, very young broad beans, and young artichokes, picked before the choke is developed.

Crudités should be accompanied by slices of rough peasant bread, fresh un-salted butter, coarse salt, fruity olive oil, and wine vinegar.

THE SHRIMP QUICHE

The shrimp and the pastry may be prepared and the pastry shell partly baked several hours in advance, which leaves nothing to be done at the last minute except to beat together the eggs and cream and put the quiche to bake.

The preliminary shrimp preparation is identical to that of crayfish (*écrevisses*) *à la bordelaise*, which in itself is a fine dish.

Shrimp Quiche

Quiche aux Crevettes

THE PASTRY
⅔ cup all-purpose flour
pinch of salt
3 ounces cold unsalted butter, cut into small cubes
about 3 tablespoons cold water

Sift the flour and salt into a bowl, add the butter, and, with a table knife in each hand, the blades crossed and touching each other, pull them apart, cutting through the flour and parcels of butter. Cross the blades and pull them apart repeatedly until the flour and butter are reduced to a coarsely pebbled mixture in which the largest pebbles are the size of peas. Work rapidly. Add only enough cold water, mashing and pulling the mixture together with a fork, to create an adherent mass that can be pressed into a compact ball in your hands. Wrap the paste in plastic film and chill it for 30 minutes in the freezer or for an hour or longer in the refrigerator. (This relaxes the paste, making it easier to roll out, and, at the same time, firms it up by hardening the butter, particularly important when working with such a large proportion of butter in relation to the flour.)

On a lightly floured work surface, preferably marble, sprinkle more flour over the ball of dough, flatten it somewhat with the palm of the hand, give it a few light blows with the side of the rolling pin to make it more supple, roll it rapidly into a strip some 4 times longer than its width, fold the two ends into the center to meet, and fold again at the center. (This is the first step in making a simple puff pastry — its purpose here is to make a flakier pastry by increasing the number of layers of flattened butter fragments.) Make certain that both sides of the folded form are lightly floured, mold it, folding under here and there if necessary, to a circular shape, and roll it out to a slightly larger circumference than that of your pie plate or tart mold. Roll it around the rolling pin, brushing off any loose flour, unroll it loosely over the mold, and press it into place with the fingertips. Trim the edges, leaving a slight overlap; if any edges are short, patch them with fragments of trimming, their borders moistened and pressed to the short edges. Roll the outer edge under, press it to the border all the way round, and crimp it with the side of your thumb dipped repeatedly in flour. Prick the bottom and sides of the lined pastry mold, here and there, with the tines of a fork and refrigerate the mold for 15 minutes or long enough to firm up the pastry. Line it with a round of parchment paper or foil, pour in enough dried beans, raw rice, or specially designed metal pellets to provide sufficient weight to prevent the crust from buckling, and bake for 15 minutes, starting in a hot oven and reducing the heat immediately to medium. Remove the weighted paper and return the pastry to the oven for 3 or 4 minutes to dry out. Put it aside.

THE SHRIMP
    2 tablespoons *mirepoix (page 55)*
    ¾ pound fresh shrimp
    1 tablespoon olive oil
    salt, freshly ground pepper
    1 pinch cayenne pepper
    1 tablespoon Cognac
    ½ cup dry white wine
    ½ cup cream

Heat the oil in a sauté pan, add the shrimp, unshelled, and the *mirepoix,* salt, pepper, and cayenne, tossing and stirring with a wooden spoon over high heat until the shrimp have turned pink on all sides. Add the Cognac, light it, and continue stirring until the flames are extinguished, then add the white wine and reduce until the liquid has nearly disappeared. Put aside to cool.

Shell the shrimp, leaving the tail segment of the shell attached to 12 of them, and pound the shells in a mortar with the *mirepoix* and cooking juices. Stir the cream into the pounded shells, transfer to a small saucepan, bring to a boil, then pass the mixture through a fine sieve, working the residue well with a wooden pestle to extract all the juices. Reserve.

Arrange the shrimp with the tail segments around the edge of the pastry shell so that they lean against the side with the tail tips protruding above the border of the shell. Cut the rest of the shrimp into pieces and distribute them in an even layer on the bottom of the shell.

THE QUICHE BATTER
  3 eggs
  salt, freshly ground pepper
  1 cup heavy cream
  1 small handful freshly grated Swiss Gruyère

Combine in a bowl the eggs, salt, pepper, reserved shrimp-flavored cream, and additional cup of cream, whisk well, pour the mixture into the pastry shell, sprinkle the surface with cheese, and bake in a moderate oven for approximately ½ hour. The quiche is done when the center of the custard is firm; it is better warm than hot.

THE COQ AU VIN

There are many traditional variations on *coq au vin:* the Jura has its *coq au vin jaune* (or Château-Chalon), often garnished with morels; in Alsace, *coq au vin de Riesling* is usually bound at the last minute with egg yolks and cream and served with fresh noodles; tomato may be joined to the white-wine moistener in Provence, black olives and red peppers garnishing the sauce with an accompanying rice pilaf; cider replaces wine in Normandy, beer in Flanders. . . .

Coq au vin, unmodified, means Burgundian red-wine chicken stew with the traditional Burgundian garnish of little onions, mushrooms, and lardons; the preparation is the same as that of *boeuf bourguignon*. It is usually made from

young chickens and, when prepared with care, it is good — but it makes sense that a 2 month-old bird, though perfect for a rapid sauté, in which succulence is sealed into the flesh by searing, should be less satisfactory in a dish whose qualities depend on the flavor and gelatinous body, which, over an extended cooking period, may be drawn from the meat into a reduced and concentrated sauce. A *coq au vin* prepared in a Burgundy peasant kitchen is made from a year-old cock, neither too tough nor too tender, that has lived in liberty and been fed liberally on grain. Its sauce is a concentration of savory, gelatinous essences that, at the ultimate point of refinement, no more than coats the pieces of chicken.

Farmers or those with farmer friends may have no trouble finding the perfect bird. If using young, commercially raised chickens, there are several points to bear in mind: 1) replace the large bird by 2 smaller ones — or buy parts and use only leg and thigh sections, which lend themselves better to braising than do breasts; 2) replace half the red wine by a mixture of red-wine essence (page 63) and rich stock (page 65) — or replace all of the wine by half red-wine essence and half stock; 3) do not overcook the chicken — 30 or 40 minutes is enough — but reduce the sauce radically after having passed it through a sieve and cleansed it by skimming, half off the heat.

A scattering of mixed dried herbs (page 52) can replace the *bouquet-garni*. Rather than dressing the dish on a platter, it may be served directly from its cooking utensil, in which case the bread is better diced, sautéed in butter until golden and crisp, and sautéed at the last minute with a crushed garlic and chopped parsley mixture that can be scattered over the surface of the stew at the moment of serving.

A *coq au vin* will not suffer from being prepared in advance, except for the addition of garnish and final reheating.

Chicken in Red Wine

Coq au Vin

2 finger-thick strips lean *pancetta*, cut crosswise into finger widths, blanched,
    rinsed, and drained
3 medium carrots, peeled, and cut into sections
3 medium onions, peeled and coarsely chopped
1 10-to-12-month-old cock (*about 6 pounds*), cut into serving pieces
olive oil (*or other cooking oil*)
salt
small handful flour
healthy dash of Cognac
1 bottle (*or more*) good red wine
bouquet-garni (*page 50*)

GARNISH

½ pound small mushrooms, trimmed, rinsed, and dried, whole, halved, or
    quartered, depending on size
30 small garnish onions, peeled
4 ounces unsalted butter
salt
6 square slices firm-textured, day-old white bread, crusts removed, each cut
    in 2 diagonally
1 clove garlic, peeled
chopped parsley

In a large sauté pan, over low heat, fry the *pancetta* strips in a bit of oil until they are golden and superficially crisp. Put them aside and, in the same fat, cook the carrots and onions, stirring regularly to avoid overbrowning, for 20 to 30 minutes. Put the vegetables aside, add more oil to the pan if necessary, and, over higher heat, cook the chicken pieces, first salted, until they are nicely colored on all sides. Sprinkle them with flour and continue to cook, turning the pieces, until the flour is lightly browned, return the carrots and onions to the pan, pour over the Cognac, then the wine, and raise the heat. With a wooden spoon or spatula, move the chicken pieces around in order to scrape all surfaces of the bottom and sides of the pan, dissolving all adherences. Tuck the *bouquet* into the middle and, if necessary, add wine or stock so that the pieces of chicken are completely covered. Bring to the boiling point, cover, and adjust the heat to maintain a bare simmer until the meat is tender but not falling from the bones. (The length of cooking time can vary from 30 minutes for a young bird that has never exercised to 1½ hours for a 10-month-old rooster, and still an hour longer for one that may be too old to have a fine flesh but will produce a marvelous sauce.)

Sauté the mushrooms, seasoned, in butter, over high heat, for 2 or 3 minutes or until their excess moisture has evaporated and they are lightly colored. Put them aside. Cook the onions in butter, seasoned, over very low heat, covered, shaking the pan from time to time, for 20 to 30 minutes, until they are tender but only yellowed. Put them aside.

Transfer the chicken pieces and the carrots to a platter, press the juices from the *bouquet-garni* and discard it, and skim any fat from the sauce's surface. Using a wooden pestle, pass the contents of the sauté pan through a fine sieve, stirring and pressing the debris to extract all liquid, and leave it to settle for a few minutes. Return the chicken and the carrot pieces to the pan, scatter over the little onions, the mushrooms, and the lardons, cover, and hold in a warm place while finishing the sauce. Remove any fat that has risen to the surface of the cooking liquid, transfer it to a small saucepan, and cleanse it, half off the heat (page 48). When it is thoroughly cleansed, reduce the sauce over high heat, stirring constantly, to bring it to a velvety, spoon-coating consistency — it should not be thick. Pour the sauce over the chicken and its garnish, return it to a simmer, and leave it, covered, at a bare simmer, for 15 to 30 minutes.

Cook the bread triangles in butter, over low heat, until they are golden and crisp, and rub each lightly with the clove of garlic. Arrange the chicken pieces on a heated platter. Dip a corner of each crouton, first into the sauce, then into the chopped parsley, and arrange them, parslied tips pointing out, around the edge of the platter. Pour sauce and garnish over the chicken and sprinkle with a bit of parsley; serve steamed potatoes separately.

Flamri with Raspberry Sauce

Flamri à la Purée de Framboises

1 cup water
1 cup dry white wine
4 ounces fine semolina
¾ cup sugar
small pinch of salt
1 egg
3 egg whites
unsalted butter
1 pound fresh or frozen raspberries, sieved and sweetened to taste

Bring the water and the wine to a boil, sprinkle in the semolina in a slow stream from well above the saucepan, stirring with a wooden spoon, and leave it, covered, to cook gently for 25 minutes. Remove it from the heat and mix in the sugar and salt. Continue stirring and, when it is slightly cooled, stir in the egg. Beat the egg whites until stiff, fold them delicately into the mixture, and pour it into a buttered 1-quart charlotte mold, the bottom of which is lined with a round of buttered parchment paper. Cover with another round of buttered parchment paper and poach in a *bain-marie* (the mold immersed by two-thirds in hot, but not boiling, water, either in a gentle oven or over low heat, in a large, tightly closed saucepan) for 40 minutes.

Leave the pudding until it is tepid before unmolding it. Remove the round of paper from the surface, run a knife blade around the edges, unmold onto the serving dish, lift off the other round of paper, and cover loosely with plastic film to protect it from the air until just before serving, chilled and coated with raspberry sauce. Serve a sauceboat of raspberry puree separately.

Two Informal Spring Dinners

MENU II *(for 4)*

MARINATED RAW SARDINE FILLETS
[FILETS DE SARDINES CRUES EN MARINADE]

*A slightly sharp, very dry white wine: Muscadet, Quincy, Pouilly-sur-Loire
(Chasselas), etc.*

• • •

GRILLED STEAK, MARCHAND DE VIN
[GRILLADE DE BOEUF, MARCHAND DE VIN]

*A hearty, fruity, young, cool red wine: Beaujolais de cru, Chinon,
Saumur-Champigny, Mercurey*

• • •

GRATIN OF POTATOES
[GRATIN DE POMMES DE TERRE]

• • •

FIELD SALAD
[SALADE DES CHAMPS]

• • •

CHEESES
[FROMAGES]

*The same as the preceding or a Burgundy from the Côte de Beaune or the
Côte de Nuits*

• • •

APPLE TART
[TARTE AUX POMMES]

A Sauternes

THE MARINATED SARDINE FILLETS

Raw sardines, straight from the net, gutted with a forefinger, rubbed gently beneath seawater to rid them of the loose-clinging scales, the fragile fillets pried from the bone with fingertips, with or without a drop of lemon juice, have always regaled French fishermen. Fashionable restaurateurs have discovered that a chic clientele will never order the homely sardine and have substituted raw salmon fillets, sliced thinly on the bias, on their menus, often sprinkled with lime instead of lemon. Most fish lend themselves to this treatment on condition that they be very fresh. Red-mullet fillets marinated briefly in lemon juice, laid out on a sauce of grilled, peeled, and seeded red-pepper puree, and seasoned with salt, pepper, lemon juice, and olive oil are wonderful — ribbons of lemon and olive-oil sauce incorporating their pureed livers (first firmed up for a few seconds in a few drops of olive oil over low heat) can be dribbled the length of the fillets. The chopped feathery leaves of fresh dill are especially suited to salmon, those of wild fennel to red mullet, sea bass, or sea bream; flat-leafed parsley, chives, or hyssop go well, together or separately, with any raw fish — and the tiny ultramarine blossoms of hyssop can be scattered in lacy patterns across the iridescent surfaces of the fillets for a presentation of unusual beauty. Sardines take well to the slightly bitter, strongly flavored herbs — fresh thyme, savory, hyssop — or a mixture, the intense flavors attenuated by that of parsley.

Marinated Raw Sardine Fillets

Filets de Sardines Crues en Marinade

12 sardines, filleted
juice of 2 lemons
salt, freshly ground pepper
olive oil
fresh herbs, finely chopped

Lay the fillets out in a shallow dish and sprinkle them with lemon juice, turning them so that all are evenly moistened. Leave them for a few minutes or up to half an hour, turning them once or twice. The flesh will lose its translucence, turning whiter and opaque as if altered by heat — they are said to be "cooked" by the lemon juice. Lift them to paper toweling to drain slightly (discard the lemon juice), then lay them out, skin sides up, on their serving dish — the pattern will be dictated by the shape of the dish. Sprinkle with salt, grind over pepper, dribble over olive oil, and scatter with herbs.

Grilled Steak, Marchand de Vin

Grillade de Boeuf, Marchand de Vin

Good beef is a deep, clear red color with a purple cast; the back cuts are finely but not excessively veined with fat. It need not be aged for long periods, but a carcass that has hung for a week in a butcher's cold room will be tenderer, juicier, and more flavorful than a freshly butchered animal.

In French butchery, beef is completely boned out except for the thin ribs, a *pot-au-feu* cut, and the occasional rib steak (*côte de boeuf*), which is always cut very thick with a single rib remaining, chined and trimmed — grilled, the rib is carved free and the meat sliced on the bias for serving. When this cut is completely boned out, it is the *entrecôte*.

The less exercise a muscle receives, the tenderer the flesh. All of the most tender grilling cuts come from the back. The fillet or tenderloin, a narrow, elongated muscle that lies inside the carcass, one to each side of the spinal column, is the least exercised and the tenderest muscle in the body. This is the French fillet; when cut up, the narrow tip becomes the filet mignon, the central section the tournedos, and the thick end the chateaubriand. Lying along the outside of the carcass, the other side of the vertebrae from the fillet, is the *contre-filet* or *faux-filet*, sometimes confusingly called *entrecôte*. From the haunch comes the rumsteak (or romsteak, from the English "rump"). These are the classic tender cuts; the fillet, most expensive and tenderest of all, also has the least flavor. The most flavorful cuts, firmer, resistant beneath the tooth without being tough, come from the abdominal wall (flank steak and skirt) and, from inside the animal, a single small cut, the joining of two skirt muscles — *onglet* in French — known both in French and English as the butcher's piece (*"le morceau du boucher,"* because the butcher keeps it for himself), known also in English as "hanging tender" or, more aptly, "bloody skirt," for it is the bloodiest and most succulent of all grilling cuts, the most sought-after in France, and the least known elsewhere. Another delicious cut, much admired in France, which undoubtedly disappears into mince elsewhere, is the *araignée* (spider), a flattened cushion of tender flesh from the pelvis, interthreaded with a web of nervous tissue that must be trimmed out.

Steaks may be grilled on heavy cast-iron grills, preheated over a gas flame or beneath an intense heat source, but genuine grilling — and by far the best — is done over embers on a preheated heavy welded iron grill. (Best of all, in winemaking regions, bundles of vine branches from the winter's pruning are burned for grilling.)

Any steak that is served with a butter or a sauce is best trimmed of all fat and tough membranes. The tenderest cuts will cook more rapidly than firmer cuts, and aged meat cooks faster than fresh. The meat should be brought to room temperature — removed at least an hour ahead of time from the refrigerator — before being grilled, rubbed first with olive oil, and, just before being thrown onto the grill, sprinkled with coarse salt and pepper, freshly and coarsely ground. There should be no lingering flames but the bed of coals should be very hot so that the meat is seared on contact with the grill. Good beef is not improved by marinating, being sprinkled with herbs, or rubbed with garlic, but the smoke of smoldering rosemary, thrown onto the embers a minute before removing it from the grill, will flavor it subtly and pleasantly. Best results will be had from steaks measuring 2 fingers or more in thickness. A very thick steak (3 inches or more), which may require as much as 20 minutes cooking time, should cook over gentle heat, once the sides (there may be 2 or 4, depending on the shape and size of the steak) have been seared; the embers can be spread out or, with a barbecue apparatus, the grill cranked higher. Very thick steaks should be carved into slices, on the bias, before being served out.

Within reasonable limits, the degree of doneness may be considered to be a question of taste, but there is no point in serving steak to a guest who professes not to like rare meat — a steak is ruined by overcooking and so is the good humor of the other guests; those who cannot bear the sight of blood (an Anglo-American phenomenon) will be happier with braised meat than with dried-out steak.

A steak *marchand de vin* is served with the *marchand de vin* butter apart, and each guest spreads a spoonful over his steak. On restaurant menus, *marchand de vin* often indicates a pan-fried steak sauced by sautéing chopped shallots in the pan in which the steak was cooked, washing the pan with red wine, and lightly buttering the reduction, which is sometimes strengthened by the addition of meat glaze.

Other "butters" often served with grilled beef are: *Bercy* (the same as *marchand de vin,* except that white wine replaces the red), *chivry* (see the recipe for grilled lambs' kidneys, page 264), *maître d'hôtel* (chopped parsley, seasoning, and lemon juice, whisked with butter), anchovy butter, etc.

MARCHAND DE VIN BUTTER

A richer *marchand de vin* butter may be prepared by substituting a somewhat smaller quantity of red-wine essence (page 63) for the red wine in the recipe and, if *glace de viande* (page 69) is at hand, a small spoonful may be melted into the shallot and wine reduction before being whisked into the butter. The butter may be prepared in advance, but should be served semisoft and not chilled.

¾ cup good red wine
1 tablespoon finely chopped gray shallot (*if unavailable, replace it with onion plus a small, finely chopped clove of garlic*)
salt, to taste
generous pinch of freshly ground pepper
6 ounces unsalted butter, softened
1 tablespoon lemon juice
1 tablespoon chopped parsley

Reduce the wine and chopped shallot, in a small saucepan over high heat, to about ⅓ cup, pour it into a mixing bowl, and, when it is just tepid, whisk it vigorously with all the other ingredients.

THE POTATO GRATIN

The simplicity of their preparations and their perfect alliances to all grilled and roast butchery meats, poultry, and game place the various potato gratins among the most precious of standbys in a home kitchen. The different textures achieved by coarsely grating the potatoes, passing them into spaghetti or macaroni thicknesses through the blades of hand *moulis* or electric processors, creating large, paper-thin slices with a *mandoline,* slices of all sizes and thicknesses with a knife, dicing or simply chopping them coarsely stamps these gratins with such different characters that, though all may be seasoned and moistened identically, they seem to taste different.

It may be important to avoid rinsing the potatoes, the superficial, clinging starch acting as a binder to create a short sauce of the cooking liquid, diminished through evaporation and absorption. On the other hand, it can be essential, to retain a clean, dry, unsticky texture, to rinse them well and dry them thoroughly in towels after giving them their chosen form. This is true when they are cooked dry except for being coated with a film of butter: 1) grated through the medium blade of a *mouli,* well rinsed and drained, rolled up in a strong towel and squeezed dry, sautéed in a large frying pan, salted and with abundant butter, for a few seconds, tossed until all strands are veiled with butter, packed into a large gratin dish, the surface pressed smooth, and baked for 30 to 40 minutes until golden, crisp-surfaced, and tender (if half a dozen unpeeled garlic cloves are tucked here and there into a shallow layer of potatoes in the bottom of the dish, sliced truffles scattered over, and another layer of potatoes pressed on top, the result is sumptuous); 2) potatoes alone — or alternate layers, salted, of finely sliced potatoes (rinsed, laid out, and rubbed dry between two towels) and celeriac, each sautéed for a few seconds in butter, finishing with a layer of potatoes — baked for 45 to 50 minutes in a moderate oven.

Of the gratins that are improved by retaining the surface starch, the simplest is *boulangère* potatoes — finely sliced potatoes and onions layered, moistened with water or stock, and baked. (A leg of lamb is often placed on top and roasted at the same time, its juices intermingling and those of the gratin spooned up for basting.) A variation on *boulangère:* finely sliced, unrinsed potatoes and onions, placed first in a saucepan, salted, moistened with barely enough water — or less than enough — to cover them, brought to the boil (stirring and scraping the bottom with a wooden spoon to prevent sticking), spread in a buttered gratin dish with their liquid, creamed sorrel (shredded, stewed, salted, in butter until melted, inundated with cream, briefly reduced) spread over the surface, and baked for 45 to 50 minutes in a moderate oven. The great classic is gratin *dauphinois,* of which there are many versions: generously garlic-rubbed gratin dish, generously buttered; large, paper-thin sliced potatoes, unrinsed, layered, overlapping, salted; heated milk poured over not quite to the top level of potatoes; thick cream spread thickly over the surface and a good hour in a moderate oven. (Don't fill the dish too full or the cream will boil over — if this happens, there is nothing to be done but place foil in the bottom of the oven to collect it until it quiets down.)

Gratin of Potatoes

Gratin de Pommes de Terre

2 cloves garlic
unsalted butter
3 cups milk
2 pounds non-mealy potatoes, peeled, passed through the medium blade of
    a *mouli-julienne* or food processor, or coarsely grated
1 egg
salt, suspicion of freshly grated nutmeg
3 ounces Gruyère cheese, grated

Choose a large shallow earthenware baking or gratin dish. Rub the sides and bottom well with the garlic cloves, wait a couple of minutes for the garlic moisture to dry, and generously butter the dish. Bring the milk, lightly salted, to a boil and parboil the potatoes for about 5 minutes. Pour the contents of the saucepan into a sieve, collecting the milk in another receptacle, beat the egg, pinch of salt, nutmeg, and half the grated cheese together in a mixing bowl, and slowly pour in the milk, whisking. Stir the potatoes into the mixture and pour it into the baking dish, smoothing the surface. Sprinkle with the remaining cheese, distribute paper-thin slices of butter, cut from a chilled block, evenly over the surface, and bake in a hot oven for 15 to 20 minutes or until the potatoes are cooked and the surface is golden.

Apple Tart

Tarte aux Pommes

1 half-baked pastry shell (*same ingredients and preparation as for shrimp quiche, page 212*)
1 pound cooking apples (*preferably russet*), peeled, cored, and sliced
2 ounces unsalted butter
pinch of cinnamon
2 eggs
½ cup sugar
1 cup heavy cream

Sauté the apple slices in butter until they are tender and translucent, but not falling apart; line the bottom of the pastry shell with the slices and sprinkle lightly with cinnamon.

Beat the eggs and sugar together until the yellow color lightens, stir in the cream, and pour the mixture over the apples. Bake in a medium oven until the custard has set and the crust is golden. Serve warm, but not hot.

Four Simple Spring Menus

MENU I *(for 6)*

*This menu will, ideally, be accompanied by a single, simple, young red wine
(Passe-tout-grains, Côtes-du-Rhône-Villages, Saint-Joseph, Bandol,
Palette, Saint-Nicolas-de-Bourgueil; Premières Côtes de Bordeaux;
Dolcetto d'Alba, Barbera d'Alba or Nebbiola d'Alba; California
Zinfandel).*

BOILED BEEF WITH VEGETABLES
[POT-AU-FEU]

. . .

FIELD SALAD
[SALADE SAUVAGE]

. . .

CHEESES
[FROMAGES]

. . .

FRESH FRUITS
[FRUITS]

THE POT-AU-FEU

"In France, the *pot-au-feu* is the symbol of family life. . . . A good *pot-au-feu* will always be a comfortable and thoroughly bourgeois dish which nothing may dethrone." — Escoffier, *Ma Cuisine*

If any single preparation merits being termed the French national dish, it is *pot-au-feu*. There are a number of regional variations: in Provence mutton is added, in the southwest a hen, often stuffed with rice, may be thrown in, and veal sometimes lends a more gelatinous quality to the broth. No soup is more succulent than the amber broth, unclarified and imperfectly degreased and poured over dried bread crusts, from a beef *pot-au-feu*.

Pot-au-feu is a meal in itself; it would be an error to attempt to correlate it with other dishes.

A perfect bouillon depends, among other things, on the meat's being started in cold water. But to guard their succulence, meats should be plunged directly into boiling liquid. Logically, then, a perfect *pot-au-feu* must really be two: the first, begun cold, produces the basic broth; the second, moistened with the boiling broth, permits the meats to retain their maximum qualities.

Cabbage greatly enriches the garnish and, in itself, is never better than when braised in the fat bouillon skimmed from a *pot-au-feu*. Because of its distinctive flavor, it should always be cooked separately so as not to destroy the delicacy of the soup. (The cabbage's leftover cooking liquid moistens to perfection a partridge braised with cabbage — see page 122.) In the past, a parsnip always lent its unique, sweet flavor to the bouillon of a *pot-au-feu*.

Oxtail is an economical cut and lends a fine rich quality to the bouillon. None of the other cuts recommended is irreplaceable, but at least one must be gelatinous (in this instance, the heel — those cuts, known as *macreuse* and *paleron,* both from the chuck section, are also excellent gelatinous cuts) and another interlarded.

Leftover *pot-au-feu* meats lose their firmness and savor if allowed to stand in the bouillon. If they are to be used in other preparations, they should be drained and stored separately, covered with a plate or plastic wrap. Possibilities for using leftover boiled beef are endless. Simply sliced and served cold, sprinkled with coarse salt, it is delicious — or prepared *à la vinaigrette* as a first course in combination with sliced green onions and potatoes, boiled in their skins, peeled, and sliced. Perhaps the commonest of the hot preparations is *miroton:* sautéed onions sprinkled with flour, moistened with bouillon and vinegar — a couple of tablespoonfuls of the latter for 1½ cups of bouillon — and simmered for 15 minutes with a pinch of herbs; they are then poured over the slices of beef, which have first been arranged in a gratin dish and sprinkled with capers and sliced sour gherkins. The surface is sprinkled with bread crumbs, dotted with butter, and gratinéed in a gentle oven.

An earthenware *pot-au-feu* or *marmite* is the perfect cooking vessel. Lacking this, use the largest pot of any kind available — 10 to 15 quarts.

Pot-au-Feu

Pot-au-Feu

THE PRELIMINARY BOUILLON

1 pound carrots, peeled
3 large onions, 1 stuck with 3 cloves
1 parsnip, peeled
1 whole head of garlic, unpeeled
handful dried cèpes (*Italian* porcini), soaked in cold water, stem tips
    trimmed, rinsed
1 or 2 oxtails (*about 4 pounds*), cut into sections and tied firmly together
1 large *bouquet garni* (*page 50*)
handful coarse salt

THE POT-AU-FEU

3 pounds shank of beef, in one piece, tied up
3 pounds short ribs, in 3 pieces, tied firmly together
2 small green cabbages, quartered, cores removed, thick ribs trimmed
1 apple, unpeeled
1 pound small spring turnips, peeled
1 pound small spring carrots, peeled
2 pounds leeks, white and light green sections only, tied in a bundle

ACCOMPANIMENTS AT TABLE

slices of dried-out French-type bread
grated cheese (*Parmesan, or half Parmesan and half Gruyère*)
dish of coarse salt
Dijon-type mustard (*and/or horseradish*)
sour gherkins or small dill pickles

THE PRELIMINARY BOUILLON

It is practical, but not necessary, to prepare this bouillon the preceding day.
Prepare it exactly as for veal stock (page 66); if the oxtail is intended to serve in
another preparation — simmered in tomato sauce and accompanied by pasta, for
instance, or *à la provençale,* with black olives, garlic, and sweet peppers added to
the tomato sauce — it should be removed after 3 hours; if not, it will continue
for another couple of hours to lend its qualities to the broth. Pass the broth.

THE POT-AU-FEU

Skim off any excess fat from the bouillon, bring it back to a boil in the cleansed
marmite, taste for salt, and add the tied-up meats and, if necessary, just enough

boiling water to ensure their being largely covered. Skim, regulating the heat to maintain a bare simmer, the lid kept slightly ajar.

Fit the quartered cabbages snugly, so that they will retain their form, into a large saucepan, pour over salted boiling water, and parboil, covered and at a simmer, for 15 minutes, drain, refresh, and squeeze the quarters. An hour and a half after the meats have been put to cook, replace the parboiled cabbage quarters in their saucepan, skim several ladles of bouillon from the surface of the *pot-au-feu,* taking as much of the fat with the bouillon as possible, pour it over the cabbages (just enough to immerse them completely), and put them to simmer, covered, until ready to serve — a good 1½ hours.

One-half hour later, add the apple to the pot in which the meat has been cooking, and 1 hour later add the turnips, carrots, and bundle of leeks.

Cooking time depends on the age of the animal and the way in which it has been raised. Usually, today, one may count about 3 hours for meat to be just right — tender, but still firm enough to be easily cut into slices.

Discard the apple. Leave the cabbage to continue cooking while the soup is being served. The easiest and perhaps the most sympathetic way to serve the soup is directly from the *marmite,* leaving meats and vegetables in the pot to keep hot. Crusts of dried bread should be placed in each soup plate before the bouillon is ladled in and a piece of Parmesan and a grater (or a dish of grated cheese) should be at the table for those who require it.

Serve the meats, strings removed, on a separate platter from the vegetables to facilitate carving. Remove the cabbage quarters from their cooking liquid and surround them with all the vegetables from the *pot-au-feu,* first removing the strings from the leeks.

A tureen of bouillon or the *marmite* should be kept at table throughout the service to moisten meats and vegetables. The usual accompaniments are a dish of coarse salt, Dijon-type mustard and/or horseradish, and sour gherkins (or small dill pickles), of which the first is obligatory. Gherkins, if not too vinegary, are good with the meat, but will annihilate any wine.

Four Simple Spring Menus

MENU II *(for 4)*

*This menu will, ideally, be accompanied by a single, simple, young red wine
(Passe-tout-grains, Côtes-du-Rhône-Villages, Saint-Joseph, Bandol,
Palette, Saint-Nicolas-de-Bourgueil; Premières Côtes de Bordeaux;
Dolcetto d'Alba, Barbera d'Alba; Nebbiolo d'Alba; California Zinfandel)*

GARDEN PEAS A LA FRANÇAISE
[PETITS POIS A LA FRANÇAISE]

. . .

BLANQUETTE OF VEAL
[BLANQUETTE DE VEAU A L'ANCIENNE]

. . .

RICE PILAF
[RIZ PILAF]

. . .

TOSSED GREEN SALAD
[SALADE VERTE]

. . .

CHEESES
[FROMAGES]

. . .

MOLDED CHOCOLATE LOAF WITH WHIPPED CREAM
[GATEAU MOULE AU CHOCOLAT, CREME CHANTILLY]

THE GARDEN PEAS A LA FRANÇAISE

Most often, peas *à la française* are prepared with a *chiffonade* of lettuce mixed in and with a certain amount of water added. Although the flavor of the lettuce braised with the peas enhances them, serving the lettuce with the peas detracts from their rare delicacy. (The onions and lettuce will make a valuable addition to a soup.) Inasmuch as the cooking liquid should be very sparse, and because with this method of cooking there is practically no evaporation, the water contained in the vegetables themselves, plus the humidity of the freshly washed lettuce, is largely sufficient.

The quantity of peas recommended for 4 people may seem overgenerous, but in order for the dish to be prepared to perfection, all the peas must be tiny, tender, and of nearly the same size. A batch of peas picked at the same time, all the pods of which are similar in appearance, never displays an altogether uniform maturity, once shelled, and the larger and harder peas should be put aside for another use. (In purees and soups, they are superior to the tiny ones because of their greater starchy binding content.) The length of cooking time may also seem surprising, but it should be remembered that their cooking is mainly a gentle steaming and that they are not even uniformly heated through until a good 15 minutes after they have been put to cook — the same tiny peas plunged into rapidly boiling water would require only a couple of minutes.

It is absolutely essential that the receptacle in which they are cooked be of a heavy material that takes the heat slowly and evenly (earthenware, heavy copper, or enameled cast-iron ware), that it be of a size just to hold the ingredients, and that it have a tight-fitting lid.

Garden Peas à la Française

Petits Pois à la Française

    1 medium head tender, leafy lettuce
    large pinch of thyme *(or a couple of branches)*
    7 or 8 little new onions, peeled
    ¼ pound unsalted butter, softened
    salt, pinch of sugar
    4 pounds tender garden peas, picked the same day, shelled just before using

Remove the outer leaves from the lettuce, keeping the heart intact, wash the leaves and the heart, and line the bottom and sides of the saucepan with lettuce leaves. Carefully open out the leaves of the heart, imprison the thyme within, close them up again, tie the heart well with thread, and place it in the center of the saucepan, with the little onions all around.

Mash the butter together with the salt and sugar, and very gently, with your hands, mix in the peas, being careful to crush none. When they are all uniformly coated with this *pommade,* pack them lightly all around the lettuce heart, cover them with more lettuce leaves, fit the lid tightly, and start them out over high heat for something less than a minute — just long enough for the saucepan to absorb a bit of heat — and leave them to cook over very low heat, gently shaking the saucepan from time to time, for 40 to 45 minutes. After half an hour, lift off the lid briefly to check their progress.

Remove the lettuce heart and all the surface leaves, and serve directly from the cooking utensil.

Blanquette of Veal

Blanquette de Veau à l'Ancienne

6 ounces small, firm, unopened mushrooms, stems trimmed, rinsed
1 lemon
water
unsalted butter
salt
2 pounds breast or rib tips of veal (*tendrons — the point at which the ribs become cartilaginous*), cut into 4 slices
3 medium carrots, peeled and cut into sections
2 medium onions, peeled, 1 stuck with 2 cloves
bouquet-garni (page 50)
about 20 small new onions, peeled
2 tablespoons flour
¼ cup cream
3 egg yolks
freshly ground pepper
pinch of freshly grated nutmeg
a few drops of lemon juice
chopped parsley

In a small saucepan, combine the mushrooms, a bit of lemon juice, very little water, a fragment of butter, and salt and boil, covered, for 1 minute.

Arrange the pieces of meat in a heavy saucepan so that, without packing them in, they take up a minimum of space, add the mushrooms' cooking liquid (put the mushrooms aside) and enough cold water to cover the meat by a finger's depth, salt, bring to a boil, and skim 2 or 3 times, adding small amounts of cold water each time the liquid returns to a boil. Add the carrots, the 2 onions, and the *bouquet-garni,* making certain that all are submerged, and regulate the heat to maintain a bare simmer, the saucepan covered, for 1½ hours.

During this time, the little onions should be seasoned and gently stewed, whole, in butter, in a saucepan, the bottom of which just holds them side by side. Count about 15 minutes, keeping them covered and tossing them from time to time; they should be soft and slightly yellowed, but not browned.

Pour the contents of the saucepan containing the meat into a large sieve placed over a mixing bowl. Pick out the 2 onions and the *bouquet* and discard them. Reserve the liquid. Return the meat and carrot pieces to their saucepan, add the mushrooms and the little onions, and put the pan aside, covered. Skim any fat from the surface of the liquid.

In another saucepan, make a *roux:* melt about 1 ounce of butter over low heat, add the flour, and leave to cook for a minute or so, stirring regularly, without allowing the flour to brown. Whisk in the cooking liquid, continue whisking until a boil is reached, lower the heat to maintain a simmer, the saucepan half off the heat, and, over a period of about 20 minutes, skim the light, fatty skin that repeatedly forms on the surface. Pour this lightly thickened sauce back over the meat and its garnish and leave to simmer, covered, for about 15 minutes.

Mix together in a bowl the cream, egg yolks, pepper, and very little nutmeg, stir in, pouring slowly, a ladleful of the sauce, and then, away from the heat, stir this mixture into the stew. Return the saucepan to medium-low heat, stirring constantly, until the sauce is only thick enough to coat the spoon lightly. It must not approach a boil or it will curdle. Sprinkle with chopped parsley and serve, accompanied by a pilaf (page 78).

Molded Chocolate Loaf with Whipped Cream

Gâteau Moulé au Chocolat, Crème Chantilly

¼ cup water
3 ounces bitter chocolate
3 ounces unsalted butter, softened
3 eggs, separated
¾ cup sugar
4 tablespoons flour
1 scant teaspoon vanilla extract
small pinch of salt
1 cup heavy cream
4 tablespoons sugar
½ teaspoon vanilla extract

Stir the water and the broken-up chocolate together in a round-bottomed metal mixing bowl, over a low flame, until melted, remove from the heat, whip in the butter, then the egg yolks, and finally the sugar, the flour, and the scant teaspoon of vanilla. If, at this point, the mixture seems to curdle or disintegrate (it is only the action of the chocolate rehardening in contact with colder ingredients), place the bowl in another bowl filled with warm water and continue stirring; it will come back together. Beat the egg whites and salt until they stand stiffly in peaks, gently fold about a third of the entire volume into the chocolate mixture, then the remainder. Pour into a buttered 1-quart mold (a savarin or a decorative jelly mold with central tube) and poach in a *bain-marie,* in a medium oven, immersed in hot water to approximately the same level as the pudding's surface, for 40 minutes. Leave to cool slightly and unmold onto the serving plate, leaving the mold over the pudding until serving time. Whip the cream with the sugar and ½ teaspoon vanilla extract. Serve well chilled, either with whipped cream separately or the central well filled with whipped cream and a decorative ribbon of it piped around the base of the pudding.

Four Simple Spring Menus

MENU III *(for 4)*

This menu, each course of which is typically Lyonnaise, is well served by a cool, fruity Beaujolais from the most recent vintage (Beaujolais-Villages, Chiroubles, Morgon, Côte de Brouilly, Fleurie, Saint-Amour, Juliénas).

TERRINE OF POULTRY LIVERS
[TERRINE DE FOIES DE VOLAILLES]

• • •

DEEP-FRIED BEEF TRIPE, REMOULADE SAUCE
[GRAS-DOUBLE FRIT, SAUCE REMOULADE]

• • •

DANDELION AND BACON SALAD
[SALADE DE PISSENLIT AU LARD]

• • •

GOAT CHEESES
[FROMAGES DE CHEVRE]

• • •

STRAWBERRIES IN BEAUJOLAIS
[FRAISES AU BEAUJOLAIS]

THE TERRINE OF POULTRY LIVERS

This terrine should be prepared the day before it is served, but, unlike many, it does not keep remarkably well, and once cut into, it should be consumed within a day or so.

Terrine of Poultry Livers

Terrine de Foies de Volailles

1 teaspoon mixed herbs (*page 52*)
2 "heads" of cloves (*the tiny ball attached to the extremity of each clove*)
1 clove garlic
1 healthy handful fresh white bread crumbs
1 medium onion, finely chopped
½ ounce unsalted butter
6 ounces fresh pork back fat, chilled
1 pound poultry livers, trimmed of greenish stains and white nervous tissue, chopped
1 egg
1 tablespoon finely chopped parsley
salt, freshly ground pepper
2 bay leaves

Reduce the mixed herbs and clove heads to a powder in a stone mortar. Add the garlic clove and pound to a paste, add the bread crumbs, mix together so that the garlic thoroughly impregnates the whole, and put aside.

Cook the chopped onion gently in butter for 10 minutes or so or until it is yellowed and soft.

Remove enough thin slices from the pork fat to line the bottom and the sides of the terrine and to cover the surface, once filled; cut the rest into little cubes.

With the exception of the slices of pork fat and the two bay leaves, combine all the ingredients in a large mixing bowl, working them thoroughly together with both hands, squeezing the mixture repeatedly, through clutching fingers, until it is completely homogeneous. Taste for salt and pepper.

Line the bottom and the sides of the terrine with slices of pork fat, pressing them to ensure their adhering, pour in the liver mixture, tap the bottom of the terrine 2 or 3 times against a wooden surface to settle its contents, place the bay leaves on the surface, and lightly press the remaining pork fat slices on top. Cover the terrine (if it does not have a lid, fit over it a piece of foil) and poach it in a *bain-marie,* either in the oven (the terrine placed in a larger, deep pan, hot water poured in to immerse it by two-thirds) or on top of the stove (in a tightly covered saucepan large enough to contain the terrine, filled to two-thirds the terrine's height with hot water), without allowing the water to boil, for 1 hour.

Place the terrine on a platter, to collect any juices that run over the edge, and remove the lid or foil. (Don't be alarmed at the quantity of liquid in which the contents seem to float — it is made up of gelatinous juices that will solidify in the terrine and of fat that will solidify on the surface.) Place a board or a plate just the size of the terrine's opening, on the surface, with a weight of about 2 pounds on top — a can of conserves, for instance. The weighting lends a firm, close texture to the body, without which it would be impossible to slice and serve the terrine neatly. When cooled, remove the weight and put the dish to chill. Serve it in slices directly from the terrine, the border of pork fat removed from each slice or not, as preferred.

Deep-fried Beef Tripe, Rémoulade Sauce

Gras-double Frit, Sauce Rémoulade

1 ½ pounds cooked tripe, cut into approximately 2-inch squares

MARINADE
    1 tablespoon *fines herbes* (*parsley, chives, chervil, tarragon — or whatever is available*)
    juice of 1 lemon
    1 tablespoon olive oil
    salt, freshly ground pepper

    flour
    3 eggs
    semifresh bread crumbs
    olive oil (*for frying*)
    1 handful parsley bouquets (*leaf bunches, stems removed, except for the part necessary to hold leaves together*)
    rémoulade sauce (*recipe follows*)

Sprinkle the squares of tripe with all the elements of the marinade and leave for an hour or so, turning them from time to time.

Arrange 3 plates on the work surface, the first containing flour, the second the eggs, beaten as for an omelette, and the third the bread crumbs. Dip the pieces, one by one, first lightly on both sides in the flour, then on both sides, being certain that they are well coated, in the eggs, then in the crumbs, placing each piece on the bed of crumbs, sprinkling crumbs generously over the surface, and pressing lightly with the palm of the hand to ensure their adhering. Lift each from the crumbs and remove it to a board that has been lightly dusted with crumbs. Should any seem imperfectly breaded, pass it a second time in egg and crumbs. If one has the time, they may be breaded an hour or so before the meal, and are then less fragile when the moment comes to handle them.

Drop them, one at a time, into very hot olive oil. Do not use a frying basket. (The heat may have to be lowered later, to prevent the oil from overheating.) Fry no more than five at a time. (If the frying pan is overcrowded, the temperature of the oil drops too radically, and at the same time the articles to be fried risk touching, sticking together, frying unevenly, and having their crisp surfaces damaged.) When they are golden and crisp on one side, turn each over carefully with the prong tips of a fork, and, when evenly browned, lift them out with a large wire skimming spoon, sponge them lightly between two paper towels, and remove them to the folded napkin in which they will be served, while treating the others in the same way. When the last are removed from the oil, drop in the parsley bouquets and, as soon as the violent sizzling has stopped (after a few seconds), remove them, drain them, without sponging, on a paper towel, and sprinkle them over the fried tripe. Serve, enclosed in a folded napkin, and accompanied by the following *rémoulade* sauce.

Rémoulade Sauce

Sauce Rémoulade

MAYONNAISE
 salt, freshly ground pepper
 juice of 1 lemon
 2 egg yolks, at room temperature
 1 cup olive oil, at room temperature

 1 salt anchovy, soaked, filleted, rinsed, dried, and finely chopped
 1 tablespoon capers, rinsed, dried, and chopped
 3 sour gherkins (*or small, firm dill pickles*), finely chopped
 1 teaspoon Dijon-type mustard
 1 teaspoon chopped *fines herbes (page 50)*

Put the seasoning into a bowl (or better, a stone mortar, whose weight will prevent it from slipping around), add a few drops of lemon juice, stir, with either a wooden spoon or a wooden pestle, until the salt is dissolved, add the egg yolks, continue stirring until they lighten slightly in color, then start adding the oil, drop by drop, evenly and fairly rapidly, turning always in the same direction. As the egg yolks begin to absorb the oil and to show signs of developing body, the oil may be poured in a steady trickle, and finally in a fine stream. From time to time, the addition of oil should be stopped and a few drops of lemon juice added. Once all the oil has been absorbed (it need not all be added if the desired thickness is obtained before), taste for lemon. Two teaspoons of hot water may be stirred in if the mayonnaise is not to be used at once — this is a safeguard against its breaking.

 Stir all the other ingredients into the mayonnaise before serving.

THE DANDELION AND BACON SALAD

It is absolutely essential that this salad be prepared the moment before it is served, that the salad bowl be hot (otherwise, the hot fat solidifies on contact with the cold bowl, and the result is distinctly unpleasant), and, in order for the dandelions to retain their freshness, that they be placed in the bowl just before the hot fat is poured in.

Dandelion and Bacon Salad

Salade de Pissenlit au Lard

2 thick slices bacon, cut crosswise into strips, parboiled, rinsed, and drained
1 tablespoon olive oil
12 ounces young dandelion plants, washed and dried
about 2 tablespoons wine vinegar
salt, freshly ground pepper

Fry the bacon in the olive oil over medium-low heat, turning the pieces around until they are lightly crisp on all sides and have rendered a couple of tablespoons of fat. Put the dandelions into the preheated bowl, pour the bacon and its fat over them, wash out the pan with the vinegar over high heat, and, the moment it boils, pour it over the salad. Sprinkle with very little salt, generously grind pepper over, toss, and serve immediately.

THE STRAWBERRIES IN BEAUJOLAIS

Strawberries in wine are a common and much-loved dessert in all wine-making countries; usually the strawberries are simply presented at table and each guest fills his wine glass with berries, pours some more wine over, sugars to taste, and lightly cuts up and mashes the berries so that their juice mingles with the wine.

Strawberries in Beaujolais

Fraises au Beaujolais

1 pound fresh, ripe strawberries
sugar, to taste
wine to cover *(the same that has been drunk throughout the meal)*

Pick over the strawberries, rinse them rapidly, drain them, and sprinkle them with sugar. Leave them to macerate for an hour or so and, shortly before serving, pour enough wine over just to cover them.

Four Simple Spring Menus

MENU IV *(for 4)*

WARM ASPARAGUS VINAIGRETTE
[ASPERGES TIEDES A LA VINAIGRETTE]

The simplest of dry white wines — Soave, Gros Plant, Muscadet, etc. — or the same wine as the following

. . .

CALVES' BRAINS IN RED WINE
[CERVELLES DE VEAU EN MATELOTE]

A light, young red wine — Saumur-Champigny, Sancerre rouge, any vin primeur *or* vino nuovo

. . .

CAULIFLOWER LOAF
[PAIN DE CHOUFLEUR]

. . .

GREEN SALAD WITH FINES HERBES
[SALADE VERTE AUX FINES I'ERBES]

. . .

CHEESES
[FROMAGES]

Same as the preceding

. . .

MOLDED APPLE PUDDING
[PUDDING MOULE AUX POMMES]

THE WARM ASPARAGUS VINAIGRETTE

Hollandaise sauce is also a good accompaniment to warm or hot asparagus. Maltaise sauce (hollandaise finished with the juice of a blood orange) is conceived uniquely as an asparagus accompaniment. Vinaigrette (or, simply, olive oil, salt, and pepper) is less an accompanying sauce than an essential seasoning that permits a total appreciation of the asparagus, unadorned.

Although best hot or warm, asparagus may also be served cold, *à la vinaigrette,* but should never be rewarmed.

Warm Asparagus Vinaigrette

Asperges Tièdes à la Vinaigrette

3 pounds fresh, firm, evenly formed large asparagus
salt, freshly ground pepper, wine vinegar, fruity olive oil

Peel the asparagus (correctly peeled, the entire stem will be tender and there is no waste — do not scrape or try to peel too thinly): cut off a short section from the end of the stalk and, with a sharp paring knife, peel from the cut end, starting thickly and peeling progressively more thinly to the point at which the skin becomes tender. Soak the asparagus for a few minutes in cold water and tie them into bundles of a dozen or so each. A single round of string is no good: hold the bunch in your hand grasping a string end between thumb and asparagus while, with the other hand, you twine the string firmly round and round the length of the bunch and back again, to tie the two ends tightly. (This not only holds the bunch firmly together, the stalks protecting one another from the movement of boiling water, but permits the easy removal of the bunch from the cooking water by slipping a tine of a long two-pronged kitchen fork beneath the rounds of string; finally, the tied bunch is placed directly on the folded napkin covering the

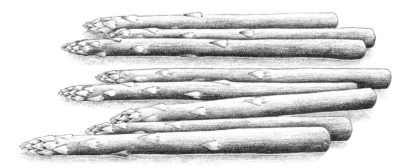

serving plate, the strings are clipped and slipped out from beneath the bunch, and the stalks of asparagus fall into a casual and attractive presentation.)

They should be cooked, well immersed in boiling water — a large oval *cocotte* is practical and, if they just fit, it will be more sensible first to lay the bundle or bundles in place, throw over a handful of coarse salt, and bring the water to a boil in another receptacle before placing the *cocotte* over high heat and pouring over the boiling water; when it returns to the boil, cover the pot with the lid ajar and adjust the heat to a light boil. After 7 or 8 minutes, test by piercing a stalk, with the grain, with a sharp knife point; the moment it penetrates with little resistance, they are done — the tips must remain firmly intact. The bunches may be permitted to drain for a minute on a towel before being transferred to the napkin on the serving platter, each divested of its strings before the other bunch is placed, in order to form overlapping rows, exposing all the tips.

Specially designed plates with a well to one side for the vinaigrette are practical; lacking these, each guest props the far side of his plate on a knife handle or the arch of a fork or spoon before first mixing salt and pepper with vinegar in the front of the plate, to dissolve the salt, and then adding olive oil. Each asparagus, taken in hand, is dipped and rolled repeatedly in the vinaigrette as it is eaten.

Calves' Brains in Red Wine

Cervelles de Veau en Matelote

2 calves' brains (*firm and moist in appearance, unstained with blood, if possible*), soaked in cold water, surface membranes peeled off, resoaked in cold water, if necessary, to remove blood stains
red-wine *court-bouillon* (*page 64*), made with 2 parts of wine to 1 of water, strained

GARNISH
20 small garnish onions, peeled, seasoned, and stewed gently in butter until tender but uncolored
½ pound small, firm, unopened mushrooms, trimmed, rinsed, dried, seasoned, and sautéed rapidly in butter over high heat
beurre manié made with 2 tablespoons flour and 1 ounce softened unsalted butter, mashed to a paste with a fork
2 or 3 slices stale white bread, crusts removed, cut into small cubes, and tossed in butter over low heat until light golden and crisp

PERSILLADE
1 clove garlic, peeled, pounded to a paste, and mixed with 2 tablespoons finely chopped parsley
red-wine essence (*page 63*) (*optional*)

Slip the brains into the boiling *court-bouillon,* return to the boil, and poach, covered, at a bare simmer for 20 to 25 minutes. Remove them, slice them, arrange them in a warmed gratin dish, scatter over the onions and mushrooms, and keep warm, covered, while finishing the sauce.

Over high heat, reduce the *court-bouillon* by about half, adding some red-wine essence, if desired, to intensify the flavor. Taste for salt. Whisk in the *beurre manié,* bits at a time, until the sauce is lightly thickened, remove it from the heat, pour the sauce into a sieve held over the brains and their garnish, pass it all through, and put the dish into the oven until the sauce begins to bubble evenly over the surface.

Add a bit of butter to the croutons in their pan, rewarm, and, over high heat, add the *persillade;* sauté for a few seconds until the croutons are all evenly coated with *persillade.* Scatter over the reheated brains upon removing them from the oven. Send the cauliflower loaf to the table at the same time.

Cauliflower Loaf

Pain de Choufleur

a few small, tender green beans
1 small carrot
1½ ounces unsalted butter
1 good-sized cauliflower
stiff *béchamel (page 76),* made with 2 tablespoons flour, 1 ounce butter, and
 ½ cup milk
2 whole eggs and 1 egg yolk
salt, freshly ground pepper, freshly grated nutmeg

Cut the string beans into approximately 2-inch lengths and split them in half. Either peel the carrot with a serrated vegetable peeler that makes ridges the length of the carrot, and slice it thinly, crosswise, or peel it smoothly, cut it into 2-inch lengths, slice these thinly lengthwise, and cut them into matchlike strips. Parboil the beans and the carrots in rapidly boiling salted water for 2 or 3 minutes or until they have lost their crispness and are pliable. Drain them in a sieve, refresh under cold running water, and sponge them dry with a paper towel.

Generously butter a quart mold (any form), arrange the carrot and bean fragments in a simple design, pressing them well against the buttered surface, and put the mold to chill to fix the decorative elements in place.

Break the cauliflower up into flowerets, cook them in boiling salted water until they are just tender, not mushy, drain them, dry them out for a couple of minutes in 2 tablespoons of butter, tossing and stirring, over medium heat, and pass them through a fine sieve. Stir in the *béchamel*.

Beat in the eggs and the egg yolk, season to taste with salt, pepper, and very little nutmeg, pour the mixture into the mold, and tap the bottom a couple of times against a wooden surface to settle the contents. Lightly press a buttered parchment paper against the surface and poach in a *bain-marie*, immersed by two-thirds in hot water, in a medium oven for about half an hour or until the center is firm to the touch. Once removed from the *bain-marie*, leave the loaf to settle for a few minutes before unmolding.

Molded Apple Pudding

Pudding Moulé aux Pommes

CARAMEL
>   3 heaping tablespoons sugar
>   3 tablespoons water
>
>   almond oil or butter
>   1½ pounds cooking apples (*preferably russet*)
>   ⅓ cup water
>   ½ cup sugar (*to taste*)
>   1 pinch cinnamon
>   3 eggs

For the caramel, combine the sugar and water in a small saucepan, bring it to a boil, and adjust the heat to a bubble. Don't take your eye off it, and remove it the instant it is a rich, deep amber color. Pour in about 1 tablespoon of hot water, stirring until it is thoroughly blended, and pour the caramel immediately into the mold, turning it in all directions to coat the mold as evenly as possible. When cooled, lightly oil or butter any parts of the inner walls of the mold that have not been coated with caramel.

Quarter, peel, core, and slice the apples. Cook them with the water, over high heat, stirring constantly with a wooden spoon, until they are just cooked — that is, reduced to a near-puree. Stir in the sugar and the cinnamon, pass through a sieve, and beat in the eggs. Pour the mixture into the mold, tap it on a wooden surface to settle the contents, and poach it in a *bain-marie* in hot, but not boiling, water, in a moderate oven, for 45 to 50 minutes. Leave to cool until tepid; then unmold and, once unmolded, leave the dessert covered by the mold and chill. Remove mold just before serving, well chilled.

SUMMER MENUS

Two Summer Dinners

MENU I *(for 8)*

ARTICHOKE BOTTOMS WITH TWO MOUSSES
[FONDS D'ARTICHAUTS AUX DEUX MOUSSES]

A light, young, dry white wine: Sancerre, Quincy, Muscadet,
Entre-Deux-Mers

· · ·

SOLE FILLETS WITH FINES HERBES
STEWED CUCUMBERS
[FILETS DE SOLE AUX FINES HERBES]
[CONCOMBRES A L'ETUVEE]

A richer, fuller, but still dry white wine, several years old: Burgundy
(Chassagne-Montrachet, Meursault), Loire (Coulée de Serrant, Vouvray),
Graves (Laville-Haut-Brion), Côtes-du-Rhône (Condrieu, Saint-Joseph),
California Chardonnay

· · ·

SPITTED ROAST LEG OF LAMB
BUTTERED GREEN BEANS
[GIGOT D'AGNEAU ROTI A LA BROCHE]
[HARICOTS VERTS AU BEURRE]

A rich, full-bodied, fairly young red wine (3 to 6 years old): Burgundy
(Nuits-Saint-Georges, Fixin), Bordeaux (Pomerol), Côtes-du-Rhône
(Hermitage, Côte Rôtie)

· · ·

CHEESES
[FROMAGES]

A wine of the same general type as that chosen for the roast, older and from
a richer vintage

· · ·

PEACH MELBA
[PECHE MELBA]

The first course and all the elements of the dessert will have been prepared far ahead of time. The preliminary preparations for the fish course (except for the actual poaching and the finishing of the sauce — 15 minutes) may be done in advance. The cucumbers may be prepared and parboiled, and the beans and roast prepared for cooking ahead of time. There is little to do at the last minute, but one must organize one's time, for neither the fish nor the green beans can wait. In the recipe I have indicated a 20-minute period of relaxation for the leg of lamb, but that time, fortunately, is flexible. The meal may be begun 15 minutes after the roast has been put to cook. Don't try to prepare the fish until the first course is nearly finished. (It is good to wait a bit between courses, and as long as the guests' glasses contain wine, everything is all right.) It is best to have the boiling water in readiness for the beans, but do not begin to cook them until after the roast has been put to relax.

ARTICHOKE BOTTOMS WITH TWO MOUSSES

Note that, in this recipe, 2 cups of veal jelly (pages 67 and 69) are required, half for the tomato mousse, the other half for coating all the elements after being dressed. The juxtaposed flavors and textures of the artichoke bottoms, the two mousses, and the jelly form an exciting ensemble, but less elaborate presentations (the artichoke bottoms simply filled with one mousse and presented, without the coating of jelly, on a *chiffonade* of lettuce or a few sprigs of watercress) are possible. To fill artichoke bottoms with tomato mousse, it must first be left to set completely before being spooned into the bottoms and molded like the liver mousse.

Artichoke Bottoms with Two Mousses

Fonds d'Artichauts aux Deux Mousses

TOMATO MOUSSE
1 medium onion, finely chopped
½ ounce unsalted butter
splash of white wine
1½ pounds firm, ripe tomatoes, peeled, seeded (*page 44*), and coarsely
    chopped
salt, cayenne pepper
1 cup veal jelly (*pages 67 and 69*)
1 cup heavy cream

CHICKEN-LIVER MOUSSE
2 or 3 shallots (*or 1 small onion*), finely chopped
½ pound chicken livers, trimmed
4 ounces unsalted butter, softened
salt, freshly ground pepper
healthy pinch of mixed dried herbs (*page 52*)
dash of Cognac
½ cup heavy cream

8 artichoke bottoms, precooked, chokes removed (*page 45*)
3 to 4 tablespoons old Madeira, tawny port, or other good-quality fortified
    wine
1 cup veal jelly (*pages 67 and 69*), melted
chervil

THE TOMATO MOUSSE

Cook the onion in the butter over low heat for 10 minutes or until it is soft and yellowed but not browned, add some white wine, reduce almost completely, add the tomatoes, salt, and a bit of cayenne, and cook, covered, at a light boil for half an hour. Over high heat, reduce the mixture, stirring with a wooden spoon, until any watery juices have evaporated, add the veal jelly, return to the boil, and continue to reduce over high heat for several minutes. With a wooden pestle, pass the contents of the saucepan through a fine sieve into a metal bowl. Taste for seasoning, remembering that the addition of cream will sweeten the taste and attenuate the salt — and that cold preparations support higher seasoning than hot. Partially immerse the bowl in ice water and stir until the puree cools and begins to thicken slightly. Half whip the cream until it is good and frothy but still pourable (stiffly whipped cream will make a mousse dry and cottony) and mix it into the puree. Pour into a deep serving platter or crystal dish and chill until firm; embedding the dish in cracked ice will hasten the process.

THE CHICKEN-LIVER MOUSSE

Cook the shallots in about 1 ounce of butter until they are softened but uncolored. Add the livers, salt, pepper, and herbs and sauté over higher heat, tossing and stirring, for a couple of minutes, only until all the surfaces are gray — they must remain rare. Add the Cognac, tip the pan to the flame (or strike a match) to ignite it, remove from the heat, and stir until the flames die out. Pass the mixture through a fine sieve (adding some of the softened butter to loosen it up if it becomes difficult to pass) and mix in thoroughly the remaining butter. Half whip the cream, incorporate it into the mixture, and refrigerate until it is semifirm. Fill the artichoke bottoms, piling the liver mousse in a dome and smoothing the surface with an overturned tablespoon. Chill thoroughly.

Arrange the stuffed artichoke bottoms on the bed of tomato mousse. Stir the fortified wine into the tepid meat jelly. In a small metal bowl, embedded in ice, place a few tablespoons at a time of the liquid jelly, stir with a tablespoon until it begins to turn syrupy, and rapidly spoon it over the liver mousse domes. (Once it begins to thicken, it jells fast — if you are stuck with solid jelly, put it aside to be remelted.) Refrigerate the dish between coatings and begin again — never cooling more than a few spoonfuls of jelly at a time — coating and recoating until the jelly is used up and the dish is masked evenly in amber transparence. If a larger dish is at hand to contain cracked ice, the dish will be best served embedded in it.

THE SOLE FILLETS WITH FINES HERBES

This is the radical version — the simplest of all the variations on fish poached in richly flavored liquid that is then reduced to form the sauce base. Practically any fish can be used. The way in which it is cut up or filleted is imposed by the size and shape of the fish. (From small, flat fish like sole, flounder, plaice, etc., 2 fillets are lifted from each side; from monkfish, the thick, gelatinous, central bone is removed and the two thickish fillets may either be sliced into long strips or cut crosswise or on the bias into thick medallions; salmon or other large, round fish — cod, hake, bass — may be unboned and cut into finger-thick cross sections or filleted and sliced, lengthwise or on the bias.) Fillets or strips are often stuffed (usually with a mousseline forcemeat, sometimes enriched by the addition of *duxelles,* chopped truffles or pistachios, pureed spinach or sea-urchin corals, finely diced cooked lobster, etc.) and folded, as here, or rolled into *paupiettes.*

The poaching liquid can be, as here, a white-wine *fumet,* wine alone, mushroom cooking liquid, leftover (or specially prepared) fish soup, or a combination.

If red wine or a red-wine *fumet* is used, it is good to reinforce the color and flavor by an addition of red-wine essence (page 63) to the reduction.

The sauce may be no more than a syrupy reduction of the poaching liquid mounted with butter; sometimes cream is added to the reduction and further reduced before the butter is whisked in off heat; the reduction may be less extreme, bound by egg yolks and a lesser amount of butter incorporated (not recommended for a red-wine sauce) or, if some *velouté* is held in readiness, the reduction may be added to it and it will then usually be creamed and buttered. Garnishes of mussels, mushrooms, diced crustaceans or pimientos, or special spices, such as saffron or curry, are possibilities.

Sole Fillets with Fines Herbes

Filets de Sole aux Fines Herbes

4 large soles, filleted (*16 fillets*), carcasses reserved
salt, freshly ground pepper
chopped *fines herbes (page 50)*
10 ounces fresh, unsalted butter
white-wine fish *fumet (page 72)*, made from the carcasses

Soak the fillets in ice water for 10 to 15 minutes, spread them out on paper towels, outsides (membrane surfaces) up, sponge them dry with more paper towels, flatten each slightly with the flat side of a large knife blade, and slit each shallowly, 3 or 4 times on the bias, with a very sharp knife — only to cut through the membrane. Sprinkle with salt, pepper, and *fines herbes,* place a blade of butter on the thick half of each fillet, fold the slender half over, and press gently.

Butter a large, heavy sauté pan, preferably copper, of a size just to hold the folded fillets placed side by side, sprinkle the bottom with *fines herbes,* lay the folded fillets on top, pour over barely enough *fumet* to cover, sprinkle over more *fines herbes,* and press a buttered round of parchment paper to the surface of the fillets. (Up to this point, they may be prepared slightly ahead of time.)

Place the pan, covered, over medium heat. As the liquid heats, check regularly, lifting the edge of the buttered paper, and, the instant the boil is reached, remove from the heat and leave, tightly covered, to poach for 7 or 8 minutes. Dice the remaining butter.

Delicately remove the fillets, one by one, to a pastry rack placed over a platter to collect the draining juices; lay the buttered paper atop to protect them. Over high heat, reduce the cooking liquid. When the fillets have drained, transfer them to a heated serving platter, add their drained juices to the reducing liquids, and, when these arrive at a syrupy consistency, a sharp, staccato bubble replacing the foamy boil, remove from the heat and whisk in the remaining butter. Give the pan a swirl, pour the sauce over the fillets, and serve immediately, accompanied by the stewed cucumbers.

Stewed Cucumbers

Concombres à l'Etuvée

2 pounds cucumbers, peeled, quartered lengthwise, seeded, and cut into
    1-inch lengths
Salt, freshly ground pepper
1 ounce butter

Plunge the cucumber sections into heavily salted boiling water for a minute, drain them well, and cook them over low heat in butter for 7 or 8 minutes, tossing from time to time, until yellowed and quite tender — they should remain slightly firm. Serve them separately or on the same platter as the fillets, scattered around the edge.

Spitted Roast Leg of Lamb

Gigot d'Agneau Rôti à la Broche

1 leg of lamb, sawed at the knuckle, with a good length of shank bone
    remaining, pelvic bone removed, fat trimmed off
2 cloves garlic, peeled and sliced thinly lengthwise
1 teaspoon mixed herbs (*page 52*)
olive oil
salt, freshly ground pepper

A good leg of lamb is proportionately short and well rounded. The fat is white and plentiful and the flesh a clear rose-tan color.

Two or three hours before roasting, pierce the meat with the point of a small knife and insert garlic at either end next to the bone and at several points in the fleshier parts of the leg. Sprinkle with the herbs and rub the leg all over with the olive oil. Leave at room temperature.

Grass, or yearling, lamb (different from baby, milk lamb, which must be well done) is never so exquisite as when roasted pink on a spit before a well-attended wood fire. Count approximately 10 minutes' cooking time per pound. With a bit of experience, one can feel the right moment by pressing the surface of the meat between thumb and forefinger. When properly cooked, it is firm and resilient to the touch. For an average-size leg of lamb, plan on an hour before an open fire (count 10 minutes less in an oven, starting it in a hot oven that is turned down to medium the moment the roast is put in), during the last 10 minutes of which the turning of the spit should be stopped so that the thick, rounded section of the leg is left facing slightly downward toward the heart of the fire; baste regularly at this point. The roast should not be seasoned until it is well seared — about 15 minutes after being put to cook — and after the actual cooking process it should always be left in a warm place for a good 20 minutes to relax. During this period, the flesh becomes firmer and the heat contained in it continues to even out the cooking of the interior. In an oven, one may leave it with the oven turned off and the oven door left slightly ajar. Before an open fire, it may be unspitted and placed, covered, in the dripping pan near the fire, or transferred to the serving platter and removed to a warm oven. When cooking before an open fire, prepare the fire in the fireplace a good hour before putting the roast to turn so that it will be blazing and a heart of coals will have formed. Nurse the outside edges to keep them flaming — there is always plenty of heat radiated from the center. Try to keep the logs in a vaguely semicircular form so that the heart of the fire is somewhat farther back than the outside parts. Construct a low wall of bricks, a strip of asbestos, etc., directly behind the dripping pan to protect it from the intense heat of the fire bed.

CARVING AND SERVING

Carve at table. A special handle that screws onto the shank bone *(manche à gigot)* greatly facilitates carving. Lacking that, grasp the shank bone with a folded napkin while carving. With the other end of the leg resting on the serving platter, slice away from your person at a sharply acute angle to the bone, first from the large, rounded cushion of flesh, removing as many slices as there are guests, turn the leg over and slice in the same way, holding the knife almost parallel to the bone, from the flatter muscle corresponding to the front part of the leg, then bring the knife back to the shank and, slicing slightly upward but still away from yourself, remove as many small slices as from each of the other two sections. (Each part has a different flavor and a different degree of doneness — the shank, being so much smaller, is always well done when the rest has cooked pink, but because of its gelatinous structure, it remains moist and succulent.) Pour a spoonful of the juices that have escaped during carving over each serving; serve the green beans at the same time.

Buttered Green Beans

Haricots Verts au Beurre

2 pounds tiny, freshly picked green beans, topped and tailed
salt
3 ounces unsalted butter, diced

Cook the beans in the largest possible quantity of well-salted, rapidly boiling water until just done — 6 to 8 minutes if they are small and fresh. Before being buttered, they should be well drained (but not allowed to cool), returned to their cooking utensil, and tossed (the pan should be held over the flame and the beans tossed constantly to avoid any possibility of sticking or scorching) over high heat until their superficial moisture has completely disappeared. Add the butter off the heat and continue tossing and swirling the pan until it has been absorbed.

Peach Melba

Pêche Melba

VANILLA ICE CREAM
    2 cups milk
    ½ vanilla bean
    1 egg yolk
    ½ cup sugar
    1 cup heavy cream

8 fresh peaches, poached in syrup (*or home preserved*)
2 pounds fresh or frozen raspberries, passed through a nylon drum sieve,
    sugared to taste
slivered fresh almonds (*optional*)

The dessert created by Escoffier to honor the singer Nellie Melba depends on three things only for it to rank among the finest of classical French desserts: the honesty of the ice cream, flavorful peaches that have been freshly poached in a syrup containing only water and sugar, and a sauce that is nothing but a puree of fresh raspberries. Whipped cream detracts. The only acceptable refinement is the sprinkling of a few sliced fresh almonds over the surface.

THE VANILLA ICE CREAM

Bring the milk to a boil with the vanilla bean, remove from the heat, and allow it to infuse for about 10 minutes. Stir the egg yolk and the sugar together and beat until the yellow lightens in color, then slowly pour in the milk, stirring all the time. Place the saucepan over low to medium heat and stir constantly with a wooden spoon, making certain to reach all corners of the saucepan, until the custard lightly coats the spoon. Above all, it must not be allowed to boil. Immerse the saucepan halfway in a basin of cold water, stirring the contents from time to time, and, when completely cooled, whip the cream until it is fairly firm and frothy, but not stiff, and stir it in. Freeze.

There is no perfect replacement for the old-fashioned hand-turned ice-cream freezer, but the small electrical apparatuses meant to be installed in the freezing compartment of a refrigerator produce respectable results with a minimum of effort. There are also electrical freezers, of the same form as the old-fashioned variety, which freeze by means of cracked ice and coarse salt; still, the movement is not the same.

THE PEACHES

Heap the ice cream in the center of a chilled, deep serving dish (crystal offers the prettiest presentation), surround it with the peaches (cut in half and pitted), and coat lightly with raspberry puree. Sprinkle the surface with peeled, sliced fresh almonds, if available, and send the rest of the sauce to the table in a sauceboat.

Two Summer Dinners

MENU II *(for 6)*

COLD CALVES' BRAINS IN CREAM SAUCE
[*CERVELLES DE VEAU FROIDES A LA CREME*]

*A young, dry, fruity white wine: Pouilly-Fumé, Sancerre, Pouilly-Fuissé,
Mercurey Blanc*

· · ·

SQUID A L'AMERICAINE — RICE PILAF
[*CALMARS A L'AMERICAINE — RIZ PILAF*]

The same as the preceding

· · ·

JELLIED POACHED CHICKEN
[*POULE AU POT EN GELEE*]

*Château-Chalon or a light young Burgundy red wine, served cool: Côte de
Beaune (Chassagne-Montrachet, Santenay, etc.) or Mercurey*

· · ·

TOSSED GREEN SALAD WITH FINES HERBES
[*SALADE VERTE AUX FINES HERBES*]

· · ·

CHEESES
[*FROMAGES*]

*An older wine than the preceding: a Côte de Nuits (following a
Burgundy) or a Côtes-du-Rhône (Châteauneuf-du-Pape, Hermitage)*

· · ·

APRICOT FRITTERS
[*BEIGNETS D'ABRICOTS*]

Sauternes, sweet Vouvray, Coteaux du Layon, etc.

Calves' Brains in Cream Sauce

Cervelles de Veau Froides à la Crème

3 fresh calves' brains, soaked in cold water, membranes removed, soaked
    again
vinegar *court-bouillon* (*page 64*)

SAUCE
    salt, freshly ground pepper
    2 teaspoons Dijon mustard
    1 lemon
    1 cup heavy cream
    1 heart fresh, crisp celery, finely diced
    1 tablespoon chopped chives

Slip the brains into the boiling *court-bouillon* and turn down the heat so that they
poach at the barest simmer for 20 to 25 minutes. Lift them out gently, one by
one, with a perforated skimming spoon, place them on a plate, and cover them
with a cloth that has been moistened in the *court-bouillon* (which prevents them
from drying out and discoloring on the surface). Put them to chill in the refrigerator until ready for use.

    Trim the brains, slice them neatly, and arrange them on a chilled serving dish.
Put salt, pepper, mustard, and the juice of ½ lemon together in a bowl and stir
until they are thoroughly combined. Pass the trimmings from the brains through
a small sieve, stir them into the sauce, then stir in the cream. Taste and, if
necessary, add a bit more lemon juice and additional seasoning. Stir in the celery.
Spoon the sauce over the brains and sprinkle with chopped chives.

Squid à l'Américaine

Calmars à l'Américaine

2 pounds squid
1 onion, finely chopped
3 tablespoons olive oil
salt, cayenne pepper
1 small glass Cognac
⅓ cup dry white wine
2 cloves garlic, peeled and finely chopped
1 pound firm, ripe tomatoes, peeled, seeded (*page 44*), and coarsely chopped
bouquet-garni (*page 50*)
2 ounces unsalted butter, diced
small handful finely torn-up fresh basil leaves (*lacking that, fresh parsley*)

Clean the squid: pull the tentacles apart from the conical body, press the outsides of the tentacles at the mouth opening to force the little pouch of clawlike teeth to pop out, remove the eyes and any soft intestinal material that clings to the base of the tentacles. Pull out the translucent pen from the body, clean out the inside of the body well, peel off the surface membranes, and wash the tentacles and the body in several waters. Cut the conical bodies into sections, put them into a colander, and leave to drain.

Put the onion to cook gently in a bit of olive oil or butter until it is soft and yellowed in color. Set it aside. Heat the olive oil in a large, heavy sauté pan and throw in the squid. Sprinkle with salt and toss the pieces or stir them around for a couple of minutes, keeping the heat high, until they have retracted in size and become firm. Add the Cognac, set fire to it, and stir constantly until the flames die down. Add the white wine, reduce a minute, still over high heat, then add the cooked onion, garlic, tomatoes, small pinch of cayenne pepper, and *bouquet-garni*. Bring to a rapid boil, scrape the bottom with a wooden spoon to be certain that nothing is sticking, and turn the heat down so that, covered, the sauce simmers. After 45 or 50 minutes, remove the pieces to a heated serving dish, discard the *bouquet-garni*, and reduce the sauce over high heat, stirring constantly with a wooden spoon, until it becomes fairly consistent. It should not be too thick, but it must lose its watery consistency. Remove the pan from the heat, add the butter, swirl the pan until all the butter is absorbed into the sauce, and pour it over the squid. Sprinkle the surface with the basil (torn only at the last minute or they will be discolored and unsightly). Serve accompanied by a rice pilaf (page 78).

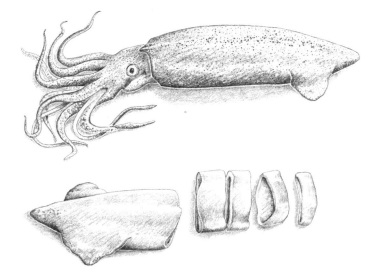

THE JELLIED POACHED CHICKEN

In the original edition of *The French Menu Cookbook*, the chicken was split the length of the back and opened out for boning; the boning and trussing method described for chicken mousseline (pages 205–207) is simpler and more satisfying.

The chicken should be prepared the day preceding the dinner; it may be decorated and glazed with jelly on the morning of the same day. If the decorative presentation does not interest you, the cooled poached chicken, its trussing strings removed, may be fitted into an oval terrine, its strained and wine-flavored jelly poured over it, and left to set.

Jellied Poached Chicken

Poule au Pot en Gelée

1 large tender roasting chicken with skin intact, including that of the neck (*a well-fed, 6-month-old farm chicken, if possible*), boned (*pages 205–207*)
veal or chicken jelly (*pages 67 and 69*)

STUFFING
    1 clove garlic
    large handful semifresh bread crumbs
    stock (*some of the above jelly*)
    10 ounces chicken livers (*plus that of the chicken being poached*), trimmed and chopped
    1 medium onion, finely chopped
    1 ounce unsalted butter
    1 teaspoon mixed dried herbs (*page 52*)
    1 tablespoon finely chopped parsley
    2 eggs
    salt, freshly ground pepper

    juice of 1 lemon
    1 small glass fortified wine: Madeira, sherry, port
    decorative elements: hard-boiled egg whites, black olives, blanched tarragon leaves, canned pimiento, etc.

THE STUFFING

Pound the clove of garlic to a paste in the mortar, mix in the bread crumbs, and stir or mash in enough stock to make a paste. Combine all the stuffing ingredients in a large bowl and mix thoroughly with your hands, squeezing the mixture repeatedly through your fingers. Taste for salt. Stuff and truss the bird as for chicken mousseline (pages 205–206). Rub the surface with lemon juice and wrap the bird firmly in a double layer of muslin, tying the two ends securely. Place it in a pot, preferably oval, and pour over melted jelly to cover. Bring it to the boil, adjust to a bare simmer, and poach, covered, the lid slightly ajar, for 1½ hours. Remove the chicken and leave it, still wrapped, to cool, then refrigerate. Pass the cooking liquid through a strainer lined with a moistened and wrung-out cloth, cool, then refrigerate and, when solidified, remove all traces of fat.

THE DECORATION

Unwrap the chicken and remove the trussing strings. With a cloth moistened in hot water and wrung out, delicately wipe any surfaces that show traces of clinging fat and place the chicken on its serving dish. Melt the jelly, cool until it is barely tepid, and stir in the fortified wine. Cool small quantities of jelly at a time, stirring with a tablespoon in a small metal bowl placed over cracked ice. First coat the chicken thinly all over with jelly and refrigerate it to set. Dip each element of the *décor* in jelly, affix all to the chicken's surface, and refrigerate again. Trickle the semiliquid jelly over the chicken, concentrating on the highest points (leg joints and breast) repeatedly, refrigerating each time, until the jelly is all used up — or, if there is enough jelly, until the outline of the chicken, softened through the undulating coat of jelly, melts into the mirror of clear jelly at its base. Chill until serving. The base may be decorated with bouquets of chervil.

Apricot Fritters

Beignets d'Abricots

    12 apricots, ripe but firm
    3 or 4 tablespoons sugar
    about 2 tablespoons Cognac

FRYING BATTER
    1 scant cup flour
    1 pinch salt
    1 egg, separated
    ⅓ cup tepid beer
    about 2 tablespoons water
    1 ounce unsalted butter, melted
    1 tablespoon Cognac
    oil (*preferably a light olive oil*), for frying
    confectioners' sugar

Cut the apricots in half, sprinkle them with sugar and Cognac, and leave them to macerate for an hour or so. Sift the flour and salt into a mixing bowl, make a well in the center, add the egg yolk, beer, and water and stir from the center outward until the flour is incorporated into the liquid. Stir in the melted butter and Cognac. It should be fairly liquid. Leave it to rest an hour or so and, just before using, gently fold in the egg white, beaten stiff. Sponge the excess liquid from the apricot halves, drop a third of them into the batter, and, being certain that each is well coated with batter, lift them out, one at a time, with a teaspoon and drop them into the deep fat. (It should be hot, but not smoking; let a drop of batter fall in, and if it sizzles immediately, the oil is ready.) When the fritters are golden and crisp, lift them out with a large wire skimming spoon and wrap them in a towel while continuing with the other 2 batches. When all have been fried, transfer them to a serving platter on which has been placed a folded napkin, sprinkle them with confectioners' sugar, and serve, the surface covered with the flaps of the napkin to keep them warm.

A Semi-formal Summer Dinner

THE MENU (*for 8*)

CANTALOUPE WITH PARMA HAM
[MELON CHARENTAIS AU JAMBON DE PARME]

*An uncomplicated dry white wine: from southern France, Cassis, Palette,
or Bellet; from Italy, Regaleali (Sicily), Frascati (Roman hills),
Vermentino (Genoese countryside); California Chenin Blanc*

• • •

BRAISED STUFFED ARTICHOKE BOTTOMS
[FONDS D'ARTICHAUTS FARCIS A LA DUXELLES]

The same wine as the preceding

• • •

GRILLED LAMBS' KIDNEYS WITH HERB BUTTER
POTATO STRAW CAKE
[ROGNONS D'AGNEAU GRILLES CHIVRY]
[PAILLASSON DE POMMES DE TERRE]

*Cool, fruity young red wine: from France, Saumur-Champigny (Loire),
Saint-Joseph (Côtes-du-Rhône); from Italy, Dolcetto or Nebbiolo
(Piedmont), Bardolino or Valpolicella (Veneto)*

• • •

TOSSED GREEN SALAD
[SALADE VERTE]

• • •

CHEESES
[FROMAGES]

*Following a French wine, Hermitage or Côte Rôtie; following an Italian
wine, Barbaresco or Barolo*

• • •

PEACHES IN RED WINE
[PECHES A LA VIGNERONNE]

The meal requires a minimum of preparation and, with the exception of the actual cooking of the artichokes, potatoes, and kidneys, everything may be done in advance. The artichokes may be put to cook 15 minutes before the diners go to table, the potatoes at the same time as the artichokes are served, and the kidneys only after the second course is finished.

Braised Stuffed Artichoke Bottoms

Fonds d'Artichauts Farcis à la Duxelles

mirepoix (page 55)
8 artichoke bottoms, chokes removed, rubbed with lemon, uncooked
    (page 45)
salt, freshly ground pepper
3 ounces unsalted butter
duxelles (page 58), made with ½ pound mushrooms
equal quantities of dry white wine and stock
chopped parsley

Choose a sauté pan of the exact dimensions, as nearly as possible, just to hold the artichoke bottoms without their being packed in. Line the bottom with the *mirepoix*.

    Season the inside of each artichoke bottom with a bit of salt and pepper and place a small piece of butter in each. Stuff them with *duxelles,* with the help of a teaspoon, packing the stuffing in firmly and smoothing the surface.

    Place the prepared artichoke bottoms, side by side, on the bed of *mirepoix,* pour in the liquids to immerse the artichoke bottoms partially, and bring to a boil. Cook, covered, at a simmer for about 1 hour. Remove the artichoke bottoms to a preheated serving dish. Pass the cooking liquid through a fine sieve into a small, heavy saucepan, pressing well without rubbing (in order to extract all the juices, without at the same time passing the solids through in puree). Reduce the liquid over a high flame, stirring constantly. The moment it begins to turn syrupy in consistency, remove the pan from the heat and whip in the remaining butter, cut into small pieces. Spoon the sauce over the artichoke bottoms, sprinkle each with a pinch of chopped parsley, and serve. (If preferred, the *mirepoix* may remain in the sauce.)

Grilled Lambs' Kidneys with Herb Butter

Rognons d'Agneau Grillés Chivry

8 to 12 fresh lambs' kidneys
mixed dried herbs (*page 52*)
olive oil
salt, freshly ground pepper
herb butter (*recipe follows*)

Beginning at the top, slit the kidneys lengthwise, being careful not to cut them completely in two. Open them out, butterfly-fashion, and, using either sharpened branches of rosemary or small skewers, skewer them across — this prevents their folding up as the flesh becomes firmer through contact with heat. Sprinkle with herbs, turn them around in the olive oil, and, just before putting them to cook, season both sides with salt and pepper. Sear the cut surface first (face up beneath a broiler or face down over hot coals). To remain moist, flavorful, and tender, the kidneys must remain pink inside. Once having been turned, the moment a rose-tinged tiny drop of liquid appears on the surface, they are done. Count approximately 2 minutes on each side.

Serve them immediately on a large, round, heated serving platter, arranged face up in a circle around the potato cake, a teaspoonful of herb butter (below) in the center of each kidney, and a tablespoonful on the potato cake. Serve the remaining butter separately.

HERB BUTTER

2 chopped gray shallots
1 large handful parsley and chervil leaves
2 tablespoons chopped chives
2 teaspoons fresh tarragon leaves
¼ pound unsalted butter, softened

Blanch the chopped shallots for a minute in boiling water and drain. Plunge all the herbs into boiling water and, after half a minute, drain and press them in a cloth to rid them of excess moisture. Pound the herbs and shallots together in a mortar until reduced to a puree, mix together with the butter, and pass through a drum sieve (page 47) or an ordinary fine sieve, using a wooden pestle. Stir the resultant puree so that the greener parts (the last to pass through the sieve) are thoroughly mixed into the butter. If not used immediately, keep covered and chilled, but remove from the refrigerator ahead of time so that the herb butter will be soft — otherwise it will chill the kidneys on contact.

Potato Straw Cake

Paillasson de Pommes de Terre

4 ounces unsalted butter
1½ pounds firm, yellow-fleshed potatoes, passed through the medium blade of a *mouli-julienne* or food processor, rinsed, drained, and rolled tightly in a towel to dry
Salt, freshly ground pepper

In a large, heavy omelette pan, over low to medium heat, melt half the butter, rolling the pan to coat the sides. Add the potatoes and pack them down with a fork, smoothing the surface. Sprinkle over salt and pepper, place small wedges of butter all around the edges, against the sides of the pan, and cover, either with a large, flat lid or with a plate that is slightly larger than the pan. The potato cake is ready to be turned after 18 to 20 minutes, when the odor of nut butter is perceptible and the edges begin to be golden and frizzled. (When removing the lid or plate to check, be careful not to tip it or all of the condensed moisture on the underside will run in a stream over the potatoes, causing them to stick after being turned; lift the lid carefully off without changing its position, then wipe the underside dry.) Give the pan a jerk to make certain that the cake is not sticking: it should slide easily back and forth in the pan. Hold the lid firmly in place with a towel or potholder and turn it and the pan upside down together to unmold the cake onto the overturned lid; return the pan to the heat, add another lump of butter, and slip the potato cake back into the pan, golden face up. Finish cooking with the lid off — about another 15 minutes — and slip it gently from the pan onto a heated round serving platter.

PEACHES IN RED WINE

In wine-making areas, this is one of the commonest summer desserts, peaches replacing the springtime strawberries. Each person prepares his own portion, adding the sliced peaches to his wine glass and sugaring to taste. An alternative to the red wine is an old Sauternes — something of a luxury, but breathtakingly beautiful and worth it.

Peaches in Red Wine

Pêches à la Vigneronne

1 pound peaches, dipped rapidly in boiling water, peeled, sliced, and
    sprinkled with sugar
red wine poured over to cover

Four Simple Summer Luncheons
à la Provençale

Meridional French cooking is a world apart. Although certain typically Provençal dishes have been adopted by classical French cooking, the general spirit remains distinctly different. What it lacks in delicacy and nuance, it largely makes up for in robust vitality, high-spiritedness, and color. Olive oil, olives, garlic, tomatoes, anchovies, saffron, cayenne, basil, and all those herbs that grow wild in profusion — thyme, rosemary, fennel, savory, oregano, and serpolet — are the characteristic elements. Lamb and mutton are more often used in Provençal cooking than veal and beef, rabbit and guinea fowl take precedence over chicken, and eggplant, zucchini, sweet peppers, broad beans, and artichokes are typical vegetables.

The Mediterranean verve that typifies most of the favorite specialties of Provence defies any attempt to compose them into elaborate menus, for other dishes in juxtaposition would inevitably suffer. Depending on the dish, it should form the entire body of the meal, with a bit of green salad and fresh fruit to finish, or, at most, it should be preceded by a simple hors d'oeuvre and the salad followed by a fresh cheese. These are dishes that seem to go with the sun, the summer, and the out-of-doors and are probably better eaten at lunchtime than at dinner.

Four Simple Summer Luncheons
à la Provençale

MENU I *(for 6 to 8)*

A single, uncomplicated wine throughout the meal: white (Cassis, Châteauneuf-du-Pape, Lirac, Côtes du Lubéron); rosé (Bandol, Lirac, Tavel); red (light-bodied, from the most recent vintage — Côtes-du-Rhône Primeur, Italian Dolcetto, California Zinfandel, etc.)

PROVENÇAL FISH STEW
[SOUPE AUX POISSONS]

• • •

TOSSED GREEN SALAD
[SALADE VERTE]

• • •

FRESH WHITE CHEESE WITH FINES HERBES
[CERVELLE DE CANUT]

• • •

FRESH FRUITS
[FRUITS FRAIS]

THE PROVENÇAL FISH STEW

In the beginning, bouillabaisse was fisherman's stew — a kettle of sea water, propped or hung over a beach fire, with aromatics and the unsalable, leftover catch thrown in. The imposed precepts and the decried heresies of gastronomic literature are no doubt drawn from its origins (it must be cooked at a high boil, luxury fish such as *langouste* are unacceptable, it must be moistened only with water, etc.). Authentic bouillabaisse country is said to be that part of the Mediterranean coast that lies between Marseilles and Toulon, and all the inhabitants agree that, without *racasses,* the local scorpion fish, bouillabaisse cannot exist; the Toulonnais are scorned by the Marseillais because they add mussels and potatoes to their bouillabaisse; the fishing port of Martigues, near Marseilles, is known for its black bouillabaisse, which differs from the Marseillaise version in that tiny cuttlefish are added with their ink sacks. Toward the end of the last century, the Marseillais writer Reboul *(La Cuisinière Provençale)* listed more than 30 varieties of Mediterranean fish commonly used in bouillabaisse. Among those always present are: several varieties of scorpion fish *(rascasses rouges, rascasses noires, chapons de mer),* many varieties of wrasse *(rouquiers,* all exotically colored, some bright green, others blotched, striped, spotted — *girelles* have a single vivid orange stripe from nose to tail tip), gurnards *(galinettes),* weevers *(vives),* "sea cicadas" *(cigales de mer* — blunt-nosed rock lobsters), John Dorys *(Saint-Pierres),* conger eels *(congres),* moray eels *(murènes)* when available, monkfish *(baudroies),* little Mediterranean crabs *(favouilles).* . . . Most cooks prefer to break with tradition by first preparing a stock from 2 to 4 pounds of the little rockfish sold under the name of *"soupe"* — small versions of the same fish used for the bouillabaisse, to which a broken-up monkfish head is a precious addition.

Away from the Mediterranean coast, goodness must prevail over authenticity; rather than offend purist sensibilities, I have preferred not to label the following preparation "bouillabaisse." Because the quality of a fish stew depends on the presence of as many different varieties of fish as possible, it is never practical to prepare it for fewer than 6 to 8 or more people. The types of fish described as fatty or oily (sardines, herring, salmon, shark, tuna, sturgeon, etc.) do not mingle well in this kind of preparation. Choose among the following, leaving the smaller fish whole (or removing their heads to add to the *fumet*) and cutting large fish

into thick slices: gurnards, groupers, drums, red mullets, ocean perch, small breams or bass, hake, whiting, wrasses, bennies, weevers; conger eels and monkfish; little crabs and mussels. If the choice is limited, add such fish as cod, haddock, pollack, ling, or plaice. Sliced squid may also be thrown in but will require some 20 minutes more cooking time than the others.

A *rouille,* made by pounding together hot chili peppers and garlic, sometimes with moistened bread crumb or egg yolk, and adding or mounting it with oil, is often served separately, either to be spread on the slices of bread before the soup is poured over them or to be mixed into the soup at the time of serving; if this is done, the slices of bread should not be previously rubbed with garlic.

Provençal Fish Stew

Soupe aux Poissons

6 pounds fish (*whatever is available — see above suggestions*), cleaned, large fish sliced thickly
1 to 2 pounds crustaceans (*small crabs, jumbo shrimp, small rock lobsters*) (*optional*)
1 to 2 pounds mussels, scrubbed
1½ pounds medium potatoes, peeled and quartered

MARINADE
½ teaspoon powdered saffron
dash *pastis* (*anisette*)
¼ cup olive oil
1 teaspoon mixed dried herbs (*page 52*)

¼ cup olive oil
1 large onion, finely chopped
2 or 3 leeks, white and light green parts only, finely sliced
large pinch whole saffron
2 or 3 cloves garlic, finely chopped
1½ pounds firm, ripe tomatoes, peeled, seeded (*page 44*), and coarsely chopped
large *bouquet-garni* (*page 50*) containing, in addition to the usual elements, fennel branches, a strip of dried orange peel, and a small hot chili pepper
3 to 4 quarts fish *fumet* (*page 72*), a cut-up monkfish head used in its preparation, if possible
salt (*depending on the saltiness of the* fumet)

GARNISH
about 20 slices French bread, dried out in the sun or in a slow oven, but not toasted, each rubbed lightly with a peeled garlic clove (*4 or 5 cloves, in all*)

Spread the fish (except for crustaceans and mussels) and the potatoes out on a large platter, sprinkle over the elements of the marinade, gently rub and smear the surfaces until evenly coated, and leave to marinate for an hour or so.

In a large kettle, cook the onions and leeks in olive oil until they are softened and yellowed, add the saffron, garlic, tomatoes, and marinated potatoes, and cook over high heat for a few minutes, stirring occasionally. Add the *bouquet* and the *fumet,* bring the mixture to a boil (taste for salt), add the crustaceans and the firmer-fleshed varieties of fish (monkfish, conger eel, gurnard, weever) and, 7 or 8 minutes later, add the mussels and all of the more fragile fish (red mullet, whiting, bass, wrasse, bream, hake, cod, etc.). After 5 minutes it is ready.

Serve, first, some soup alone into the warmed soup plates, pouring it over slices of bread. Arrange the fish and potatoes on a huge platter and serve into the same plates, pouring a ladle of soup over each serving. Finger bowls and a container to collect skeletons and shells will be appreciated.

THE CERVELLE DE CANUT

A specialty of Lyons, *cervelle de canut* is basically a fresh white cheese made of cows' milk (homemade cottage or pot cheese — that is to say, freshly curdled milk, put to drain in muslin), beaten with a whisk, seasoned with salt, pepper, and finely chopped *fines herbes,* and enriched by the addition of a certain amount of cream. The essential herb is chives. Parsley, chervil, and tarragon may be used, but chives should dominate.

A *canut* is — or was — a worker in a silkworm factory at the time when silk was one of Lyons' important industries.

Four Simple Summer Luncheons à la Provençale

MENU II *(for 4 to 6)*

*Appropriate wine: a light, dry, well-chilled rosé throughout the meal — or
a rustic white wine with the sardines and a light, cool, young red wine with
the* pieds et paquets *and the cheeses*

FRESH SARDINES IN VINE LEAVES
[SARDINES FRAICHES DANS LES FEUILLES DE VIGNE]

• • •

LAMBS' TRIPES ("FEET AND PACKAGES") A LA MARSEILLAISE
[PIEDS ET PAQUETS A LA MARSEILLAISE]

• • •

WILD SALAD
[SALADE SAUVAGE]

• • •

FRESH CHEESES
[FROMAGES FRAIS]

• • •

STRAWBERRIES IN ORANGE JUICE
[FRAISES A L'ORANGE]

FRESH SARDINES IN VINE LEAVES

The grapevine leaves lend a pleasant, subtly acrid flavor to the sardine flesh while, at the same time, protecting it from drying out in direct contact with heat; when the charred leaves are unwrapped, the skin and scales of the fish cling to the leaves, exposing the moist and delicate fillets. The mixed herbs go wonderfully with fresh sardines or anchovies but will mask the taste of more delicate flesh; small red mullets, prepared in the same way, with the chopped feathery leaves of wild fennel replacing the mixed herbs, are lovely. Any small fish can be prepared in this way — *fines herbes,* dill, or oregano are other herb possibilities.

Fresh sardines are rigid, often arched, with glinting metallic blue reflections and bright eyes.

Fresh Sardines in Vine Leaves

Sardines Fraîches dans les Feuilles de Vigne

4 fresh sardines per person, gutted but not scaled
mixed dried herbs (*page 52*)
olive oil
salt, freshly ground pepper
large, freshly picked grapevine leaves, stems removed

In a large bowl or deep, wide dish, scatter the sardines, herbs, oil, and salt, grind over pepper, and mix well but delicately, lifting and turning the fish with your hands until they are evenly coated, inside and out. They may be left to marinate for an hour or so or grilled immediately.

Prepare a very hot bed of coals. Roll each fish in a vine leaf, first placing the leaf glossy side down, with the fish on top at the stem end of the leaf. As each is rolled, place it, flap-side down, on a large, double faced fish grill. Close it and grill the fish for approximately 2 minutes on each side, turning the grill as soon as the leaves are charred on the first side. Slip the wrapped sardines onto a platter and serve, accompanied by lemon halves, a cruet of olive oil, finger bowls, and a bowl to receive the leaves and bones.

LAMBS' TRIPES A LA MARSEILLAISE

The seductive *daube* of lambs' tripe, known as "feet and packages" (*pieds et paquets*), is such staple and admired fare in Provence that butchers and tripe merchants make up the packages in advance, each stuffed with diced green bacon and garlic *persillade,* and sell the feet and packages (4 feet and about a dozen packages to a 2-pound parcel), all ready to be braised.

Like all ruminants, sheep have four stomachs, identical in appearance (but in miniature — thinner and more fragile) to beef tripe. The first three stomachs (or whatever is available) are used in this preparation. Lambs' tripe can be had or ordered from specialty butchers but few butchers outside of France are willing to clean lambs' feet. (A great pity, for another of the great dishes is *pieds de mouton en poulette* — feet poached for several hours in a *court-bouillon* and finished in an egg yolk–bound *velouté* with mushrooms and a dash of lemon.) For this reason, calves' feet have been substituted in the following recipe; if you can't find calves' feet, substitute pigs' feet, and if you can't find lambs' tripe, substitute sections of a pig's large intestine, usually used as sausage casing (or for *andouillettes* — chitterling sausages) — or forget about the packages and simply cut beef tripe into strips, combine it with whatever feet you can find, and braise the lot in the same ingredients.

If the lambs' stomachs appear not to have been impeccably cleaned by the butcher, brush them well under running water, then soak them and rub the surfaces well in tepid vinegar water. The ideal cooking vessel is a 4-quart potbellied earthenware pot known as a *daubière*. The dish may be prepared in advance and gently reheated.

Lambs' Tripes à la Marseillaise

Pieds et Paquets à la Marseillaise

4 pounds lambs' stomachs *(2 sets)*, well cleaned and cut into diamond shapes
    3½ inches on each side

STUFFING
    7 ounces lean *pancetta,* diced
    4 cloves garlic, pounded to a paste with a pinch of coarse salt
    1 teaspoon mixed dried herbs *(page 52)*
    handful chopped parsley
    tripe trimmings, chopped

    mirepoix (page 55)
    1 pound firm, ripe tomatoes, peeled, seeded *(page 44)*, and coarsely chopped
    4 cloves garlic, finely chopped
    4 calves' feet, large bone removed, split, parboiled briefly, and rinsed
    salt, cayenne pepper
    bouquet-garni (page 50)
    1 bottle dry white wine

Mix all of the stuffing ingredients thoroughly. To stuff the tripe sections, lay one out before you, place a teaspoonful of stuffing in the lower (acute angle) corner, and, with a sharply pointed small knife, cut a 3-to-4-inch buttonhole, on the diagonal, in the opposite half of the diamond shape. Fold the side flaps (obtuse angles) over the stuffing, fold the lower corner up over the side flaps, roll up the package toward the slitted end, and pull that corner gently to one side in order to encircle the package within the slit, being careful not to tear it. (The tripe is elastic and the slit will stretch to accommodate the package — if it should tear, tie it up with a bit of thread.)

Mix together the *mirepoix,* tomatoes, and garlic. Put half the mixture in the bottom of the pot, place the feet on top, sprinkle with salt and a suspicion of cayenne, place the *bouquet-garni* in the middle, and begin to tuck the packages around to leave no empty spaces, but without packing tightly. Spoon in the remaining chopped mixture as you go. When all the packages and mixture are placed, sprinkle with more salt and very little cayenne and pour over white wine until the liquid is visible but the top layer of packages not quite covered. Cover as hermetically as possible, a sheet of foil over the top of the pot before pressing the lid into place. Use an asbestos pad or other heat disperser to protect the earthenware from direct heat (or put into a cool oven — 250°F) and cook over very low heat, adjusting it during cooking, if necessary, to maintain a bare simmer for 8 to 9 hours. Carefully skim all fat from the surface, taste for salt, and serve into shallow soup plates, as is or accompanied by new potatoes, boiled in their skins. (If prepared one day to be served the next, be certain that the surface is thoroughly degreased before reheating and reheat very slowly, counting a good two hours to return to the simmer.)

Strawberries in Orange Juice

Fraises à l'Orange

2 pounds strawberries
sugar
juice of 3 oranges

Wash the strawberries rapidly without letting them soak, and remove the stems. Place them, whole, in the bowl or deep dish in which they are to be served, sprinkle them generously with sugar, pour the orange juice over, and leave them to macerate, covered, in the refrigerator for a couple of hours before serving. Simple, delicious, and refreshing.

Four Simple Summer Luncheons
à la Provençale

MENU III *(for 6)*

Appropriate wine: a light, dry, well-chilled rosé throughout the meal — or a rustic white wine with the beans and a light, cool, young red wine with the beef and macaroni and with the cheeses

WARM SALAD OF SMALL GREEN BEANS
[HARICOTS FINS CHAUDS EN SALADE]

• • •

PROVENCAL BRAISED BEEF
[DAUBE A LA PROVENCALE]

• • •

MACARONI IN BRAISING LIQUID
[MACARONADE]

• • •

TOSSED GREEN SALAD WITH FINES HERBES
[SALADE VERTE AUX FINES HERBES]

• • •

CHEESES
[FROMAGES]

• • •

FRUIT
[FRUITS]

Warm Salad of Small Green Beans

Haricots Fins Chauds en Salade

2 pounds young, freshly picked green beans

ACCOMPANIMENTS
   olive oil
   coarse salt, freshly ground pepper
   cold unsalted butter
   crusty white bread

For this or any other preparation of green beans served whole to be exquisite, the beans should be tiny and freshly picked. Snap off the tips, but leave them whole, and wash them quickly in cold water. Plunge them into a large quantity of well-salted water at a churning boil and cook, uncovered, at a continued rapid boil, until tender — 4 to 8 minutes. Serve them, well-drained and undecorated, accompanied by a cruet of the finest and freshest olive oil available, a pepper mill, a salt mill, cold unsalted butter, and rough, crusty white bread. The contact of the olive oil with the hot beans produces a delicious olfactory explosion.

THE DAUBE

A *daube,* like most rustic dishes that require a long, slow, even cooking process, is never so good as when prepared in seasoned earthenware — the *daubière* recommended for *pieds et paquets* (page 274) is perfect; earthenware absorbs heat more evenly and holds it longer than any other kitchen vessel, and the potbellied form of the *daubière,* with its relatively narrow neck, not only cuts down on evaporation because of the reduced surface, but concentrates the fat that rises to the top, making it easier to skim.

Like many long-cooking dishes, a *daube* will improve with a gentle reheating the day following its preparation. Leftover *daube* is often served in its jelly, the meats and other solid material arranged in a metal mixing bowl or simple mold, the degreased cooking juices poured over, chilled overnight, unmolded, and cut into slices at table. If any of this remains, it is traditional to melt the juice free of the solid elements, chop the latter to be mixed with parboiled, squeezed, and chopped spinach or chard, some *brousse* (ricotta), and an egg, to make a stuffing for ravioli, which is then parboiled, drained, spread in a gratin dish, the melted juices poured over, a bit of Parmesan grated over, and reheated rapidly in a hot oven.

Provençal Braised Beef

Daube à la Provençale

4 pounds gelatinous cuts of beef (*shank, chuck*), cut into approximately 3½-
 ounce pieces, respecting the natural muscular structure when possible
larding elements: 2 cloves garlic, pounded to a paste with a pinch of coarse
 salt and a large pinch of mixed dried herbs (*page 52*)
small handful chopped parsley
4 ounces fresh pork back fat, cut into lardons approximately 1 inch long by
 ⅓ inch square

MARINADE
 2 tablespoons olive oil
 about 1 bottle dry white wine (*or red — or any bottle ends of any color*)

MIXTURE
 5 ounces pork rind, parboiled, rinsed, and cut into squares
 8 ounces *pancetta,* thickly sliced, cut crosswise into finger widths, parboiled
 for a few seconds, and rinsed
 2 carrots, finely chopped
 2 onions, finely chopped
 4 cloves garlic, finely chopped
 8 ounces mushrooms, finely chopped (*or 1 ounce dried* cèpes — *Italian*
 porcini — *soaked, stem ends trimmed, rinsed, and finely chopped*)
 1 pound ripe, firm tomatoes, peeled, seeded (*page 44*), and coarsely chopped
 handful pitted black olives (*unpitted if they are the small niçoise olives*)
 large pinch mixed dried herbs (*page 52*)
 salt

 2 *bouquets-garnis* (*page 50*), each containing a dried strip of orange peel
 brandy (*Cognac, Armagnac, marc, etc.*)
 stock (*page 66*) (*plus any leftover jellied roasting juices*)

Add the chopped parsley to the mortar in which the garlic and herbs have been
pounded, mix well, add the lardons, and toss with your hands until they are well
coated with the mixture. Pierce each piece of meat, with the grain, using a sharply
pointed small knife, open the vent with your finger, and force in a lardon. Each
piece may be larded once, twice, or three times, depending on its shape and
structure. Make certain that the lardons are well embedded in the flesh. Put all
the pieces of meat (as well as any lardons that may be left over and any of the
mixture that is left in the mortar) into a large bowl, dribble over olive oil, pour
over wine to cover, and leave, covered, for several hours in a cool place or
refrigerated overnight, turning the meat a couple of times in its marinade.

Be sure that your pot is large enough to leave about 2 inches' distance from the brim when filled with all the solid elements. (The liquid will expand as it heats — with less space, it may brim over.) Combine the mixture ingredients and ladle some of the mixture into the bottom of the pot, add a layer of meat, sprinkle over some salt, and continue making alternate layers, placing the two *bouquets* somewhere in the middle and finishing with a layer of mixture. Add a healthy dash of brandy, pour over the marinade, and finish with enough stock to cover. Cover tightly, placing first a sheet of foil over the pot before pressing the lid into place, keep the pot from direct contact with heat by means of a heat disperser, bring it slowly to a simmer, and adjust the heat to maintain a bare simmer for 5 to 6 hours (or cook in a cool oven — 250°F — checking for the degree of simmer after an hour or so). Carefully remove as much surface fat as possible. (If, toward the end of skimming, you are picking up juices as well as fat, refrigerate the bowl of skimmed fat; it will solidify and can be lifted free of the jellied juices and discarded, the juices being added later to any leftover *daube*.) At the end of cooking, the *daube* will be swimming in juices; if you wish to concentrate the flavor, a portion of the juices may be ladled into a saucepan, reduced over high heat by about two-thirds, and poured back over the meats. Serve the *macaronade* at the same time.

Macaroni in Braising Liquid

Macaronade

1 pound large macaroni (*ziti, rigatoni, pennoni, etc.*)
cooking liquid from the *daube*
freshly ground pepper
freshly grated Parmesan cheese

Cook the macaroni in abundant salted boiling water, keeping it slightly firm (10 to 20 minutes, depending on the size and quality of the macaroni). Drain it well and layer it, with sprinklings of cheese and a few grinds of the pepper mill, in a deep gratin dish or casserole. Ladle *daube* juices, lifting them from the surface of the *daube* to pick up any remaining fat, over the macaroni to cover it barely, sprinkle the surface with cheese, and put it into a hot oven for 8 to 10 minutes, until the juices arrive at a boil and the cheese is melted, but not colored.

Four Simple Summer Luncheons
à la Provençale

MENU IV *(for 5 or 6)*

*Appropriate wine: a light, dry, well-chilled rosé throughout the meal — or
a rustic white wine with the ratatouille and a light, cool, red wine with the
beef and potatoes and with the cheeses*

COLD RATATOUILLE (MIXED VEGETABLE STEW)
[RATATOUILLE FROIDE]

• • •

BLANQUETTE OF BEEF TRIPE WITH BASIL
[BLANQUETTE DE GRAS-DOUBLE AU PISTOU]

• • •

STEAMED POTATOES
[POMMES DE TERRE A LA VAPEUR]

• • •

TOSSED GREEN SALAD
[SALADE VERTE]

• • •

CHEESES
[FROMAGES]

• • •

CHERRIES AND FRESH ALMONDS
[CERISES ET AMANDES FRAICHES]

This menu may be prepared in such a way, if desired, that at the last minute only the potatoes have to be steamed and the *blanquette* sauce thickened. The ratatouille is best prepared in advance, and the *blanquette* may, except for the addition of the final thickening agent, be prepared a day in advance, rewarmed gently, and finished as described.

THE COLD RATATOUILLE

Ratatouille, although often served hot as an accompaniment to pork and veal dishes, gains through being savored cold as an hors d'oeuvre. If the tripes were not prepared with basil, it could replace the parsley in the ratatouille.

Cold Ratatouille (Mixed Vegetable Stew)

Ratatouille Froide

1 pound medium onions, peeled and quartered
⅔ cup olive oil (*in all*)
1 pound sweet red peppers (*or red, yellow, and green, mixed*), seeded and cut
    into squares
1 pound small eggplant, cubed
4 large, firm, ripe tomatoes, peeled, seeded (*page 44*), and coarsely cut up
6 cloves garlic, peeled and chopped
salt, cayenne pepper
1 teaspoon mixed dried herbs (*page 52*)
2 bay leaves
1 pound small zucchini, thickly sliced
freshly ground pepper
chopped parsley

In a large casserole, cook the onions gently in half the olive oil until they are softened and yellowed, but not colored. Add the peppers and the eggplant and continue to cook over low heat for 10 minutes or so, stirring from time to time with a wooden spoon. Add the tomatoes, garlic, salt, a pinch of cayenne, the dried herbs, and the bay leaves. Continue to cook over low heat, moving the contents of the pot gently around, until the vegetables have given up enough of their juices to be nearly immersed. Raise the heat somewhat, still stirring occasionally, until a boil is reached, adjust the heat to a bare simmer, and cook, covered, with the lid slightly ajar, for about 2 hours, adding the zucchini after 1½ hours. At the end of this time, the vegetables should all be meltingly tender but intact — above all, one does not want a boiled mush.

Place a colander over a large bowl and pour the contents of the pot into it to drain. Permit the vegetables to drain a good 10 minutes before returning them to their casserole. Transfer the juices to a saucepan and reduce them over high heat, stirring regularly, until they become syrupy and the foaming boil has changed to sharply punctuated surface bubbling. Pour it back over the vegetables, simmer for a few minutes to bring everything back together, transfer to a non-metallic container, and leave to cool. Taste for salt, grind over pepper, add the remaining olive oil and the chopped parsley, stir carefully to avoid crushing the vegetables, and pour into a serving dish. Sprinkle with a bit more parsley.

THE BLANQUETTE OF BEEF TRIPE

The term *pistou* ("pestle" in Provençal) refers to the pounded *pommade* of garlic and basil leaves (this usually contains much more garlic), grated Parmesan cheese, worked into a thick paste, and thinned with olive oil; it is customarily used to add an explosive, last-minute perfume to a minestrone, which then takes the name *soupe au pistou*.

Blanquette of Beef Tripe with Basil

Blanquette de Gras-double au Pistou

2 pounds honeycomb tripe, pre-cooked but not bleached, cut into 2-inch
    squares
2 large onions, finely chopped
2 tablespoons olive oil
2 tablespoons flour
½ bottle dry white wine combined with approximately the same quantity of
    stock (*page 66*)
salt
bouquet-garni (*page 50*)

PISTOU
    1 clove of garlic, peeled
    1 handful of fresh basil leaves
    salt, freshly ground pepper
    1 tablespoon olive oil
    4 egg yolks
    juice of ½ lemon

Cook the onions gently in the oil, in an earthenware casserole or large, heavy saucepan, for about 10 minutes, without allowing them to brown. Sprinkle with the flour and leave to cook for another minute or so, stirring several times so that the flour cooks evenly. Away from the flame, add slowly, stirring the while, a ladleful of the wine and stock mixture, then stir in the rest. Return to the heat and, over a medium flame, bring to a boil, without ceasing to stir.

Add the tripe, salt, and *bouquet-garni* and leave to cook very gently for approximately 2 hours. (Tripe actually needs 6 or 7 hours of cooking, but it is precooked when one buys it — the time necessary depends on the extent of its precooking.)

Pound together in a mortar the clove of garlic, the basil, a pinch of salt, and some pepper, until the mixture is reduced completely into a puree. Stir in the tablespoon of olive oil and the egg yolks.

Remove the pot containing the tripe from the heat and discard the *bouquet*. Set aside a ladleful or small bowlful of the cooking liquid and allow it to cool somewhat, then stir it slowly and thoroughly into the basil mixture. Pour the contents of the mortar slowly into the pot, stirring the while, and return it to a moderate heat. Stir without stopping until the sauce begins to thicken; it should coat the spoon. Above all, it must never come to a boil after the egg mixture has been added. Stir in a bit of lemon juice, taste for seasoning, and serve in its cooking utensil, accompanied by steamed potatoes, served apart.

Cherries and Fresh Almonds

Cerises et Amandes Fraîches

The green almonds, in the process of maturing, contain a gelatinous material that eventually becomes the nut. Sometime between the months of May and July, depending on the variety of almond and the climate, the nut solidifies. At this point in its development the outside hull and the unformed shell are easily cut through with a knife, and the almond, from which one first peels the soft, spongy skin (which later becomes the dried, brown covering of the shelled almond), is of a delicacy unrelated to that of the matured nut.

Serve the almonds whole with the cherries and leave your guests to do the work. It is a fine marriage.

Index

Index

A NOTE ON THE ILLUSTRATOR

Judith Eldridge is a graduate of the Massachusetts College of Art and attended botany classes at the University of New Hampshire. Combining those interests, she wrote and illustrated Cabbage or Cauliflower? *(Godine, 1984). She divides her time between intaglio printing and horticultural illustration.*

THE FRENCH MENU COOKBOOK

was set in Galliard by Dix Typesetting Company, Syracuse, New York. Introduced in 1978 by the Mergenthaler Linotype Company, Galliard is based on a type made by the sixteenth century's Robert Granjon, and is the first of its genre to be designed exclusively for phototypesetting. The name Galliard stems from Granjon's own term for an 8-point font he cut about 1570. It undoubtedly refers to the style of the face, for the galliard was a lively dance of the period.

Galliard possesses the authentic sparkle that is lacking in the current Garamonds. It is a type of solid weight, which will bring good color to the printed page — an asset in offset printing, in which the more delicately constructed romans appear to disadvantage. The italic of Galliard is particularly felicitous and reaches back to the feeling of the chancery style, from which Claude Garamond in his complementary italic had departed.

The book was printed and bound by Halliday Lithograph, West Hanover, Massachusetts. The paper was 70# Glatfelter Offset, an entirely acid-free paper.

Designed by Richard C. Bartlett